RED CLOUD AND THE INDIAN TRADER

Red Cloud and the Indian Trader

The Remarkable Friendship of the Sioux Chief and JW Dear in the Last Days of the Frontier

Marilyn Dear Nelson

Christopher Nelson

TWODOT®

ESSEX, CONNECTICUT
HELENA, MONTANA

A · TWODOT® · BOOK

An imprint of Globe Pequot, the trade division of
The Rowman & Littlefield Publishing Group, Inc.
4501 Forbes Blvd., Ste. 200
Lanham, MD 20706
www.rowman.com

Distributed by NATIONAL BOOK NETWORK

British Library Cataloguing in Publication Information available

Library of Congress Cataloging-in-Publication Data
Names: Nelson, Marilyn Dear, 1948- author. | Nelson, Chris, 1941- author.
Title: Red Cloud and the Indian trader : the remarkable friendship of the Sioux chief and
   JW Dear in the last days of the frontier / Marilyn Dear Nelson, Chris Nelson.
Other titles: Remarkable friendship of the Sioux chief and JW Dear in the last days of the frontier
Description: Essex, Connecticut : TwoDot, 2023. | Includes bibliographical references.
Identifiers: LCCN 2023032137 (print) | LCCN 2023032138 (ebook) | ISBN 9781493073900
   (paperback) | ISBN 9781493073917 (epub)
Subjects: LCSH: Dear, J. W. (John William), 1845-1833. | Indian agents—South Dakota—
   Biography. | Red Cloud, 1822-1909—Friends and associates. | Red Cloud Band of Sioux
   Indians—History. | United States. Office of Indian Affairs. Red Cloud Agency—History. |
   Dakota Indians—Government relations. | Black Hills War, 1876-1877. | Fur traders—United
   States—Biography. | Confederate States of America. Army. Virginia Cavalry Battalion, 43rd—
   Biography. | United States—History—Civil War, 1861-1865—Regimental histories.
Classification: LCC E78.S63 .N457 2023 (print) | LCC E78.S63 (ebook) | DDC 973.7092/2
   [B]—dc23/eng/20230811
LC record available at https://lccn.loc.gov/2023032137
LC ebook record available at https://lccn.loc.gov/2023032138

♾™ The paper used in this publication meets the minimum requirements of American National Standard for Information Sciences—Permanence of Paper for Printed Library Materials, ANSI/ NISO Z39.48-1992.

To the many who have helped bring this story alive

Contents

Illustrations

Photos

MAPS

PREFACE

John William Dear was born in 1845 into a close-knit farming family in Northern Virginia. He was known by his family and Virginian friends as "Willie," but on the Great Northern Plains, where he lived most of his adult life, he was known simply as "JW." After the Civil War, when he fought with Mosby's Rangers as a Confederate guerrilla, he went West. For fifteen years, until his premature death, JW lived a tumultuous life as one of the last fur traders on the Upper Missouri and as the longest-serving, government-appointed Indian trader to the Oglala Lakota Sioux.

In the summer of 1871, JW met Red Cloud, the powerful leader of the Oglala, who at that time was the most respected Indian chief in America. For the next twelve years, the two men lived alongside each other on the vast Northern Plains. This was one of the most turbulent, violent, and controversial periods in the history of the American West. The end of the Civil War saw tens of thousands of emigrants brave the two-thousand-mile journey across Indian territory in search of a better life in California and Oregon. It saw the coming of the transcontinental railroad across Indian land, the wanton slaughter of millions of buffalo the Indians depended upon for survival, the end of the fur trade, the discovery of gold in the Black Hills of Dakota, the Great Sioux War of 1876, Custer's last stand at the Battle of Little Bighorn, and the forcing of the Lakota onto reservations.

This book tells the story of two men caught up in these momentous events—Red Cloud, whose life has been well researched, and JW Dear, my great-grandfather, whose story has never been told. Historical events for the period are well documented, but JW's life has been pieced together from the lost voices of history found in previously unseen material in private collections, letters, diaries, images, archive centers, press reports, and my family's archive.

What has emerged is a story that covers twenty-five tumultuous years of American history that includes the Civil War, the abolition of slavery, the opening of the Old West, and the process of nation building, driven by great vision, sacrifice, and human endeavor. But it is also a story of mismanagement, avarice, corruption, bigotry, extreme violence, and injustice. It is a story of how Red Cloud and JW became caught up in these life-changing events, which bound the two men together as they fought for their survival. Theirs is an authentic story of the Wild West, true and tragic.

I have attempted to tell their story as they experienced it—seen through their eyes and the prism of Indian and American views of their country *at that time*, and not judge their actions, thoughts, or deeds by today's standards. Similarly, wherever possible, I have used the language and terminology current *at that time*.

—Marilyn Dear Nelson
August 2023

Prologue

Saturday, October 9, 1875, was ration day for the Indians at the Red Cloud Agency, and hundreds gathered in all their holiday finery.[1] As the afternoon sun set in the clear Nebraskan sky, shadows lengthened on the beaten earth, the temperature fell, activity around the agency and JW Dear's trading store subsided, and a colorful cast of characters prepared to wend their way home.

Groups of Indians wrapped in blankets against the chill of the early Nebraska winter headed for the hundreds of tepees scattered among Indian villages surrounding the agency. Some walked, others rode, and a few led their ponies, their travois laden with goods bumping behind them on the rutted ground. Frontiersmen, scouts, mixed-race interpreters, agency personnel, and civilian staff from the nearby army cantonment of Camp Robinson chatted in groups, while their horses stood patiently, harnessed to buggies, waiting to carry them home. As teamsters finished hitching their mules and oxen to an assortment of sturdy wagons, they leaned back against them, warming themselves in the last rays of a wintry sun.

A handful of customers were still in JW's trading store making last-minute purchases; others drifted toward his saloon and restaurant for a drink or a meal and perhaps a game of cards or billiards. But many braved the cold and remained outside to watch a photographer from St. Louis, Albert Guerin, and his assistant, set up a tripod and camera in front of the trading store to capture an image that marked a pivotal moment in the history of the American West.

Standing left to right in front of JW's store at Red Cloud Agency are Red Cloud, JW Dear, and Blue Shield. Majestic buttes dominate the background. Photographed by Albert E. Guerin, October 9, 1875. Dear Family Collection

The Red Cloud Agency was the largest and most troublesome of the seventy agencies the government had established to dispense Indian rations and supervise the welfare of three hundred thousand Indians. Red Cloud; more than six thousand Oglala; agency personnel; and JW, the licensed Indian trader to the Oglala, had all moved to the site in August 1873. The seeds of the tension and unrest that currently gripped the agency were sown a few weeks before this photograph was taken. Gold had been discovered in the Black Hills of Dakota, which was legally owned by the Lakota, but at a meeting at the agency in September, Red Cloud and his fellow chiefs failed to reach agreement to sell the Hills to the United States.

This put President Ulysses Grant in a difficult position, caught between the legal title of the Indians to the land, ceded to them by treaty, and overwhelming public opinion that believed the Indians should not be allowed to halt the rightful progress of thirty-five million Americans. Grant eventually decided to force the Lakota to relinquish ownership, whatever the consequences, and non-reservation Indians were given an impossible ultimatum, which expired at the end of January 1876—to leave their winter quarters spread over tens of thousands of square miles of inhospitable terrain, and brave snow and sub-zero temperatures to report to their designated agencies or be hunted down. When the photograph was taken the tension at the agency was palpable, and although Grant had yet to make his fateful decision, the threat of an all-out Indian war felt unmistakably real.

Guerin was the official photographer to the Jenney Expedition, which had traveled to the Black Hills to survey for gold. He arrived at the agency with other members of the expedition on October 9 and immediately enlisted JW's help to stage the photograph in front of his trading store. Indians were reluctant to be photographed, and this was the first known occasion that Red Cloud allowed himself to be photographed at his agency—a tribute to his trust in JW.

Guerin's image graphically captured daily life at the agency, but this was the calm before the storm. Many Indians failed to meet the government's deadline, heralding the start of the Great Sioux War and the most violent year in the history of the American West. Months of mindless violence followed, and unspeakable atrocities and depredations were carried out by both whites and Indians, culminating in June in the Battle of Little Bighorn and the massacre of Colonel Custer and two hundred sixty-five men of the 7th Cavalry, an event that had a profound impact on the future of the Lakota.

JW sent this photograph to his future wife, Mary Ann Rogers, in Virginia, and it is still in the possession of the Dear family. Little has changed. If you stand today where JW and Red Cloud were photographed, the magnificent sandstone buttes and the surrounding plains remain unchanged. And remarkably, the relationship between the Red Cloud and Dear families, which began with the two men meeting on the Great Northern Plains over one hundred fifty years ago, still continues to this day.

PART I

INDIAN TROUBLES, THE CIVIL WAR, AND RECONSTRUCTION: 1861–1868

CHAPTER 1

Red Cloud, the Oglala, and the Great Northern Plains

IN 1845, THE YEAR JOHN WILLIAM DEAR WAS BORN, RED CLOUD WAS twenty-three years old and roaming the Great Northern Plains of present-day Nebraska, Wyoming, and South Dakota, seventeen hundred miles west of Virginia.

The plains were home to more than one hundred thousand Indians. Over forty tribes, each with its own traditions, rituals, language, or dialect—like Red Cloud's Oglala Lakota Sioux, the Crows, Utes, and Pawnees—shared the rich grasslands of that vast territory which stretched north to the Canadian border.[1]

The Sioux were divided into three regional groups, the Lakota, Dakota, and Nakota. In the eighteenth century the Lakota Sioux settled on the Great Northern Plains west of the Missouri River. They were subdivided into seven tribes, of which Red Cloud's Oglala was the largest and most warlike.[2]

There was an abundance of game: ten million buffalo roamed the plains, providing Indians with food, clothing, and shelter, that was supplemented with deer, elk, and antelope and fish from the many rivers that crisscrossed their land.

Ponies were their most valuable and treasured possession, and they were accomplished and fearless horsemen. They were an oral society that did not read or write, and knowledge was passed from generation to generation by word of mouth, often through the medium of storytelling, song, and dance.

In those days only a few white men ventured west of the Missouri, and the Indians had little understanding of the white man and his culture and values. The only whites they encountered were occasional fur trappers and the brave and adventurous souls who made a precarious living trading with the Indians.

The way of life of Red Cloud's tribe had remained virtually unchanged since they had crossed the Missouri and settled on the plains a hundred years before. The tribe was divided into a number of bands, each made up of a number of kinsmen and followers who traveled and camped together. Each band was led by a hereditary chief or by someone who had gained leadership through respect. The affairs of the tribe were settled by consensus; a chief could influence a discussion but was ultimately bound by the collective wish of his people.

The Oglala spent their days hunting game and fighting. Skill and bravery in the hunt and in combat established rank and precedence. "Work" as it was defined by the white man was not part of their culture. A few tribes farmed, but the majority were nomadic and moved frequently, their lives governed by the seasons and the movement of game. For the Oglala, their land was wherever the buffalo roamed. The concept of land ownership was alien to them—land was something to be used and shared, like the air they breathed.

Every aspect of the environment was part of their very being. They believed everything had a spiritual essence, a sacred or mystical power or energy: the earth, plants, animals, and humans, which came from one shared source, Mother Earth. They believed in an afterlife, and that there was no separation between the physical and spiritual worlds. That belief was underpinned by tribal traditions and elaborate rituals orchestrated by a medicine man or shaman. The spiritual world of the Indians was an integral part of their daily life.[3]

Fighting and cruelty were also ingrained in their culture. One of the most feared and warlike of all the Northern Plains tribes was the Oglala, whose hunting grounds ranged from the Platte River in the south to the Yellowstone and Upper Missouri Rivers in the north. Their sworn

The earliest known portrait of Red Cloud, head chief of the Oglala Lakota Sioux. Photographed in June 1872. George W. Ingalls Photograph Collection, The Huntington Library, San Marino, California

enemies who shared the plains with them were the Crows, Utes, and Pawnees.

Red Cloud's maternal uncle was Old Smoke, the hereditary chief of the Bad Face Band of the Oglala. In the winter of 1841–1842, when he was nineteen, Red Cloud killed his uncle's bitter rival.[4] That brought him great respect, and during the 1840s and 1850s his influence within the tribe steadily grew as he established himself as a ruthless and charismatic warrior.

By his late twenties Red Cloud was ready for marriage. An Oglala man could take as many wives as he could afford, and Red Cloud was in love with two women, Pretty Owl and Pine Leaf. The question was who he should marry first? Whoever he chose would always hold a slight edge in status. He chose Pretty Owl, with every intention of marrying Pine Leaf when the appropriate amount of time had passed. But that never happened. The day after his wedding to Pretty Owl, a distraught Pine Leaf committed suicide. This made a profound impression on Red Cloud, and he resolved to never take a second wife, and, unusual for an Oglala, there is no evidence he ever did.[5]

Western emigration across the Great Plains increased to a flood when gold was discovered in California in 1849. Tens of thousands of miners and their followers streamed across Indian land. For years Indians had hunted and feasted on the buffalo and game which thrived along the fertile Platte valley, but now this was threatened as the vast influx of emigrants drove away the buffalo and game, brought white man's diseases, and introduced alcohol to the Indians on an unprecedented scale. The Indians responded aggressively to this threat to their way of life. Clashes between whites and Indians became regular occurrences, and military force was drafted to protect emigrants and other travelers from Indian depredations.

Forts were established along the Platte and Missouri Rivers.[6] One of these was Fort Laramie, which had started life as a trading post where trappers, hunters, and Indians met to trade robes, skins, and furs.[7] During the 1840s the nature of the fur trade changed, and in 1849 the fort was sold to the army and converted into a military post. Located five hundred miles west of Omaha it was ideally placed to protect the emigrant road known as the Oregon Trail, running along the Platte River. However, the presence of the army generated a violent response from the Indians.

The Office of Indian Affairs (OIA) was established in 1824 to bring a more disciplined and focused approach to the management of Indian tribes, which was becoming an increasingly complex and controversial task. Initially it reported to the War Department; however, by 1849 there was a growing feeling that the army's handling of the Indians was insensitive and unnecessarily brutal.[8]

As a result, responsibility for the Indians was transferred to politicians, much to the War Department's annoyance, who reported to the newly created Department of the Interior. The army's criticism of the politicians was that personnel changed frequently depending on the political party in power and that they were weak, inefficient, often corrupt, and more interested in furthering their own interests than those of the nation or the Indians they served. Since the army was required to resolve problems that could and should have been avoided, often at great expense, it wanted to reassume responsibility for the Indians. The "Transfer Issue" as it became known, was the subject of heated and acrimonious debate in US politics for the next thirty years.[9]

To stem the violence and bloodshed along the Oregon Trail, the government brokered a deal with the Northern Plains Indians in 1851. The agreement, known as the Fort Laramie Treaty, provided for $50,000 of rations annually to be issued to the Northern Plains tribes by the forts

Fort Laramie on the banks of the North Platte River, five hundred miles west of Omaha. The Oregon Trail passed within half a mile of the fort. A sketch by Frederick Piercy in 1853. Courtesy of the Library of Congress, LC-USZ62-8152

located along the Missouri and Platte Rivers.[10] In return the Indians allowed emigration along the Oregon Trail and agreed to live in clearly defined tribal territories, which the government hoped would put an end to intertribal warfare.[11]

The treaty was only marginally successful, and throughout the 1850s clashes between Indians and whites continued, as did the squabbling and fighting between rival tribes. Red Cloud thrived in such an environment, and with Old Smoke's tacit approval, he became the acknowledged war leader of the Oglala.

By early 1861, the growing threat of civil war in the East had temporarily stemmed the flow of emigrants heading west. The army's presence on the plains was reduced as Union troops were moved east in preparation for the potential engagement with southern Confederate rebels. The federal government's primary focus was on uniting the country, not managing the Indians.

As a result, the level of violence on the Northern Plains and along the Oregon Trail fell, and a degree of normality returned to Red Cloud's life. At the same time, a fifteen-year-old boy whose life would become intertwined with Red Cloud's, was preparing for war in Virginia.

CHAPTER 2

JW Dear, Mount Gilead, and Virginia

JOHN WILLIAM DEAR WAS A FIFTH-GENERATION VIRGINIAN, ROOTED IN the rolling hills and wooded valleys of the northern counties where his family had farmed for a hundred years. He was of German blood on his father's side, and English on his mother's.[1] A century before, his paternal ancestor, twenty-five-year-old Johannes Hirsch, struggling to survive in his war-torn and disease-ravaged homeland, made the decision to brave the perils of a long ocean crossing to seek a new life in America. He traveled five hundred miles from his home in Täbingen in southern Germany to the great trading port of Rotterdam on the North Sea, where he boarded the *Snow Charlotta* bound for America.[2]

During the eighteenth century seventy thousand German immigrants arrived in colonial Pennsylvania.[3] Johannes landed in America on September 5, 1743, where he swore the Oath of Allegiance to his new country in front of the Philadelphia Courthouse. He moved south to what is now Madison County in central Virginia, married a German-born widow, worked hard, and did well. By the early 1750s he had become a successful farmer and landowner and changed his name from Hirsch to Deer. *Hirsch* is German for deer, which morphed in time to Dear. In his will, written in 1781, Johannes left the fruits of his hard work, his farm and large estate, to his children.[4]

Two generations later his direct descendants, JW's father, the patriotically named George Washington Dear, and his elder brother Amos, were born twenty-five miles away in Little Washington, a small farming community in Culpeper County.[5] Both brothers married well. Amos married

9

Phoebe Spiller, who came from an affluent English family.[6] The couple owned more than twenty slaves, a large farm on the outskirts of the village, and the hostelry in the village center, known as Dear's Ordinary, which survives to this day.[7] This branch of the Dear family continued to live and farm in Little Washington until the early 1930s.

In 1839 George married Sarah Ann Rowles.[8] Her well-connected, patrician family lived twenty miles away in the village of Markham, and JW, their third child, was born on July 6, 1845.[9] But whereas Amos made a success of his life and prospered, George struggled. George must have been a man of charm and some charisma to capture the affluent and refined Sarah Rowles—and to keep her, despite the tribulations of their life together. He was a likable rogue, but a risk-taker who was not good with money and was often in debt.[10] In 1854 and again in 1855, he was convicted and fined for selling alcohol without a license. As a result, his exasperated wife took the unusual step of legally protecting the assets she had inherited from her father and grandfather from her husband.[11]

In spite of this they continued to live together, seemingly happily, and had two more children. The 1850 census recorded George as a tenant farmer owning nine slaves, but a decade later he was a laborer with no slaves and was clearly struggling financially, surviving only by his wife's inheritance.[12] George's inability to provide adequately for his family and their penury by comparison with their wealthier relations weighed heavily on young JW and molded the man he would become. His single-minded drive to succeed at least partly stemmed from his troubled childhood, moving from tenancy to tenancy as his father inexorably sunk down the social scale.

George, Sarah, and their seven children, Frances, Thomas, JW, Clay, Richard, Jennie, and Luther, moved to Mount Gilead in Loudoun County, Northern Virginia, where, in the fall of 1860, George took yet another tenancy. In the 1860 Federal Census, the county had a population of 21,000, and 607 families owned 5,501 slaves. Most of the population, like the Dears, lived on farms. A few toll roads and a network of bridle paths connected the scattered communities. Leesburg, seven miles northeast of the Dears' cottage, was the largest town in the county with a population of sixteen hundred and was served by a railroad which connected it to Alexandria to the south, and from there it was a ferry ride across the Potomac to Washington, DC.

Mount Gilead was a small hamlet of one hundred thirty souls perched astride a ridge of the Catoctin Mountain, fields and woodland dropping away on either side. The road from Leesburg, which bisected the village and formed its main street, led down to the ford across the North Fork of Goose Creek at Coe's Mill. Washington was forty miles to the east, and this proximity to the capital made the area a constant battleground throughout the coming Civil War. The largest local landowners were John Simpson and his three sons, James, John Jr., and Henson. Between them they farmed over fourteen hundred acres and owned more than forty slaves who lived in three slave houses spread across their estates.[13]

George leased a portion of James Simpson's land and one of his cottages for the next ten years as a tenant farmer.[14] The farm lay adjacent to the main street, and the Dears' modest cottage was conveniently located "in a quiet retired portion of the neighborhood," a few hundred yards from the village center.[15] The family had easy access to the village shop, which was owned and operated by their landlord, and to a post office, blacksmith, and carpenter.[16] Just behind Main Street was a small timber-framed village school, which the Dear children attended.

The North Fork Baptist Church, a mile from their home, was easily reached by the country path that crossed the North Fork of Goose Creek as it meandered gently through the valley to the west of the Dears' cottage. The church, built in 1785, was a functional red brick building where the community gathered for both religious and social activities and where Sarah, who was a staunch Baptist, worshiped throughout the 1860s. And it was probably the church that awakened JW's lifelong love of music and singing.

Three wealthy families who lived within a few miles of the Dear household were destined to play an important part in JW's life. The Rogers family lived at Willow Cottage a few miles north on the road leading to Hamilton; the Megeaths, three miles to the west in Philomont; and the Richards, at Green Garden estate on the outskirts of Upperville.[17] Over the coming years JW became linked to all three families, initially through friendships forged by fighting together for the Confederate cause in the Civil War, then through business, and later by marriage.

The Dear family arrived in Mount Gilead during the lead-up to the November 1860 presidential election. President James Buchanan's Democratic Cabinet was split over the issue of slavery, and the little-known Republican, Abraham Lincoln, was elected the sixteenth President of the United States.

In Loudoun, with a white population of fifteen thousand, only a handful of people voted for Lincoln. The staunchly Democratic South was concerned that under the new president increased federal control would limit the freedom to determine the destiny of their democratically elected state politicians. The question of slavery and federal involvement in state affairs was an increasingly debated and divisive topic. Lincoln and the Republican Party's view on slavery was well known. They, and the North in general, opposed slavery and were committed to preventing it spreading into non-slave states—they would not accept a territory into the Union if it allowed slavery. Many Southern states saw this as an infringement of their democratic rights, and as a result, between December 1860 and June 1861, eleven Southern states seceded from the Union. On February 18, twenty-four days before Lincoln became president, Jefferson Davis was sworn into office in Montgomery, Alabama, as Interim President of the Confederacy.

Initially, opinion in Virginia was divided. Although the state had voted overwhelmingly against Lincoln in the presidential election, they were loath to leave the Union. In effect Virginia was pro-Union and pro-slavery. On April 4, Virginian delegates voted against secession, but in those states that had already declared secession tensions were rising, and just before dawn on April 12, 1861, Confederate artillery bombarded the Union-held Fort Sumter in South Carolina marking the start of the Civil War.

The start of hostilities became the major topic of conversation, as people argued for and against secession and debated what practical effect it would have on their lives. President Lincoln's immediate response was to call for seventy-five thousand volunteers to help crush the opposition in the South. The question raised at the Virginia Convention was whether Virginia should provide her quota of troops to fight against the South or secede from the Union. On April 17, the Convention voted to secede.[18]

The Dears and the residents of Mount Gilead were staunch Confederates and committed to fight for their state's rights. In a statewide Secession Referendum held in May, their precinct voted 102 to 19 in favor of leaving the Union.[19]

Throughout the US Army, Southern officers and men were deciding where their allegiance lay—to serve state or nation. General Robert E. Lee was recognized by both Democrats and Republicans as one of the most able officers in America. He was a Virginian, but he opposed secession. However, he also firmly believed in a state's democratic right to determine its own destiny. When faced with the choice between state and nation, Lee chose state, and after a period as military adviser to the Confederate president, he took command of the Army of Northern Virginia in June 1862.

CHAPTER 3

The Civil War, the Early Years: 1861–1863

THREE WEEKS AFTER VIRGINIA LEFT THE UNION, THE GOVERNOR OF Virginia granted Eppa Hunton, an attorney from Prince William County, the commission of colonel and ordered him to raise, organize, and train a company of infantry from the Loudoun area.[1] Recruitment posters were displayed around the county and temporary recruitment centers were set up. One center was in Mount Gilead.

This was an emotional and traumatic time for the Dear family. On July 6, JW celebrated his sixteenth birthday; six days later Sarah gave birth to her eighth child, Frank, and the next day their eldest son, Thomas, signed up to fight for the Confederacy. The eighteen-year-old joined Company I of the newly formed 8th Virginia Infantry under the command of the Dears' landlord, Captain James Simpson.[2]

A week later Thomas Dear was twenty-two miles away taking part in the first battle of the Civil War, the Battle of Manassas. Much to the Dear family's relief the raw Confederate army prevailed, and the demoralized Union army returned to Washington, DC, in disarray.[3] When young men like Thomas joined the Confederate army to serve their state and fight for a cause they and their families passionately supported, most thought the war would last for no more than a few months. They were confident the issues would be resolved before Christmas; few thought it would last for four long, brutal years and take the lives of more than six hundred thousand Americans.[4]

During the early days of the war the Army of Northern Virginia made steady progress, and as news of its successes filtered through to the local population, this, coupled with the knowledge that Thomas had survived, gave cause for optimism and hope in the Dear household. But that was replaced by a growing acceptance that it was likely to be a long, drawn-out struggle which would involve much hardship and sacrifice on the part of the civilian population, particularly for those who lived on the front line, like the Dear family.

By mid-March 1862, Union troops occupied Loudoun. Schools and churches were forced to close, and supplies of goods of all kinds were disrupted. Sarah had four children under the age of thirteen to care for, and, with her eldest daughter Frances's help, she made most of the family's clothes. She had the further responsibility of homeschooling her children. She encouraged them to read, and JW in particular devoured books voraciously; he was hungry for knowledge and even at that young age, loved poetry and was driven to better himself. Newspapers and public gatherings were banned, and food shortages became a major problem. The family also worried about Thomas, who was now risking his life fighting for the South. Life for the Dears and many families like them was a constant struggle.

In addition to the fall in living standards, residents lived in fear of their neighbors spying on them and reporting them to the authorities. Loudoun was bound on three sides by Union states and the county's loyalties were divided between the two rival national governments: in the south there was strong support for the Confederates; in the north, where the German and Quaker communities had settled, there was more pro-Union sentiment. As the war progressed, sympathy for the Union cause in northern Loudoun translated into the formation of a local militia, which became known as the Loudoun Rangers, or sometimes as "Means's Men" after their commander, Captain Samuel Carrington Means.[5]

In August, Captain James Simpson and his brother John returned to Mount Gilead on a recruiting campaign. The brothers stayed at the home of the Dears, and on the morning of August 16, just after John Simpson had left, a detachment of Means's Men approached the cottage looking for the brothers.[6] The *Alexandria Gazette* reported that:

Sarah Dear rushed to warn James Simpson, shouting Captain, the Yankees are coming! This so alarmed him he ran out of the house . . . bareheaded and still carrying the newspaper he was reading. The rogues had no sooner seen him than they began to yell the foulest execrations such as "there is the damned rebel—shoot the damned rascal—shoot him, shoot him," and not once did they call him to halt but began firing. One bullet hit him in the knee which threw him to the ground where he lay on his face until the murderers rode up, and without any sense of shame or humanity, fired a volley at his head, six shots of which took effect in the back of his head and neck. And after that one villainous rascal went to him, and finding some sign of life yet remaining, placed his revolver at his head and fired again, and then remarked to a gentleman whom the noise had attracted to the scene [George Dear, who was later brought to Richmond to testify against the perpetrator of this crime], that his name was Alfonzo Webster, and he wished the world to know that he assisted in killing the rebel Simpson. The party then turned out his pockets and took $2,000—Simpson's recruiting expenses and his gold watch. They sent word to his wife to come and bury him and rode on pilfering, arresting peaceable citizens and stealing all the horses they could find on their march.[7]

Simpson was buried in the cemetery of the North Fork Baptist Church, a mile from the scene of his murder, where his gravestone can still be seen today. His family and friends later gained their retribution when twenty-five-year-old Alfonzo Webster went to the gallows at Camp Lee in Richmond the following April, tied to a chair, as he had fractured his ankle and crippled his spine while trying to escape from imprisonment.[8]

At the start of the war JW was a skinny, fifteen-year-old youth with a mop of unruly black hair. He attended the local school, where evidence suggests he was an able and diligent student who led a happy, carefree existence, riding, playing with friends, and helping his parents around the farm.

But JW witnessed Simpson's brutal murder. Exposed to the horrors of war he matured rapidly and by early 1863 was unrecognizable from the callow teenager at the start of the war. As he approached his

The earliest known photograph of JW in 1864, age nineteen. Given to James J. Williamson by JW's brother Clay for his book, *Mosby's Rangers* (New York: Ralph B. Kenyon, 1896), 84.

eighteenth birthday, he began to think how best to serve the Confederate cause. Should he join his brother Thomas and the 8th Virginia Infantry, or should he follow the lead of his Uncle Amos's eldest son, his cousin Charlie Dear, and other friends who had joined a recently formed partisan resistance force under the command of Captain John Singleton Mosby?

He knew from Thomas's stories that life in the regular army meant low pay, hardship, and weeks, often months, of inactivity and boredom, interspersed only by an occasional set piece battle. Mosby on the other hand offered the exciting prospect of daily engagement with the enemy, with the added benefit of being able to live at home and support his family. As JW was pondering his options in the spring of 1863, Thomas, and the 8th Virginia Infantry, which was now part of Brigadier General Garnett's Brigade, were ordered to join General Lee and the main Confederate army at Culpeper for its planned advance into the Union stronghold of Maryland and Pennsylvania.[9]

CHAPTER 4

Mosby, JW, and the Rangers

OVER THE CHRISTMAS OF 1862, WHILE CORPORAL THOMAS DEAR WAS serving with Garnett's Brigade defending Richmond, and General Lee and the main Confederate army were enjoying a series of successes against the Union army, a young Confederate officer was about to change how the war was fought in the Northern Virginia counties of Fairfax, Prince William, Fauquier, and Loudoun, a Confederate stronghold of sixty-six thousand souls, of which 40 percent were slaves.[1]

Twenty-nine-year-old Captain Mosby was convinced that a partisan guerrilla force would make a significant contribution to the Confederate war effort. His concept was that well-disciplined patriots on horseback, making lightning strikes and then melting away into civilian life, could inflict serious damage on Union troops and their supply lines and tie up valuable Union resources.

Mosby's command was conceived on December 29, 1862, in the drawing room at Oakham, Hamilton Rogers's grand Greek Revival building on his large plantation east of Middleburg, and eight miles south of JW's family home in Mount Gilead. The Rogerses were well established in the commercial and agricultural worlds of Northern Virginia and were fiercely loyal to the Southern cause. Therefore, it was to the Confederate stronghold of Oakham that General J.E.B. "Jeb" Stuart and his staff retreated after a raid behind enemy lines in Fauquier County. On that morning Mosby, then a scout on Stuart's staff, broached the subject of taking a few men under his direction to continue to scout and

Captain John Singleton Mosby in 1863. He single-handedly changed the face of warfare in Northern Virginia. Courtesy of *Documenting the American South*, Libraries of the University of North Carolina, Chapel Hill.

harass the Union army over the winter when the cavalry went into winter quarters.

Mosby had already proved the value of a small band of men moving undetected and with speed in gathering intelligence. He had in the past proposed similar ventures to Stuart, but this time Stuart agreed, and when the cavalry departed Oakham on December 30, nine men stayed behind with Mosby. He told them to find lodgings in the vicinity, no more than two men to a family, and to report to him ten days later. In the meantime, he would scout alone to spy on the enemy and look for opportunities to engage. This established the peculiar pattern of warfare he adopted, where his formidable fighters dispersed among the local population, ready to be summoned at any moment mounted in uniform on some of the best and fastest horses in the district.

This small band grew into the 43rd Battalion of the Virginia Cavalry, more commonly known as Mosby's Rangers, and became one of the most famous units—celebrated and reviled in equal measure—in either army. It was the brainchild of a singular man, a small, slight, wiry individual, apparently unassuming, but whose restless energy, careful planning, and ferocious appetite for the fray made him a formidable opponent and imbued in those he commanded an unusual devotion. His relentless attrition on wagon trains, army camps, pickets, stragglers, and railroad lines and the frequency of his attacks—often miles apart and in the early hours of the morning—multiplied his attributes in the eyes of the enemy until his reputation became as feared as his actual achievements. He was the "Gray Ghost" of the Confederate army in Northern Virginia, emerging out of the darkness of the night or the early morning mist, an avenging force of rangers at his heels, six-shooters blazing, the air rent with the blood-curdling rebel yell.

The first engagement of Mosby's little band was a success, with three strikes over two days in mid-January 1863. They were on outposts of various cavalry units yielding Union prisoners, horses, and equipment, which Mosby took to Stuart's camp near Fredericksburg. A clearly delighted Stuart allowed Mosby to increase his band of marauders to fifteen.[2]

Not long after those initial raids, and with press reports on Mosby's exploits building, men from neighboring counties and those home on leave sought to join his command. This loose, changing formation of up to fifty men became known as "Mosby's Conglomerates." On March 23, Mosby's position was formalized when President Davis appointed him Captain of Partisan Rangers with the instruction to "proceed at once to organize your company."[3]

By the end of the war, two thousand men had served with Mosby. Many were from the farms of Loudoun, Fauquier, Fairfax, and Prince William Counties, but they were leavened by university-trained men, men from wealthy mercantile and plantation families, and professional men. There were even a few foreign adventurers. Charlie Dear, JW's cousin, was the first of JW's family and friends to join Mosby. Charlie left the Virginia Military Institute to reputedly become Mosby's nineteenth recruit.

The Conscription Law, passed in April 1862, declared that all able-bodied white male Southern citizens between the ages of eighteen and thirty-five were required to serve the Confederacy for three years. During the spring of 1863, JW's family and friends spoke of little else than Mosby and the success of his Rangers. Cousin Charlie had already signed up, and several of JW's friends were planning to enlist. By midsummer, JW had made up his mind. He was attracted by the action and excitement offered by the Rangers and by the opportunity to fight alongside fellow Northern Virginians in defense of their homes. On July 6, his eighteenth birthday, JW joined Mosby.

Three days earlier General Lee's fateful decision to advance into Union territory had been halted at one of the most famous battles in the history of war: the Battle of Gettysburg. On the third day of the battle Brigadier General Garnett's Brigade, which included Thomas Dear and the 8th Virginia Infantry, attacked the Union-held Cemetery Ridge. By the end of the day more than seven thousand young men lay dead, scattered over fields, hills, and in the woods around Gettysburg. Colonel Hunton, Thomas's regimental commander, wrote:

> [General] Garnett was killed when near the first line of the enemy, gallantly leading his men. They got up to within a few yards of the first line of the enemy . . . [but] Federal reinforcements came up, and thus ended the charge of July 3—a charge that will go down in history as the most gallant ever made by any army. . . . My dear old regiment, [The Bloody Eighth], laid down under fire during the artillery duel 205 strong. Five of them were killed in the artillery duel, and 200 responded promptly

Charlie Dear, JW's cousin, took part in many of the Rangers' most dangerous raids.
Eugenia Newberg

and bravely to the order to charge. After the charge . . . only 10 of those who went in responded to the roll call—190 out of 200 were gone.[4]

News of the defeat and the enormity of the Confederate losses reached the Dear home on July 9, but it would be weeks, probably months, before the family knew for sure that Thomas would never return home; until then they lived in hope. No one who survived, in the smoke and mayhem of the battlefield, saw Thomas die, and his body and that of his brigade commander, General Garnett, were never identified. For seven months after the battle the muster rolls of the 8th Virginia Infantry listed Thomas as missing, hoping he would be found on a list of wounded in a Union hospital. In February 1864, the family finally accepted he was dead. Thomas's death left its mark on JW but did nothing to dampen his commitment to the Confederate cause.

Those wishing to join Mosby were first subjected to his scrutiny: each recruit was interviewed by him personally. "He would stare into a man's face, watch his eyes, and instinctively judge his worth."[5] JW passed muster in July 1863 and was initially assigned to the conglomerates, those waiting to join a company. During the next eight months he was involved in numerous raids and skirmishes, but it was not until March 28, 1864, when Company D was formed in Leesburg, that JW was officially registered as a Mosby Ranger.[6]

Such was the attraction of joining Mosby that officers from other commands resigned their commissions to enlist as privates. In Company D among JW's fellow privates were a former captain of his brother's old regiment, the 8th Virginia Infantry; five doctors; two future judges; and two grandsons of US presidents.[7] For JW, hailing from a small farming community, becoming part of this eclectic mix of people from all walks of life and social backgrounds broadened his horizons and gave him a confidence and polish that stood him in good stead in the years to come.

The Ranger pattern of warfare, constant raiding, engaging the enemy sometimes daily, was far removed from the experience of those in the regular army, with their infrequent set piece battles followed by months of boredom and inaction.[8] On their way to a raid, Mosby encouraged informality, with Rangers riding up and down the line talking to friends, telling stories, and singing together; they only ever formed a line when masquerading as Union cavalry.[9] When faced with the enemy, the style of battle of the Rangers was the opposite of every tactical manual, a horse race as each man vied to beat the other to the enemy lines, adrenalin pumping, pistols firing, the rebel yell a fearful accompaniment. Mosby encouraged individuality and rewarded bravery with an additional share from the spoils of war.

Three other young Virginians who joined Mosby at the same time as JW would become his friends and play important roles in his life. Walter Whaley, who lived with his parents on the Royal Oaks estate in Centreville, which Rangers occasionally used as a safe house, joined Mosby in July.

Sam Rogers, another of Mosby's early recruits, was JW's neighbor and closest friend. He lived with his widowed mother and four siblings at Willow Cottage, a two-story, stone farmhouse a few miles from the Dears' home at Mount Gilead, where they farmed one hundred fifty acres of prime land. The Rogerses' ancestors had emigrated from Ireland in the middle of the eighteenth century, and Sam's branch of the extended family had lived in Willow Cottage since the 1780s—the house is still owned by the family today. They were well-established and respected members of the local community, who, like the Dears, worshiped at the North Fork Baptist Church. Sam and JW were the same age; both were outstanding horsemen and soon became inseparable.

During the war years, when both JW and Sam fought with Mosby, JW was a regular visitor to Willow Cottage, where he got to know Sam's sister, Mary Ann, who was affectionately known by her family and JW as Mamie, and sometimes Mollie. Although the pattern of their lives after the war meant they saw each other infrequently, over the years their friendship blossomed.

Sam's friend, Adolphus "Dolly" Richards, came from a monied and influential local family who lived at Green Garden, a fine country estate outside Upperville in Fauquier County. He was a charismatic character and a natural leader, who, despite his youth, rose to become Mosby's third

Sam Rogers, JW's friend and fellow Mosby Ranger, who lived at Willow Cottage a few miles north of JW's home in Mount Gilead. Patty Rogers

in command. Three years after the end of the war, Dolly's elder brother, Burr, was instrumental in helping change the course of JW's life.

The last of JW's immediate circle to join Mosby was his younger brother, Clay, who despite being underage persuaded his parents to allow him to join Mosby toward the end of the war. After the war he wrote:

Sam's sister, Mary Ann Rogers. Eugenia Newberg

I went to Captain Glascock shortly after I saw my brother captured and asked to be allowed to take his place in Company D. He refused on account of my youth (I was then but a schoolboy), but finally gave me permission to go with the company, which I did, up to the end of the war. Through the kindness of the men I was given a place behind my big cousin, Charlie Dear, which always brought me into the second or third "fours" in time of danger.[10]

JW's younger brother, Clay Dear, in uniform, aged seventeen. Photographed in December 1864. Given to James J. Williamson by Clay for his book, *Mosby's Rangers* (New York: Ralph B. Kenyon, 1896), 84.

The lives of these six young men, JW, Charlie, Clay, Sam, Walter, and Dolly, were shaped by Mosby's leadership style and the unique demands of being a Ranger. For Mosby, with his loose band of "renegades and cutthroats," as they were called by Union soldiers, complete control over his men was essential. He needed his officers to be bold, fearless, as aggressive as he was, and to be beholden to him only and not to the men under them.[11]

To join the Rangers, a man had to have his own horse. Unlike their Union counterparts, most Southerners were good riders from boyhood who needed no training. Those from rural communities, like JW, Clay, and their cousin Charlie, had been raised with horses. Now they were their lifeline: the faster and more robust the animal, the better to overhaul the enemy in the charge or to escape from pursuit. Many Rangers had excellent animals with famous pedigrees; Loudoun County was a breeding ground for fine horses.[12]

There was little or no drill. The saber, the classic weapon of the cavalry, was abandoned early in favor of the five- or six-shot pistol, and most Rangers carried at least two, giving them ten or twelve shots before reloading. Pistol practice was one of the few drills they were happy to indulge. "It was no uncommon thing for one of our men to gallop by a tree at full tilt, and put three bullets into its trunk in succession."[13]

"These . . . conditions . . . demanded that men should be expert in the use of their weapon. Uncle Sam's ordnance department supplied them abundantly with ammunition and much of it was consumed in target practice. This deadly aptness with the revolver not only reacted on our men and gave them nerve and self-confidence, but it increased their efficiency and formidability."[14]

There is little doubt that JW's skill as a horseman and prowess with a six-shooter stood him in good stead in later years when he lived among the Indians and the iron men of the Western frontier.[15]

For the first few years of the war the Union cavalry, never given much credence as an offensive force and largely confined to scouting and picket duties, was no match for Confederate horsemen and was easily broken. By mid-1863 it was a very different matter, as the Union cavalry had become a formidable, well-trained force.[16]

The average age of a Ranger was twenty-three, but ages ranged from sixteen to late fifties.[17] Mosby had a fondness for his youngest Rangers. Bad habits had not been instilled in them by other commands; their only way was his way.

Mosby's command was in existence for twenty-eight months, but it had a lasting impact on the social and political development of "Mosby's Confederacy" in the period immediately after the Civil War, when old animosities and grudges often continued for many years. Although around two thousand served with Mosby, his command at any one time never exceeded four hundred.[18] For those who joined Mosby, like JW's circle of six, it was an experience that marked them for life. They were treated as heroes by the local community, and the camaraderie forged by shared experiences and their utter reliance on each other made lifelong friendships. For many it was the most exciting period of their lives. Their post-war reunions were always well attended, and some rangers, fifty years after the war had ended, chose to be buried in their Confederate gray uniforms. Many years later, in the remote West, JW was still described by a local newspaper as "once one of the most daring of Mosby's men."[19]

CHAPTER 5

JW's War: 1863–1865

AFTER THE DEFEAT AT GETTYSBURG, THE ONCE INVINCIBLE ARMY OF Northern Virginia was on the defensive. With Union troops once more on Virginian soil, life for the Dear family became increasingly difficult. Thomas was dead and JW, their eldest surviving son, was involved in a particularly brutal guerrilla war. Summoned by Mosby to a command meeting, he disappeared, sometimes for days on end, to return saddle-weary and hungry, dusty, muddy, or frozen as the seasons changed, before mounting up once again. The war was taking its toll not only on the combatants but also their families as they struggled to put food on the table while regular troops and gangs of deserters pillaged local farms.

As the two armies settled in for a more static war the Rangers found the conditions for their style of warfare ideal. Throughout the fall of 1863 and into 1864 Mosby and his partisan guerrillas harried and harassed Union troops, whether they were billeted in the county or passing through to support the war effort farther south. They tied up valuable Union resources and caused such disruption that the reputation of Mosby and his men rose in tandem with the anger and irritation his attacks caused the Union high command.

In August 1864, things came finally to a head. That month, five hundred twenty fully loaded, lightly guarded wagons trundled slowly south from Harpers Ferry in West Virginia to resupply General Philip Henry Sheridan's army as he fought to remove Confederate troops from the Shenandoah Valley. The wagons and their accompanying troops were allowed to stretch out, making them vulnerable to attack, which was reported to Mosby's scouts. When the wagon train reached Berry-ville twenty miles south of Harpers Ferry, Mosby struck, and three hundred Rangers swooped down on the wagons yelling and firing their six-shooters. The resulting Union loss was six dead, nine wounded, and two hundred captured. More than forty wagons were looted and burned, and four hundred mules, two hundred cattle, and thirty-six horses taken. Two Rangers were killed and three wounded. Mosby's strike unleashed a hornet's nest in retaliation.[1]

Before the wagon train had set out, Sheridan, who had just been pro-moted from Cavalry Corps Commander to Commander of the Army of the Shenandoah, had heard from his garrison command at Harpers Ferry that "Mosby is already between Harper's Ferry and your command." He reacted savagely, ordering the cavalry to head without delay south toward Middleburg to "exterminate as many of Mosby's gang as they can."[2]

The Commander of the Union Army, General Ulysses Grant, was also annoyed by the persistence in harrying federal supply lines by the Rangers and the number of men required to guard against their depreda-tions. Hearing of the wagon train raid, he wrote to Sheridan on August 16 in an equally ferocious vein. "The families of Mosby's men are known and can be collected. I think they should be taken and kept at Fort McHenry or some secure place as hostages for good conduct of Mosby and his men. When any of them are caught with nothing to designate what they are, hang them without trial."[3]

The gloves were off, and the war descended into savagery. Sheridan replied the next day: "Mosby has annoyed me and captured a few wagons. We hung one and shot six of his men yesterday." Three days later he wrote again that "Guerrillas give me great annoyance but I am quietly disposing of numbers of them."[4] It transpired later that none of the men, in Sher-idan's chilling phrase, "quietly disposed of" were members of Mosby's command. Retaliation shaded into revenge. As a scorched-earth policy took effect, tensions heightened as crops were burned and livestock taken to prevent the resupply of the Confederate army.

In the first weeks of September, the Rangers killed and captured many Union soldiers. Mosby was wounded by a bullet in the groin and left the command in the hands of his second-in-command while he

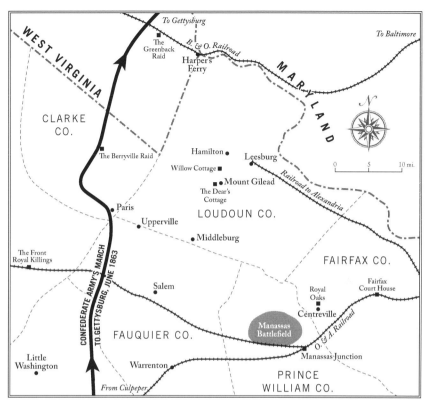

Map 1. JW's Virginia and Mosby's Confederacy.

recuperated at home. On the morning of September 23, six Rangers, three of them from JW's Company D, were captured in a brief engagement a few miles south of Front Royal. With hatred of the Rangers at a fever pitch they faced summary execution. Three were shot dead. Two others were first taunted by their captors and having refused to divulge Mosby's whereabouts, were hanged. Union troops hung a placard on one of the dead men that read "Such is the fate of all of Mosby's men."

The sixth to die that day was a seventeen-year-old from Front Royal, Henry Rhodes, who, having heard the Rangers were nearby, had borrowed a neighbor's horse to ride with them. The horse broke down and he was captured. Two cavalrymen tied Rhodes's arms to their saddles and dragged him through the town past his home, where his distraught mother ran out to plead for his life. The troopers cantered on, the barely conscious body bucking and bumping in the roadway between them. In a field north of the town he was cut loose, and a large crowd of soldiers gathered. As a band played "Love Not, the One You Love May Die," a soldier emptied his pistol into the prostrate boy. Three weeks later the execution of a seventh Ranger, a Baptist ministerial student, was particularly barbaric. He was tied to the top of a bent-back poplar tree, which was then released, catapulting him into the air and breaking his neck.[5]

The deaths of the seven men and the manner of their dying were never forgotten. Thirty-five years after the killings, more than two hundred Rangers returned to Front Royal to dedicate a monument that bears the names of the men who were executed that day. It was the largest gathering of Mosby's men since the disbandment in 1865, and a crowd of more than five thousand watched the ceremony.[6]

Three weeks after the Front Royal executions, Mosby, with a force of eighty-four Rangers, which included Company D, struck the railroad near Duffield's station in West Virginia, derailing a train. JW, Clay, and Charlie all took part in the audacious raid, with Charlie playing a crucial role. The incident became known as the Greenback Raid and was to become one of the most celebrated and talked about of all of Mosby's engagements.

Among the booty from the train, Charlie discovered and took $173,000 contained in a strongbox and satchel from two army paymasters. After the raid Charlie and two others crossed the Shenandoah into Loudoun County, where the next day the men who had been on the raid shared the proceeds at the Ebenezer Church near Bloomfield, eight miles from the Dear home in Mount Gilead. The following day Mosby wrote to his wife, Pauline, describing the raid: "A great many ludicrous incidents occurred. One lady ran up to me and exclaimed, 'Oh, my father is a Mason!' I had no time to say anything but, 'I can't help it.'"

Mosby's letter continued, "Charlie Dear and West Aldridge . . . reported that they had two U.S. Paymasters with their satchels of greenbacks. Knowing it would be safer to send them out by a small party, which could easily elude the enemy, one of my lieutenants . . . was detailed with two or three men to take them over the ridge to our rendezvous."[7]

Mosby justified such actions in his memoirs. "My command was organized under an act of the Confederate Congress to raise partisan corps; it applied the principle of maritime prize law to land war. Of course, the motive of the act was to stimulate enterprise."[8] Each man received over $2,000, a vast sum when compared with a Confederate private's pay of $18 per month, if he was paid, and in Union money, not quite so susceptible to hyperinflation as the Confederate dollar, which was virtually worthless by the end of the war.

The Front Royal killings and other brutal executions outraged Mosby. He was convinced that a member of General Sheridan's senior commanders, George Armstrong Custer, was responsible. Whenever his men captured Union soldiers, he ordered them to separate those belonging to Custer's command. Toward the end of October, Mosby wrote to General Lee describing the execution of seven of his men and asked Lee's sanction for the execution of an equal number from Custer's command. Lee concurred, as did Secretary of War James Alexander Seddon, who approved "[Lee's] instructions to hang an equal number of General Custer's men in retaliation."[9]

On November 5, Captain "Dolly" Richards returned from a raid with fourteen men from Custer's command to add to thirteen already held. The Rangers met the next day at Rectortown, and the twenty-seven prisoners were drawn up in a line and told seven were going to be selected for execution by drawing lots from a hat.

The condemned men were taken to a spot on the Valley Turnpike, as close to Sheridan's headquarters as was safe, to be executed. They were roped together and set off into a dark and rainy night. Things did not go according to plan. Three were hanged, two shot, and two escaped, but the two who had been shot had not been killed and were taken in due course to a federal hospital. A note was pinned to one of the hanged men that said "These men have been hung in retaliation for an equal number of Colonel Mosby's men hung by order of [Colonel] Custer at Front Royal. Measure for Measure."[10]

In the fall of 1864, in a desperate attempt to crush the Rangers, Sheridan established a unit of one hundred men operating along the Blue Ridge between Loudoun and the Shenandoah River with specific orders to "clean out Mosby's men." They were armed with seven-shot Spencer carbines and lived off the land like their guerrilla opponents, often wearing Confederate gray uniforms to mask their identity. They were under the command of Captain Richard Blazer and became known as Blazer's Scouts. Blazer and his men caused considerable damage to the command, and Dolly Richards and three hundred Rangers were dispatched to hunt them down. On November 18, they found Blazer and his unit of sixty-two scouts near Kabletown in West Virginia. Blazer was captured and twenty-two of his men killed or wounded.[11]

Three days later JW was in the saddle again and on the move with Company D, capturing nineteen prisoners and seventeen mules, and a week later he was involved in a skirmish just outside Leesburg between Company D and three dozen of Means's Men. His commander was shot in the head and killed, a brutal reminder of the precarious life he was living.

General Grant was becoming increasingly irritated by Mosby's activities. Specially created units and constant cavalry sweeps of Mosby's Confederacy had proved ineffective in eradicating his command, so in late October he wrote to Sheridan "there is no doubt of the necessity of clearing out [Western Loudoun County] so it will not support Mosby's gang. . . . So long as the war lasts, they must be prevented from raising another crop."[12]

Sheridan was occupied with his battles in the Shenandoah Valley, so it was not until late November that he had the necessary troops ready to act on Grant's instructions and to switch from hunting partisan guerrillas to targeting the civilians who supported them. On November 26, with Abraham Lincoln reelected and Thanksgiving over, Sheridan wrote to Grant's chief of staff stating: "I will soon commence work on Mosby. Heretofore I have made no attempt to track him up, as I would have employed ten men to his one. . . . Now, there is going to be an intense hatred of him in that portion of the Valley which is nearly a desert. I will soon commence on Loudoun County, and let them know there is a God in Israel."[13]

He was going to starve them, and their families. The next day Sheridan ordered Colonel Wesley Merritt, commander of the 1st Cavalry Division, to proceed to an area comprising Loudoun and parts of Fairfax and Fauquier Counties, which he described as a "hotbed of lawless bands, who have, from time to time depredated upon small parties on the line of army communications, on safeguards left at houses, and on small parties of our troops . . . you will consume and destroy all forage and subsistence, burn all barns and mills, and their contents, and drive off all stock in the region." The Dear family, in the heart of Loudoun County and already suffering from the deprivations of war, now faced destitution.

Sheridan gave Merritt five days to complete his task. The Burning Raid had begun, and Merritt's Second Brigade struck Mount Gilead and Circleville on Wednesday, November 30.[14] As news of the approaching troops reached the area, the Dear family and other residents hid their horses in nearby woods. Merritt's men descended upon them, corralled their livestock, which was moved on the hoof along the turnpike to West Virginia, and burned everything they could, sparing only—but not always—private homes. That evening local miller Will Brown counted one hundred fifty fires in the area as mills, barns, and crops were razed to the ground, and a local farmer's daughter described what she saw from a hill behind the family farm:

> I beheld a sight I hope I may never look upon again. The barns and stockyards of all our neighbors and some of their dwellings were burning as far as the eye could reach, towards Mount Gilead, Leesburg and Waterford smokes were rising in volumes, telling the work of destruction that was going on. And now at night the sky, all round the horizon, looks like a sunset reflection in the sky.[15]

As several thousand troops in three brigades methodically swept the country, dense columns of smoke marked their progress. Returning to camp on December 2, Merritt reported to Sheridan, "from 5,000–6,000 head of cattle, 3,000–4,000 head of sheep, and 500–700 horses had been driven off, while 1,000 head of hogs had been slaughtered." Only one of the three brigades gave a detailed report, which listed as destroyed 230 barns, eight mills, a distillery, 10,000 tons of hay, and 250,000 bushels of grain. In Mount Gilead, Coe's Mill was burned, and crops and livestock taken.

Mount Gilead's residents and the Dear family lost most of what they owned, and the Rangers could only watch helplessly, shadowing the Union troops from afar. Here and there they managed to save livestock from capture by driving them into hiding ahead of the marauding troops. The number they saved was very small, but the sense of injustice and loathing they felt toward their aggressors was great, and it was a long time before the wounds healed.

The winter of 1864–1865 was particularly severe, and "with the County . . . almost cleared of provisions [the people suffered] all the miserable privations of war."[16]

Early in January, JW and Company D under Dolly's command were in action again in freezing weather, harassing enemy troops. A few weeks later sixty men derailed a train on the Baltimore and Ohio Railroad garnering a welcome cornucopia of delicacies, taking as much food, drink, and coffee as they could carry. It was dubbed the "Coffee Raid" by the men. It would also be JW's last raid of the war.

CHAPTER 6

Fort McHenry and the End of the Rangers

THE RANGERS WERE LARGELY MADE UP OF YOUNG MEN WHO, GIVEN THE returns made from the spoils of war, particularly those who had benefited from the Greenback Raid, had money to burn. As a result, with most of the other young men of the district away in the regular army, they had free rein with the belles of the Confederacy. "When not on duty the men enjoyed various diversions—horse-races, card parties and dances principally. The belles of Virginia were abundant, and beaux were plentiful. The dangers that surrounded them gave zest and piquancy to their sports and frolics. There was not an unmarried man in Mosby's Confederacy who did not have one sweetheart at least, and some had more than their share."[1]

Part of their bounty was spent on dressing up, ordering fancy uniforms at great cost to impress their ladies.[2] JW became caught up in the excitement and "sent north" for his own suit, and it was in this splendid outfit, on his way to an assignation with a lady, that he was shot and captured. On February 3, he and his friend and fellow Ranger Tom King were within sight of JW's home when they encountered a troop of Means's Men. After the war Clay recounted:

My brother . . . and Tom King, were captured by Means's Men near our home in the vicinity of Mount Gilead, in February 1865. . . . They had just decked themselves out in their new $200 suits smuggled from Baltimore, to call on some ladies in Leesburg, when the enemy came upon them. They took to the woods, but finding escape impossible, made a stand-up fight before surrendering. Willie had previously been shot in the leg. For their gallant resistance they were sent to Fort McHenry, not to be exchanged during the war.[3]

A few days after JW's capture Union troops ransacked Green Garden, Dolly Richards's family home, while he and another Ranger hid in a secret closet. Among the booty the soldiers took were their clothes, including Dolly's new uniform, also just received from Baltimore.

Two days after JW's arrest a bellicose General Sheridan issued instructions: "That neighborhood has of late been infested with guerrillas. . . . The commanding officer . . . will send out parties to scour the country and dispose of the *lawless ruffians* who are committing the outrages spoken of. No quarter will be given these persons who have destroyed by their actions the right to be treated as prisoners of war." Around this time two eighteen-year-old Confederate soldiers, James Washington and Herbert Alexander, were caught while on leave visiting their mothers. Sheridan demanded that their families should be punished, their stock should be driven off, and their fence rails burned.

The two young men joined JW, Tom King, and thirteen other Confederate prisoners on their sixty-mile journey to Fort McHenry in Baltimore Harbor, where the sad little group arrived on February 8, 1865. Five days later the *Baltimore American* reported that they had arrived in the city and were listed by name and regiment and being "considered of the worst character," were to be kept in confinement and receive "nothing but the army ration." The conditions they had to endure were horrific and proved to be too much for Washington and Alexander, who were "cast into a cold, damp and cheerless dungeon at Fort McHenry, and so cruelly and inhumanely treated that in a few weeks death relieved them of their sufferings."[4]

JW was, as far as the Federals were concerned, a guerrilla who had been captured after a gun battle and was the only known Mosby Ranger among the seventeen prisoners.[5] His treatment was considerably harsher than theirs.

The only records that survived JW's four months in prison are his signing in and out dates and his purchases at the prison store—tobacco,

Fort McHenry in 1864, showing a detachment of Confederate prisoners being escorted into captivity. JW marched down this avenue on February 8, 1865. Anne S.K. Brown Military Collection, Brown University Library

pints of molasses, coffee, stamps, envelopes, candles, and five buttons. It is surprising he had money to pay for them when normal practice was for a prisoner to be stripped of anything valuable: his watch, boots, money, even his uniform if better than his captor's.[6] Life for a guerrilla in a federal prison was not comfortable.

JW's prison, Fort McHenry, was completed in 1800 on a peninsula south of Baltimore as a pentagonal star fort to defend the approach to Baltimore Harbor. Bombarded by the British fleet in 1814, it withstood the siege and the following morning defiantly flew the "Stars and Stripes." The sight of the flag flying in "the dawn's early light" prompted Francis Scott Key to write the poem "Defence of Fort M'Henry," which when set to music became the national anthem of the United States, "The Star-Spangled Banner."

During the Civil War the entrance to the army camp and the fort beyond was an imposing gate set in a wall at the end of a dead straight road leading southeast from the city. JW and his fellow prisoners were marched through these gates and down the broad gravel avenue that led to the fort. To the left, a pair of two-story brick buildings stood within a stockade on the outer face, of which a wooden walkway had been constructed for armed soldiers to patrol.

A Confederate prisoner described the conditions in those buildings. "Our quarters were in an old brick stable. . . . In the dark hole, on the first floor, were confined some of the most villainous cutthroats it has ever been my misfortune to meet. They were convicted of different crimes and had different terms to serve. All of them wore balls and chains, and they made night hideous with their curses, screams, and the rattling of the chains."[7]

While JW was imprisoned at Fort McHenry, President Abraham Lincoln was assassinated on April 14, 1865. A week later his body reached Baltimore on its way home to Springfield, Illinois, for burial. He lay in state on a decorated catafalque in the Baltimore Merchants Exchange building, the coffin opened to allow a portion of the vast crowds to view their assassinated president. All the city's buildings were draped in black, flags were enveloped in black crepe, and "the weather . . . was in consonance with the sad event . . . heavy clouds hung like a leaden pall over the city."[8]

In the afternoon Lincoln's remains were conveyed, without music, to the railroad's Washington Street depot. His body had been placed in a plate glass funeral car with the coffin on view to citizens who thronged the streets. The hearse was decorated with black plumes and pulled by four black horses. The 11th Indiana Volunteers, who were stationed at Fort McHenry, were part of the escort. Given the highly emotive events of the day, the body of the slain president, the grief of many thousands, the draped buildings and flags, the solemn tread of the thousands of troops, one wonders in what mood the 11th Indiana returned to Fort McHenry and their Confederate charges—and how JW fared on that day.

A bridge spans the moat and leads to the arched gateway of the fort. Immediately inside is a courtyard and guardroom off which a narrow corridor leads to three cells, each nine feet long by four feet wide. These cells could, at a severe pinch, each hold three men. The records do not list where in Fort McHenry JW was imprisoned. As a guerrilla he was probably placed in one of the three cells.

As JW struggled to survive in Fort McHenry, and the cold harsh weather of early 1865 gave way to spring, it was clear the once vaunted Army of Northern Virginia, without rations and for long unpaid, was no longer a formidable force. At the end of February, Sheridan had marched south to join Grant threatening Richmond, his cavalry divisions decimating the Confederate army and capturing railroads and canals that cut essential supply lines.

The noose gradually tightened around the Confederate army, but the Rangers remained active. On April 5, after years of provocation, they took their revenge on JW's nemesis, Means's Men, when a small command finally tracked them down and despite being outnumbered two to one, charged and routed the enemy, taking sixty-five prisoners and eighty-one horses. That was the end: "and thereafter . . . [Means's Men] . . . ceased to exist."[9]

The last action of the war for any of Mosby's command took place three days later on April 8. It was to be an inglorious end. Seventy-five Rangers, including Sam Rogers, Charlie Dear, and Clay Dear, met at Upperville, where they were briefed by Mosby. At daybreak the next day, under the command of Captain George Baylor, they arrived at their intended target. But the enemy had been forewarned, and they retreated the way they had come. Five miles into the return journey they were charged from the rear by Union soldiers who had been lying in wait. The Rangers were outnumbered, and they fled for the Occoquan River ten miles away. The various accounts of this last fight of the war differ, but Sam, Charlie, and Clay feature in all of them.

When the Rangers rallied to make a stand, all three stood their ground. A Ranger recalled that "in the retreat . . . a few determined men . . . H.C. Dear and a few others, formed a rear guard and saved many from death or capture. This brave little band, for four or five miles of the chase, exposed themselves, with reckless daring to save their comrades."

Captain Baylor's horse was shot in the nostrils and foreleg, which nearly unseated him. As he let go of the reins they trailed under the horse's hooves, tripping the animal and impeding Baylor's escape. Clay rode up alongside him and, stooping low in the saddle, secured the reins to allow his Captain to get away.[10] As they fled, Charlie's great friend Joe Bryan, looking behind him at the pursuit, saw Charlie fall from his saddle as his horse went down. Bryan thought, "Poor Charlie, you've gone at last."[11] Charlie had taken part in most of the great fights of the command, going back almost to the very beginning of operations in the Confederacy. But Charlie was remarkably lucky and tumbled down a steep depression in the ground where he was hidden from his pursuers. He eventually made it back to his safe house near Paris. Sam was not so fortunate; he was captured by the Federals and imprisoned in Elmira Prison in upstate New York. Remarkably, his horse returned home alone.

The following day, Sunday, April 9, General Lee surrendered at Appomattox. It was another two weeks before General Joseph Johnston, Lee's counterpart and the Confederate Commander of the South, signed surrender terms with General William Tecumseh Sherman in North Carolina. The process of returning Confederate prisoners to their homes began.

With conflicting rumors of what was happening in the different Confederate commands, most Rangers, like Charlie and Clay, stayed in their safe houses. JW, imprisoned in Fort McHenry, and Sam in Elmira Prison, heard from their captors of the Confederate surrender and waited to learn their fates.

On April 17, Mosby called his command together at Salem to discuss what course to take.[12] He briefed the men of developments, urged them to maintain the truce until the situation was clearer, and said those who wished to be paroled were free to do so. The next day, at a meeting of Union officers he was described as "like a highland chief coming to a lowland council."[13]

Three days later, Mosby again summoned his command to Salem. It was their last gathering as a Confederate army battalion. Mosby knew that the Federal army was hunting for them and that both the Rangers and citizens of Fauquier and Loudoun Counties, who had protected them for so long, were once more in danger.

The Rangers arrived in the mist and drizzle in their smartest uniforms and riding their best horses. Shortly before noon, when roughly two hundred men had gathered, they were ordered to form in ranks by company in a field just west of the village. A further two hundred

Rangers were still held in various federal prisons. Mosby inspected his troops for the last time and then, without a word, placed himself between William Chapman and Dolly Richards, in the center of the command, facing the men. His brother, William, the adjutant of the battalion, then read Mosby's farewell. "Soldiers! I have summoned you together for the last time. The vision we have cherished . . . has vanished. . . . I disband your organization. . . . I am now no longer your commander."[14]

At its conclusion the Rangers uttered three cheers for their commander. Tears flowed freely as each man said goodbye to his comrades and then turned his head toward home, and a very different life to come. Mosby stood at the edge of the roadway shaking the hand of each man as he passed. His fierce composure had at last cracked and he was "crying like a child." But he was not done yet, and he declared his intention to ride south to join Johnston's embattled army, which was still fighting. Fifty men elected to go with him. But before they could reach Johnston, he had surrendered, and the little force disbanded for the last time.[15]

More than two hundred Rangers rode to Winchester on April 22 to obtain their paroles. Many loyal Confederate soldiers held in POW camps delayed signing their parole papers, unsure of what was the right thing to do since some of their regiments were still active. It would be more than two months until the last of the Confederate commands surrendered.[16] Clay took the Oath of Allegiance five days later; JW signed on May 3 at Fort McHenry; Charlie waited until May 17 before traveling to Winchester to be paroled; and it was not until July 7 that Sam Rogers signed his Oath of Allegiance at Elmira Prison, the last of JW's group to be allowed home.[17]

JW's parole document stated, "J.W. Dear, Private, 43rd Virginia Cavalry of the County of Loudoun, State of Virginia, aged 19, dark complexion, 5 foot 9 ½ inches, black hair, black eyes, solemnly swore, in the Presence of Almighty God, to henceforth faithfully support, protect, and defend the Constitution of the United States." This acted as JW's passport home, to use for federal transportation and to draw food.[18]

He was released from Fort McHenry on May 23, a civilian once more, but a very different person from the young man who had joined Mosby in 1863. Over the preceding two years JW had experienced fear and excitement in equal measure, and this had tempered and matured him. He had formed lifelong friendships with the scions of established local families and had proved to himself that he was their equal. He left Fort McHenry with newfound confidence and a determination to use the money he had acquired as a Mosby Ranger to lift his struggling family out of poverty.

CHAPTER 7

Reconstruction and the *Virginia Sentinel*: 1865–1868

THE VIRGINIA THAT JW, CLAY, SAM, AND CHARLIE RETURNED TO WAS a desolate wasteland with barns and mills burned, homes plundered, and many farms totally destroyed. Fence rails had been used for firewood, crops had been taken or burned, livestock driven off, and all means of subsistence destroyed. Roads had been churned up and bridges demolished. Inflation was rampant, and prices, where goods were available, had risen to unaffordable levels.

The South, and Virginia in particular, had been devastated by war. Twenty percent of all Southern men between eighteen and forty-five were dead. Nearly everyone had lost someone close to them.[1] The South's plantation and slave-based economy had been decimated, and four million former enslaved people were now free; exports of tobacco, cotton, and molasses were down 90 percent; and the Confederate currency was worthless. The economic and political power of the South was a distant memory, and its citizens were struggling to survive in their war-ravaged states.

On his return home, JW found the residents of Mount Gilead starving and their farms a wasteland. His father had proved, in the best of times, incapable of providing for his family, his elder brother was dead, and his family now depended on him.

The majority of Confederate soldiers returning from the war had nothing. Colonel Eppa Hunton, Thomas Dear's former commanding officer, recorded in his memoirs that in December 1865 he could not afford to rent a house for his family and "was forced to room-keeping, which was then quite fashionable with the poor Confederates, and rent four rooms."[2] By contrast, under the Partisan Ranger Act in force during JW's time with Mosby, he had received a share of any booty acquired on a successful raid. Captured wagons produced household goods, coffee, canned foodstuffs, bolts of cloth, boots, shoes, and shirts. Livestock was turned over to the commissary. Captured cavalrymen yielded horses, bridles and saddles, revolvers, rifles, boots, and personal items like watches and cash. The going rate from the Confederate quartermasters (paid in gold or Union dollars) was $110 for a cavalry horse, at least $12 for a revolver, a little less for a rifle.

Mosby had ensured that the proceeds were distributed fairly to each Ranger participating in a raid. Given the number of Union cavalrymen captured, JW's share of the spoils over the length of his service was considerable—one Union prisoner would have earned him more than a year's pay for a private in the army.[3] JW's involvement in the Greenback Raid alone had earned him $2,000. Within a few weeks of his release JW had decided how to invest the money he had acquired. He and a friend bought a local newspaper.

Before the war the *Virginia Sentinel*, "an advanced and able State Rights paper," was published in Alexandria.[4] The war had forced the paper to close, and in May 1861 the proprietors moved their printing press to Warrenton, the county seat of Fauquier County, in the hope they could resume publishing. But that never happened, and the newspaper was put up for sale.[5]

JW had met James Gibson Cannon, a twenty-seven-year-old Marylander, through his friendship with the many Marylanders who had fought in Company D. The two men joined forces to purchase the title and machinery of the newspaper.[6]

The position of a newspaper proprietor was traditionally the preserve of educated, well-connected men, often with a particular social or political agenda to pursue. Managing and funding a newspaper with a strident point of view was not for the fainthearted. The very nature of the job required social standing and influence within a community, and it was therefore remarkable that JW, who was only twenty, should have taken it on; it says a great deal about the character of the man he was fast becoming. With the publication of the *Virginia Sentinel*, JW was taking center stage in the social and political life of Warrenton and Fauquier County, which had not seen a local Confederate newspaper since the early days of the war.

A newspaper business depended largely on its subscribers and advertising revenue, but the *Sentinel* was also a jobbing printer for letterheads, invoices, bills, and posters. JW clearly hoped that investing some of his bounty money in the paper would generate sufficient income to enable him to support his family. Cannon, an experienced journalist, edited the paper, while JW, with no experience of the publishing industry, was responsible for administration, securing advertising and subscription revenues, and any other business.

Warrenton had a population of eight hundred and was located twenty-eight miles south of his home in Mount Gilead, so JW needed to find a suitable place to board. His office was in the town center, a plain, eighteenth-century brick building "one door to the left" of the historic Warren Green Hotel.[7] Today there is nothing there but grass.

Within weeks of his arrival, two other Confederate war veterans made Warrenton their home and began practicing law. JW's former commander, Colonel Mosby, arrived on August 22 to open his law office close to the premises of the *Sentinel*, and Colonel Eppa Hunton arrived the following month and opened his law practice in the same building.[8]

Union troops had occupied Fauquier County from March 1862 until the end of the war, and the residents of Warrenton had become used to their presence. Due to its strategic importance to the Union army, the town had been spared the bombardment, devastation, and havoc endured by neighboring communities. Nevertheless, its residents still suffered: Union officers, as they did everywhere in the occupied South, appropriated private homes, fences and outbuildings were torn down to build temporary accommodation for enlisted men, and churches were used as hospitals. After the war, 30 percent of former enslaved people had fled the county seeking better opportunities elsewhere. Land values plummeted and many farmers struggled. It would be five years before the county's agriculture fully recovered.[9]

The federal government's Reconstruction Program, devised to help Confederate states gain readmission to the Union and emancipate enslaved people, did not go as planned. Most white residents of Loudoun and Fauquier Counties had openly supported Mosby and his men. They had provided food, shelter, and military intelligence at great risk. For four long years their energy had been focused on the war effort, and wartime loyalties remained the defining characteristic of the white population during the immediate post-war years. Many white residents remained hostile to the federal government and resisted assisting African Americans.

On Saturday, October 28, 1865, a mere five months after JW was released from prison, the first edition of the *Virginia Sentinel* rolled off the press, printed and published in Warrenton by Cannon & Dear. The *Sentinel*'s logo was the Seal and Flag of the Commonwealth of Virginia, a powerful indicator of the paper's political leaning, which was in tune with most of its readers, and its motto was "Democratic at all Times and under all Circumstances." It was critical of the government's Reconstruction Program, and more strident in its opposition to military occupation than its rival *The True Index*, which was launched a fortnight later.

Over the next two years, JW, Mosby, and Hunton lived and worked within two hundred yards of each other and met often. Both Mosby and Hunton advertised regularly in the *Sentinel*, and the paper reported their courtroom battles, Mosby for the Commonwealth and Hunton for the defense. Hunton remained loyal to his old regiment, the "Bloody Eighth," and perhaps Thomas's death at Gettysburg established a link between him and JW. Mosby was well acquainted with the Dear family, and he is reported to have often visited "his boys" as he called them, JW and Clay, after the war.[10]

As a newspaperman JW's job involved a considerable amount of travel. Law offices and trading houses, spread as far afield as Washington, DC; Baltimore; Alexandria to the east; and Middleburg, Leesburg, and Little Washington to the north and west; regularly advertised in the *Sentinel*, which meant JW, while on his travels to see customers, was able to visit his family and friends. During his visit to Mount Gilead he often ran errands for his parents; brought provisions for them; and spent time with Sam and his sister, Mary Ann, at Willow Cottage.

Direct military control in Fauquier ended on January 1, 1866; the size of the US Army was reduced significantly; and most soldiers mustered out and returned to their homes.[11] Of those that remained in the regular army, the majority were sent to the Great Plains west of the Missouri River to help pacify and subdue Indians and protect the growing number of emigrants who were moving into traditional Indian territory. The rest were assigned to the South to support reconstruction, which had the daunting task of rebuilding the South's shattered economy and integrating formerly enslaved African Americans into American society.

President Andrew Johnson's policy toward the South was one of moderation and compromise. He sought the quickest way to secure reconciliation and the restoration of federal control with the least possible

The first edition of the *Virginia Sentinel*, "published by Cannon & Dear," appeared on Saturday, October 28, 1865. In this edition of December 23, both Eppa Hunton and John Mosby advertised their law practices. Image courtesy of Virginia Museum of History & Culture

intervention. The Freedmen's Bureau was established in April 1865 to help the four million newly freed African Americans by providing food, housing, medical aid, and education and, most importantly, by helping them find their way in a new, free-labor society.

Warrenton soon experienced its first practical example of reconstruction. An office of the Freedmen's Bureau was opened to help free African Americans' transition from slavery to a prosperous freedom.[12] Almost immediately posters were circulated and advertisements placed in local newspapers like the *Sentinel*, dispelling the belief held by some formerly enslaved people that they were entitled to their former master's property and that their former master had to support them whether they worked or not. The circular stated: "blacks had to be self-supporting and recognize the fidelity of a contract."[13]

A freedmen's school for fifty-five children opened in Warrenton in February. It was financed and operated by Northerners and consequently not popular with some locals. On the first day of school a threatening note was slipped under the door; the next month the school was attacked with rocks, and troops were called to restore order. They stayed for two weeks, and after that no further trouble was reported.[14]

Tensions between the North and South continued to rise, and several Southern states took advantage of Johnson's liberal policies by severely restricting freedmen's rights. In 1866 the 14th Amendment protecting the rights of African Americans was submitted by Congress to the states for ratification, but on January 9, 1867, it was rejected by several Southern states, including Virginia. This incensed radical Northern Republicans, and on March 2, in a vengeful mood, the Republican-dominated Congress passed the Military Reconstruction Act, which placed the South under military administration. That marked the end of Johnson's liberal approach, and thereafter it was Congress, not the president, that controlled reconstruction until it ended in 1877. Virginia eventually signed both the 14th and 15th Amendments, which allowed all men to vote regardless of "race, color, or previous condition of servitude," and on January 26, 1870, Virginia became the eighth Southern state to be readmitted to the Union.

For the first two years of its existence JW's *Sentinel* did reasonably well, but when military rule was reintroduced into the South in March 1867, JW became restless.[15] It was clear the newspaper alone would not generate enough money to support his parents and siblings, so he decided to sell his stake in the paper and look for opportunities elsewhere. Cannon and Dear's last masthead together was published on April 12. The following month, after two years in Warrenton, JW moved twenty miles east to Centreville in Fairfax County, where he worked for one of the patriarchs of the village, John Daniel DeBell.[16]

It was a difficult year for the South and for Virginia in particular. President Johnson's Reconstruction Program was not working; military rule had been reintroduced; the economy was still in tatters; and many Virginians, including JW's family in Mount Gilead, were struggling. In June the *Loudoun Mirror* reported that one of the committees appointed "to solicit contributions for the suffering people of the South in the Mount Gilead district" had shipped quantities of corn and bacon to help alleviate their suffering.[17] JW was driven to find a way to help his family.

Warrenton, although traumatized by the war, had emerged almost physically unscathed, but Centreville had not been so fortunate. Before the war it was a small, sleepy village serving the local farming community, but its proximity to major turnpikes; railroad lines; and Washington, DC, made it of key strategic importance during the war. Confederate forces had built massive fortifications around the village at the start of the conflict, and many village houses were demolished to provide lumber to construct winter quarters for the troops of both sides.

At the heart of one of the most heavily impacted regions of the conflict, Centreville had a slow recovery after the war. In 1870 a correspondent for the *Alexandria Gazette* found the village "improving yet bearing marks painfully visible."[18]

The village was dominated by a handful of prosperous landowning families connected by marriage, trade, farming, or the church or simply by being neighbors. Two of the most prominent families were the Whaleys and the DeBells, who owned the nearby five-hundred-acre Sunnyside Farm and ran the local village trading store. For nine months JW boarded with John DeBell and worked as a salesman in his store, during which time he made friendships and forged a relationship with the village that lasted a lifetime.

John DeBell was connected by marriage with another large land-owner, James Cross, and it was through him that JW met James, his wife, and their nine children. Over the fall and winter of 1867, JW spent many hours at their home. He quickly established a "father-and-son" relation-ship with James and was able to unburden himself by discussing personal issues he found difficult to raise with his own father. James became his mentor and sounding board, and for many years, although they lived over a thousand miles apart, JW regularly wrote to James describing his life with its ups and downs, often seeking his advice. In later years JW helped James's eldest son establish himself in business.[19]

The opportunity that JW had been looking for presented itself in early 1868. Major Dolly Richards introduced JW to his elder brother, Burr. In 1855, Burr had gone West to Omaha, Nebraska, where he and his brother-in-law, James Megeath, started a wholesale business. Their business was spectacularly successful, and by 1868 Burr was one of the richest men in Omaha. He was impressed by JW's energy and business acumen and offered him a job as a salesman in his fur and Indian whole-sale business.

It was a difficult decision for JW to make. He loved Virginia, was close to his mother and siblings, and was worried about leaving his unre-liable father. He would also be leaving behind many close friends, includ-ing the girl he was becoming increasingly fond of, Mary Ann Rogers. He was mixing in circles with people like the Rogerses, who came from a more privileged background, and this fueled his ambition to succeed. He had seen the success that other Mosby Rangers had enjoyed out West. Opportunities for young Civil War veterans in Virginia were limited, but fast-growing Omaha offered excitement, adventure, and the opportunity to make something of himself, and maybe enable him to provide for his family in the way he believed they deserved.

On a cold, bright, spring morning in mid-March 1868, JW started his westward journey from Fairfax Station on the Orange and Alexandria

Railroad, seven miles from his lodging at Sunnyside Farm.[20] His sister Frances, her husband, and a few friends gathered on the platform to wish him a safe and speedy journey. The next phase of his life was about to begin.

CHAPTER 8

Red Cloud's War and the 1868 Fort Laramie Treaty

DURING THE FIRST TWO YEARS OF THE CIVIL WAR, RELATIONS BETWEEN the Indians and whites on the Great Plains of Nebraska and Wyoming were relatively peaceful. However, by the time of Thomas's death at the Battle of Gettysburg in July 1863, Indian attacks along the Platte River and Oregon Trail had once again become an increasingly regular occurrence.

The escalation in hostilities was triggered by an influx of European emigrants crossing the Great Plains in search of a better life in California and Oregon; young men moving west to avoid the draft; and settlers who had been given conditional access to free (Indian) land by the Homestead Act, which came into effect on January 1, 1863. Each year tens of thousands of settlers, pioneers, and miners and their wagons scythed an ever-increasing swathe of destruction across the fertile plains, killing the buffalo and game the Indians depended on.

An already delicate situation was further aggravated when gold was discovered in Montana in 1862. A year later, ex-miner John Bozeman pioneered a trail through the Powder River Country of eastern Wyoming. The trail cut four hundred miles off the original route from Fort Laramie to the goldfields and reduced travel time by four to six weeks. However, the five-hundred-thirty-mile trail also cut across the traditional hunting grounds of the Lakota Sioux and Northern Cheyenne and was used by miners, settlers, and their followers, who further disrupted the Indian way of life.

Red Cloud, the Oglala, and other Plains Indians were angered by this resurgence of white encroachment on their land. Stagecoaches were ambushed, telegraph operators killed, ranches burned, and pioneers attacked. Smoldering discontent exploded into outright hostility in November 1864 when Colonel John Milton Chivington and a force of Colorado cavalrymen massacred a village of Cheyenne and Arapaho Indians—an incident that became known as the Sand Creek Massacre.

The Indians were flying a Union flag with a white flag beneath it to show they were friendly and under the protection of the army. Chivington was a hardliner who believed in extermination. He infamously proclaimed: "Damn any man who sympathizes with Indians! . . . I have come to kill Indians, and believe it is right and honorable to use any means under God's heaven to kill Indians. . . . Kill and scalp all, big and little; nits make lice."[1] And his men did, killing and mutilating women and children indiscriminately.[2] The inevitable result was that many peaceful Cheyenne joined their more belligerent brethren and moved north to the Powder River Country, where they terrorized travelers on the Bozeman Trail.

In response the army built Fort Reno in July 1865, to protect miners using the trail. A year later the government, still under pressure to protect the goldfields and the route through Indian lands, opened negotiations with the Indians at Fort Laramie. At the meeting the authorities offered to pay compensation if the Indians allowed a road through the Powder River Country, and they also confirmed the army had no wish to garrison soldiers on the trail. This was clearly a deception, and when Red Cloud and his fellow chiefs learned the army planned to establish two new military posts, they were outraged. Despite Indian opposition, the army carried out its plan and built Forts Phil Kearny and C. F. Smith, which heralded the start of what became known as Red Cloud's War.[3]

The head chief of the Oglala Sioux, Old Smoke, died in 1864 and was succeeded by his eldest son, Old Man Afraid of His Horses. But it was Red Cloud, who had established himself as the undisputed war leader of the Oglala, who led the opposition to white encroachment on Sioux lands.

Red Cloud was forty-four years old, with a quiet and dignified presence and a steady gaze that commanded obedience and respect. In the summer of 1866, while JW was busy publishing his newspaper in Warrenton, three thousand Sioux, Northern Cheyenne, and Arapaho Indians embarked on a guerrilla war against the intruders under Red Cloud's strategic leadership.[4]

Indian war parties mounted simultaneous attacks on civilian wagon trains and army supply columns. They attacked wood-collecting patrols, cut off food supplies to the forts, and killed and mutilated miners and settlers. Army resources were stretched to the limit, and the army was continually on the back foot, reacting to events rather than taking the initiative.

The Indians struck fear and terror into whomever they encountered, and many chose to take their own lives rather than fall into Indian hands. Extreme cruelty was part of their culture and way of life. During the Sioux's secretive annual Sun Dance ceremony, young braves tortured themselves, inflicting horrendous pain to prove their bravery in a way that was incomprehensible to whites.

Indians treated all prisoners of war alike, whether fellow Indians or whites. Prisoners and the dead and dying were routinely scalped. The mutilation of their victims was driven by the Indian belief that the condition of the body at death continued into the afterlife. A sightless man with no arms, legs, or penis would therefore be at a serious disadvantage. Unsurprisingly, soldiers, miners, and settlers lived in fear of falling victim to an Indian war party.

A critical moment in Red Cloud's War occurred on December 21, 1866, at a location near Fort Phil Kearny, forty miles from the Wyoming/ Montana border. Captain William Fetterman, a boorish Indian-hater in the Chivington mold, who was alleged to have declared, "Give me eighty men and I can ride through the whole Sioux nation," got his wish when he volunteered to lead eighty-one soldiers and civilians to protect a civilian wood-collecting patrol.[5] Fetterman's patrol was lured into an ambush by decoys led by one of Red Cloud's key lieutenants, a twenty-two-year-old Oglala brave called Crazy Horse, and in less than forty minutes they were massacred to a man.[6]

In response to Indian aggression, an investigatory committee into Indian affairs reported to Congress in June 1867, recommending the creation of Indian reservations. A month later Congress appointed a high-level commission with the mandate to negotiate peace with the Indians and to concentrate them on reservations, thus ensuring the safety of overland transportation routes. If the commission failed to achieve its objectives, the bill provided for force to be used.

The commission met Spotted Tail, Chief of the Brulé Lakota Sioux, but Red Cloud made it clear there could be no peace negotiations until the forts along the Bozeman Trail had been abandoned and the army had left the Indian hunting grounds. Red Cloud continued to harass the forts, and the commission was forced to disband for the winter. In March 1868, in an effort to break the deadlock, the head of the army, General Grant, wrote to General William Tecumseh Sherman: "I think it will be well to prepare at once for the abandonment of the posts."[7]

The following month the commission convened at Fort Laramie and bowed to Red Cloud's demands. Red Cloud did not appear and let it be known he would not meet the commission until the forts had been abandoned. However, some chiefs did sign the Fort Laramie Treaty, the most important of which were Spotted Tail of the Brulé and Dull Knife of the Northern Cheyenne.[8]

Dull Knife and his much-feared warriors were allies of Red Cloud and the Oglala, a closeness that was strengthened by frequent intermarriage between the two tribes.

Spotted Tail was also a contemporary of Red Cloud, and like him had fought against the whites. But after going to war again in 1864, Spotted Tail began to realize the futility of fighting against the government and, to prevent the needless suffering of his people, became a determined advocate of peace.[9]

He and Red Cloud had an uneasy relationship. Spotted Tail refused to take part in Red Cloud's War; signed the Fort Laramie Treaty before Red Cloud had secured the physical closure of the forts on the Bozeman Trail; and agreed, albeit reluctantly, to move three hundred fifty miles east

General Sherman and the Peace Commissioners negotiating the Fort Laramie Treaty with the Northern Plains Indians. April 1868. Courtesy of Library of Congress, 111-SC-95986

to collect his rations. As a result, Spotted Tail was seen by the authorities as being the more accommodating of the two Lakota leaders. It was clear, however, that Red Cloud's word carried more weight, and although they shared many common objectives, this caused tension and a rivalry between the two chiefs.

It was not until early August 1868 that the last troops and their wagons finally rolled out of Forts C. F. Smith, Phil Kearny, and Reno, and as they did so the victorious Indians burned them to the ground, a further humiliation for the authorities. The most southerly of the forts, Fort Fetterman, which had been built in 1867 following the Fetterman Massacre, was, however, allowed to remain. It was another two months before Red Cloud deigned to travel to Fort Laramie to sign the historic Fort Laramie Treaty on November 6, 1868, marking the end of Red Cloud's War. The same week General Grant, commander of the victorious Northern Army in the Civil War, was elected the eighteenth President of the United States.

Spotted Tail, Chief of the Brulé Lakota Sioux. He was one of the first to sign the Fort Laramie Treaty. Photographed in 1870. Courtesy of Library of Congress, LC-USZ62-131515

The treaty established the Great Sioux Reservation for the exclusive use of the Sioux and undertook to ensure whites would not pass over or settle on the reservation. Most importantly, it included the Black Hills of Dakota, an area of great spiritual importance to the Lakota. The vast reservation occupied more than thirty-five thousand square miles of what is now the whole of South Dakota west of the Missouri River. An important condition of the treaty was that it could only be amended with the agreement of 75 percent of adult male Indians.

Sitting Bull, the chief of the Hunkpapa Lakota Sioux, was the fiercest opponent of white encroachment onto Sioux land and refused to sign the treaty or have any contact with whites. Crazy Horse decided to follow Sitting Bull's lead and opted to retain his band's traditional

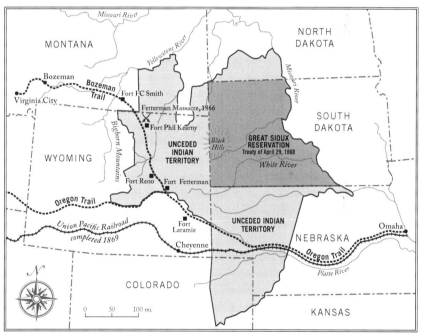

Map 2.   Sioux Lands, 1868, an area of 110,000 square miles over which the Lakota Sioux were free to hunt.

way of life. Over the coming years Sitting Bull, Crazy Horse, and other non-reservation Indians were collectively referred to by government officials, the army, and the press as the "northern hostiles."

To compensate the Indians for giving up their nomadic lifestyle and dependence on buffalo, the government established agencies on the reservations, where an Indian agent and his staff were responsible for the welfare of a tribe, like the Oglala, and for the issue of government-financed annuities: beef, blankets, coffee, flour, tobacco, and other basic rations. Indian agents were expected to keep a record of the number of Indians in their charge and encourage them to take the "White Man's Road," by replacing hunting with farming, sending their children to school, and relinquishing tribal traditions in favor of Christianity.

The government also appointed Indian traders. They were located alongside the agency stockade where Indians could trade furs and robes in exchange for ammunition, food, fabric, trinkets, and other goods not provided directly by the government. Enterprising traders often created a hub of entertainment for those living on the agency, officers and men from nearby military camps or forts, and food and accommodation for those passing through on the various stage or freight trails. Some also won government and army contracts to provide forage, wood cutting, and haulage using their own teams of oxen. One or two licensed traders had the exclusive rights to trade with up to ten thousand Indians, and a trader who worked hard, was canny, and made the most of the opportunities that came his way, could retire a rich man.

In addition to the terms set out for Indians who accepted reservation life, the Fort Laramie Treaty also recognized the rights of non-reservation Indians like Sitting Bull and Crazy Horse. It agreed they could hunt in the unceded Powder River Country in northeastern Wyoming and in the hunting grounds in Nebraska north of the Platte River, "so long as the buffalo may range thereon in such numbers as to justify the chase."[10] This amounted to another seventy thousand square miles where the Indians believed they would be free to roam forever. However, the government knew that with the coming of the railroad and buffalo hunters, and with more settlers moving into the area, buffalo and other game would become increasingly scarce, eventually forcing Indians, if they wished to avoid starvation, to accept government annuities and to move onto reservations. For the government, food was a key weapon of control.

Red Cloud was the only Indian to win a war against the United States, forcing acquiescence to all his demands. From the moment he signed the Fort Laramie Treaty the government recognized him as the leader of the Oglala and the man they had to deal with. This profoundly influenced Red Cloud's relationship with Old Man Afraid of His Horses and his son, Young Man Afraid of His Horses. In later years the authorities used the tension between them to "divide and rule," in an endeavor to implement policies they wished to impose.

After a lifetime of warfare and wandering freely on the open plains in the pursuit of game, Red Cloud, with the touch of a pen, committed to lead his people into life on a reservation. It was a pragmatic decision. He recognized his people could no longer withstand the surging westward tide of the white man nor the power of the government and that compromise and negotiation were the only way forward. And, mistakenly as it turned out, he trusted the US government to honor the agreements to which it had committed. He was to be "maddeningly disruptive" over the next forty-one years, but never again would he go to war.[11]

PART II
FUR TRADER ON THE WESTERN FRONTIER: 1868–1871

CHAPTER 9

JW Goes West: 1868

JW LEFT VIRGINIA AND MOVED WEST SIX MONTHS BEFORE RED CLOUD "touched the pen" and committed his people to reservation life. The twelve-hundred-mile train journey from his home in Virginia took JW three days to complete, and he arrived in Omaha in late March 1868.

The city, located on the west bank of the Missouri River in Nebraska, had become one of the most important cities in the country.[1] Founded just fourteen years before JW's arrival, Omaha had started life as a small settlement, a handful of buildings housing three hundred souls clustered around the levee where the ferry docked. An increasing number of European emigrants, miners, and Mormons, lured by the promise of a new life in California, Oregon, and Salt Lake City, chose to start their journey west from Omaha, which fueled the city's expansion and increased its wealth. Astute businessmen, like JW's employer Burr Richards and his partner James Megeath, quickly identified opportunities. Pioneers needed equipment and supplies for their two-thousand-mile, five-month journey across the plains, so warehouses were built and wholesale businesses established to provide for them. As more and more pioneers passed through Omaha the town grew and its commercial base widened. Land that had been worthless began to have value, and money was made from real estate and speculation. Land that previously had little or no value changed hands for considerable sums as property developers and speculators moved into the area, attracted by the prospect of making a quick profit.

By the early 1860s other developments had boosted Omaha's commercial and business fortunes. Because of Omaha's strategic position on the Missouri River, the city competed for river trade business that had traditionally been handled by Kansas and St. Louis, servicing fur trading posts and army forts. In 1859 when gold was discovered in Colorado, thousands of miners began their journey to the goldfields from Omaha, where wholesalers were delighted to sell the supplies and equipment they needed.

Three years later gold was discovered in Montana, and the easiest and most cost-effective way to equip and service the goldfields was by a twelve-hundred-mile steamboat journey along the Missouri from cities like Omaha to the head of navigation at Fort Benton. Boats went upriver laden with miners and their supplies and equipment and returned with gold from Montana and furs and buffalo robes that had been traded with Indians and trappers along the river. The roundtrip took up to four months to complete, but it could be immensely profitable. Steamboat owners also benefited from government contracts to ferry annuities to various Indian tribes along the Missouri as provided for in the 1851 Fort Laramie Peace Treaty.

A further boost to the local economy came in June 1862 when the Senate passed the Pacific Railroad Act, making Omaha the eastern terminal of the two-thousand-mile transcontinental railroad linking Omaha with Sacramento in California. The Union Pacific Railroad Company won the contract to build the eastern section of the line and the Central Pacific Company, the western sector. The project involved a workforce of ten thousand laborers, comprised mostly of unskilled Irish immigrants and Civil War veterans, who moved across the Great Plains of Nebraska and Wyoming in a tented city laying, at first, half a mile of track a day. Work started in 1865, and by November 1867 the track had reached Cheyenne, five hundred miles west of Omaha.[2]

As a result, Omaha's economy boomed. By 1868, when JW arrived in the city, many of the founding fathers were extremely wealthy, and two of the richest and most respected were Burr Richards and James Megeath. It was, however, still a rough and basic place to live. The newly consecrated

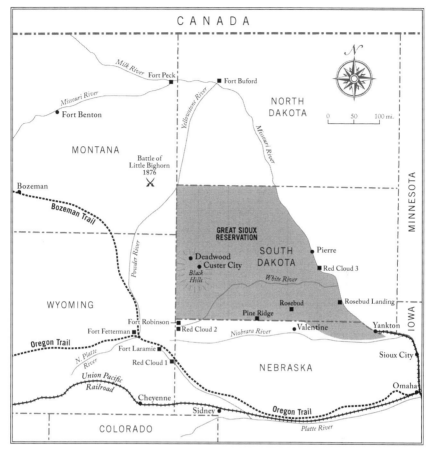

Map 3. JW's American West.

bishop of Montana visited Omaha in the spring of 1867 and described its rudimentary infrastructure:

> The [Missouri] river itself, turbid and sullen, well deserved the name the natives gave it, "The Big Muddy." The ferry-boat was flat, rude, unclean, more like a raft than a boat; the approach to it on the Iowa side was a steep bank of sticky, slippery black mud, down which we all walked or slid as best we could, our baggage and blankets being pushed and hurled after us in indiscriminate confusion. The same kind of paths

of departure from the deck existed on the Nebraska side. . . . There are no trees here, and no rocks, and I feel lonesome. A few hills behind us, however, relieve the lonesomeness somewhat. The streets are very muddy, and the whole town new, formless, and dirty. They say they suffer here greatly from high winds, and in summer time, almost intolerably from dust.[3]

Rudimentary as it might have been, Omaha was nonetheless the fastest growing and most dynamic city in America, and it began to challenge St. Louis as the "Gateway to the West." It was a male-dominated society, where corruption and cronyism were rife and everybody was focused on making money. By 1868 the population had grown to seventeen thousand, and, as the *Omaha City Directory* of that year stated, it had everything to support a booming economy.[4]

As often happens when wealth is generated over a short period of time, a veneer of sophistication and refinement soon coated many of the city's institutions. Gentlemen's clubs flourished, Masonic lodges were established, magnificent mansions built, and exclusive neighborhoods began to emerge; lavish dinner parties, balls, and wedding receptions competed for attention; and the arts, music, and theater were encouraged by the rich and influential.

Beneath the veneer, however, there was another side to the city. Aggressive and ambitious young men, driven to emulate the city's successful founders, did whatever it took to make their own fortunes. Such a heady cocktail attracted many talented and honorable men, but also swindlers, crooks, and the flotsam of society on the lookout to get rich by whatever means they could. Gambling, prostitution, and investment scams all flourished in an environment of easy money, greed, and corruption.

The city's infrastructure struggled to keep up with its success.[5] Raw sewage was discharged into the Missouri, the main streets were muddy or dusty depending on the weather, and wooden planks on the sidewalks provided the only respite from the thick mud in winter. Every block had a saloon that never closed, and many streets sported a brothel and a pawn broker. Faro banks, keno, and poker rooms ran day and night. Drunks littered the sidewalks, while assaults and robberies became so frequent that vigilante groups were formed.

JW had to adapt to this world if he wished to survive. Omaha offered opportunities that were not readily available to him in war-ravaged Virginia, and the city also catered to his taste for the finer things in life—good food and wine; fine tobacco; and well-cut, fashionable clothes. According to the *Omaha City Directory*, JW rented a room between 15th and 16th on Farnam Street South and worked as a salesman for the wholesaler Richards & Whitney at 247 Douglas Street, a four-hundred-yard walk from his lodgings.[6]

JW joined Richards & Whitney at a time of change. Beginning in 1856, the company had traded under the Richards & Megeath banner, and the partners were Burr Richards; James Megeath; and James's elder brother, Sam. In 1867, James sold his share in the company to his partners and became the sole forwarding agent for the Union Pacific Railroad Company, an enormously profitable business.

The following year, Burr Richards and Sam Megeath merged their business with another Omaha wholesaler, Whitney & Co. Sam died shortly after the merger, and the new company became known as Richards & Whitney.[7] They continued equipping pioneers for the two-thousand-mile trek west, but with the coming of the transcontinental railroad, that part of the business was in rapid decline. By contrast the trade supplying the forts and trading posts along the Missouri and Platte Rivers was doing well, as was their reciprocal fur trading business with the Indians.

JW's job as a salesman involved visiting army forts and trading stores spread along the Oregon Trail, selling goods from the company's extensive inventory, and buying furs and robes traded with the Indians. One of his most important customers was William Bullock, a bluff Virginian known as "The Colonel." Bullock had managed the army's sutler store at Fort Laramie since 1857 for Seth Ward, his partner who held the sutler's license, which authorized a civilian trader to sell goods on a military establishment.

Located on the Oregon Trail near the confluence of the Platte and Laramie Rivers and hundreds of miles from the nearest continuously inhabited white community, the sutler's trading store did a thriving business. From the late 1850s to the late 1860s, up to fifty thousand pioneers passed the fort each year on their arduous journeys to California, Oregon, and Utah. They all needed supplies for the next stage of their journey, which would take them over the Rockies into the promised land. Thousands of miners en route to the goldfields of Colorado and Montana also paused there, and more than thirty thousand Indians brought their robes and furs from their hunting grounds in Nebraska and the Powder River Country of eastern Wyoming to Fort Laramie to trade at Bullock's store. The store also did a thriving trade with officers, their wives, and enlisted men stationed at the fort.

Saloons, brothels, and gambling dens sprang up around the fort to cater to those who had spent months away from their homes and families surrounded by Indians. They needed an escape from the boredom of living on the plains with little or no female company. Inevitably such establishments attracted some of the less salubrious members of society and were frequented by outlaws, hustlers, swindlers, professional gamblers, and prostitutes. Drunkenness and violence were the norm.

By 1868 a long and profitable era for Bullock's store was ending. Recent changes in government regulations stipulated Indians could only trade with civilians who had received a license from the OIA. This meant that army sutlers, or post traders as they were now known, were excluded from this lucrative trade and civilian traders were banned from military land. Bullock's business suffered a further loss a year later when the railroad linking Omaha to Sacramento, California, was completed. As a result, the number of pioneers using the Oregon Trail dropped from tens of thousands a year to a trickle.

It was against this background that JW first traveled from Omaha to Fort Laramie by train, which, in the summer of 1868, was still seen as a daring adventure. The departure depot was a cavernous shed, where a disparate collection of JW's fellow travelers, miners, trappers, frontiersmen, officers destined for Fort Laramie, and businessmen milled about waiting for the order to board the train. Once seated, their baggage carefully stowed, and with a final call from the conductor to close the doors, the train pulled slowly out of the depot on its journey west.

An hour after they left the Missouri River and the bluffs of Omaha they passed onto the wide-open plains of Nebraska, and that flat, unrelenting landscape remained with them for the rest of their journey, broken only by occasional glimpses of the Platte River. Those hoping to see the vast herds of buffalo that once graced the plains were disappointed, but elk, deer, and prairie dogs were often seen.

It was a long and boring journey. The train moved sedately covering twenty miles an hour, and the passengers looked forward to relieving the tedium at small towns where the train was scheduled to stop for a comfort break and a very basic meal provided by the railroad company.

After thirty-six hours, if they were lucky and there had been no unforeseen mishaps, they arrived in Cheyenne, which was still a crude shanty town. Most of the buildings were roughly constructed in board and canvas, and three hundred businesses served the flotsam of society who had made the town their home, "dangerous looking miners in big boots, broadbrimmed hats, and revolvers, gamblers, prostitutes, professional gunmen and members of the Sioux, Cheyenne and Pawnee tribes." It was a place where "liquor was cheap, pay was good and the stakes high for gamblers and robbers."[8]

JW stayed overnight at what was to become his favorite haunt, the recently built Railroad House Hotel, before traveling the next morning by horse-drawn buggy the ninety miles to Fort Laramie. His first visit was always to the sutler store.

An officer's wife stationed at the fort captures a flavor of what JW encountered when he entered:

> The long counter of Messrs Bullock and Ward was a scene of seeming confusion not surpassed in any popular, overcrowded store in Omaha itself. Indians, dressed and half dressed and undressed; squaws, dressed to the same degree of completeness as their noble lords; papooses, absolutely nude, slightly not nude, or wrapped in calico, buckskin or furs, mingled with soldiers of the garrison, teamsters, emigrants, speculators, half-breeds and interpreters. Here, cups of rice, sugar, coffee or flour were being emptied into the looped-up skirts or blanket of a squaw; and there, some tall warrior was grimacing delightedly as he grasped and sucked his long stick of peppermint candy. Bright shawls,

William Bullock's sutler store at Fort Laramie in 1877, little changed from JW's first visit in 1868. Archives, Fort Laramie National Historic Site

red squaw cloth, brilliant calicoes, and flashing ribbons passed over the same counter with knives and tobacco, brass nails and glass beads, and that endless catalog of articles which belong to the legitimate border traffic. . . . To all, however, whether white man, half-breed, or Indian, Mr Bullock, a Virginia gentleman of the old school . . . gave kind and patient attention.[9]

Several of the buildings around Bullock's store have been demolished or are in ruins, but the store itself is virtually unchanged. The original mahogany counter remains, and one can feel the presence of those early pioneers and visualize William Bullock bartering with JW and his other suppliers. A mile from the store the ruts in the rock, carved by the constant passage of the steel-shod wheels of the pioneer wagons, are still clearly visible and give a hint of the hardship thousands of families endured in search of a better life.

By early 1869, as Red Cloud and the Oglala were pressing to trade and draw their rations from Fort Laramie, JW had gained a sound understanding of the wholesale trade and how the Indian and fur trade along the Missouri and Platte Rivers was organized. He had built a wide circle of friends and contacts, and, most importantly, he had earned the trust and respect of his employers and was fast becoming a valued member of the community.

The studio portrait of Richard Dear taken during his visit to Omaha in 1869. Eugenia Newberg

Occasionally, family and friends came to visit. A year after JW had left Virginia, his nineteen-year-old brother, Richard, spent some time with him. It was Richard's first visit to Omaha, and the two brothers explored the city together. JW introduced Richard to his friends, and they visited JW's favorite haunts. Richard had his photograph taken by a fashionable Omaha photographer and gave JW a small bible, which is still owned by the Dear family.[10] During their time together JW reconfirmed that he intended to stay in the West for the foreseeable future, as it offered more opportunities than Virginia, which still had not been accepted back into the Union. The reaction of his parents and loved ones is not known.

Two months after Richard left Omaha, the dream of a transcontinental railroad was realized when, on May 10, the Union Pacific and the Central Pacific tracks met at Promontory Point in Utah. Omaha proclaimed a general holiday. One hundred guns boomed a salute on the banks of the Missouri to announce to the world "The Pacific Railroad is completed," a symbolic moment in the history of the American West. Private homes were draped with bunting, flags, and banners, and Omahans, together with JW and his friends and colleagues, celebrated. It was a memorable day.[11] However, Omaha may have been connected to Sacramento, but the much-needed bridge over the Missouri linking Omaha to Council Bluffs, Iowa, was not completed for another four years.

Although JW received a good salary from Richards & Whitney, he soon realized that that alone would not make him rich nor enable him to adequately support his parents and siblings. During his first year in Omaha, JW met adventurous young men who traveled to the Upper Missouri to buy furs and robes from the Indians. It was hard and dangerous work, but for those who were skillful, or lucky, and returned to Omaha with sufficient furs and robes to sell to wholesalers like Richards & Whitney, it paid handsomely.[12]

In July 1869, JW had a lucky break. Charles Larpenteur, a vastly experienced fur trader who had a fur trading post next to Fort Buford on the Upper Missouri, visited Richards & Whitney's office in Omaha and struck a deal that was to transform JW's fortunes.[13]

CHAPTER 10

Fort Buford and the Fur Trade

JW's FUTURE PARTNER, CHARLES LARPENTEUR, WAS BORN IN FRANCE in 1803 and moved with his parents to America in 1818.[1] In his early thirties he joined the American Fur Trading company in St. Louis and for the next thirty years worked in the fur trade, much of the time at Fort Union, a civilian fur trading post on the Upper Missouri, built in 1829 to trade with the Assiniboine Indians, a tribe from northern Montana and southern Canada.[2] It was a bleak and remote location, eight hundred miles upriver from the future site of Omaha and eighty miles south of the Canadian border.

In the early nineteenth century the fur trade was the largest and most profitable industry in America, and the most successful company was John Jacob Astor's American Fur Trading Company, which he founded in 1809.[3] By the mid-1830s, however, fashions were changing, and the great herds of buffalo and other game in the south were declining. In 1834, recognizing the trend and concerned it would impact his business, the canny Astor sold his fur trading interests along the Missouri River, including Fort Union, to Pierre Chouteau Jr., a wealthy St. Louis businessman.[4]

Until the early 1860s, Chouteau's business on the Upper Missouri continued to flourish, and in a good year Fort Union handled more than forty thousand robes and as many skins and pelts. In July 1864, Chouteau appointed Larpenteur as the *Bourgeois* (manager or superintendent) at Fort Union, where he lived in some style in the Bourgeois's fine house in the fort's compound.[5] He supervised approximately twenty-five "upper-class" employees, consisting of clerks and bookkeepers and their families, and around a hundred "lower-class" *engagés*, or contract laborers. It was a hard life; living conditions were unsanitary and the threat of disease was ever present.

Indians came to the fort to trade toward the end of the hunting season, which lasted from November to February when furs and buffalo robes were in their prime. They exchanged their furs and robes for coffee, sugar, flour, blankets, beads and trinkets, ammunition, and tobacco. Although it was strictly illegal, alcohol was also bartered at many trading posts—either it had been smuggled upriver on steamboats or as happened at Fort Union in the early days, it was distilled at the trading post using an illegal still. By the time the first boat of the season arrived at the fort in early May, much of the trade had been completed. Robes, pelts, and furs were packed in great, tightly bound bundles and shipped downriver to wholesalers in Omaha, Kansas, and St. Louis.[6]

The end of the Civil War brought major changes to the Upper Missouri fur trade and to the fortunes of the Chouteau family. In July 1865, after thirty years of trading, the OIA did not renew Chouteau's license. He was a Democrat and Confederate sympathizer, and thus a casualty of the Union victory in the Civil War. As a result, he was forced to sell his trading posts along the Missouri.[7] Fort Union was bought by the Chicago-based North West Fur Company, and the new owners arrived at the fort on September 17.

During this period Indian attacks on the steamboats, as they slowly threaded their way up the Missouri, were also becoming a problem. To protect the river trade, the army built Fort Buford, two and a half miles downriver from Fort Union. The fort opened in December 1866, heralding the start of a new era.

The changing economic and political environment encouraged the emergence of independent traders who disrupted the old order and often bypassed traditional channels of doing business. These so-called free traders tended to be old-style frontiersmen like Larpenteur or young, battle-hardened, Civil War veterans attracted by the romance of the West and looking for adventure and the opportunity to make a quick fortune. Many were backed by merchants from Omaha, Kansas, and St.

Louis who were happy to share the profits without being exposed to any physical risk or moral approbation. By 1867 the fur trade on the Upper Missouri was controlled by a few small trading companies, like Durfee & Peck of Kansas, and free traders and their merchant backers, like Richards & Whitney, all focused on making as much money as quickly as possible.[8] As the new wave of traders scrambled to secure deals, discipline broke down, and the use of alcohol and ammunition to barter with the Indians became more widespread. US marshals were employed to police the situation and to stamp out the illegal use of whiskey, but they faced an impossible task and made little impact.

Larpenteur chose not to work for the North West Fur Company, and in the fall of 1865 he traveled to St. Louis to wind up his affairs with Pierre Chouteau. He returned to his farm in Iowa, but it was not long before he missed the excitement of his old trade. In the spring of 1867, he was employed by Durfee & Peck to set up a business in direct competition with the North West Fur Company, which had not made a success of its new acquisition. Durfee & Peck had already committed to exploiting the gap left by Chouteau's demise and a year earlier had built Fort Peck, a large fur trading post on the confluence of the Milk and Missouri Rivers, one hundred thirty miles upriver from Fort Buford.

Larpenteur oversaw the building of Durfee & Peck's trading store close to Fort Buford. It started trading on November 25, and over the next few months handled 2,000 robes, 1,800 deer skins, 1,000 wolf pelts, and 900 elk hides. Larpenteur's success, however, was short lived, and, for reasons that are unclear, on May 18, 1868, when the first steamer of the season arrived at Fort Buford, he was fired by Durfee & Peck. Undaunted, he went home to Iowa, raised $8,000 by selling his farm, and returned with his brother-in-law to Fort Buford as a free trader. Their adobe store, made from earth and straw just outside the fort's stockade, opened for business on October 13, and for the next six months did brisk business.

Within a year Larpenteur needed to refinance his business, and on June 3, 1869, he left Fort Buford for Omaha with the aim of securing a new backer and "bringing up another outfit."[9] He met Richards & Whitney in their office on Douglas Street, and they agreed to underwrite his business over the coming year in return for a share of any profit he made.

JW, who had been working for the firm for sixteen months, and who had impressed them with his hard work and sound judgment, was given the task of overseeing their investment.

It was a dangerous and physically demanding assignment. For more than six months he would be living in one of the most remote locations in America, surrounded by thousands of Indians—many of them hostile. But this was the break he had been looking for. In addition to his basic salary, as a partner he also received a share of the profit the venture generated.

In mid-July JW and Larpenteur left Omaha by train for the ninety-mile journey to Sioux City, Iowa. The railroad depot was close to the river, and they made their way to the levee, where the steamers were docked. A casual observer would have seen a tall, sixty-five-year-old man with receding hair and muttonchop whiskers, dressed in the traditional garb of a successful frontiersman—a well-cut frock coat, white shirt, and black string tie—and his fit-looking, twenty-four-year-old companion picking their way along the dusty, rutted streets. JW was the younger man. Of medium height with jet-black hair, the oil he used glistening in the sun, he sported a carefully trimmed moustache and matching small beard, both as black as his hair. Carefully dressed, there was something of the dandy about him. His dark, piercing eyes were taking everything in as he looked around at the bustle of activity on the levee. Derricks were swinging cargo onto the decks of steamboats lined up against the bank as their crews scuttled backward and forward across the slippery, bouncing timbers that served as gangplanks.

The two men stood on the levee braving the heat and humidity, waiting to board a stern-wheeler to Fort Buford. The boat was already laden with two hundred tons of cargo, made up of Indian annuities, supplies, and equipment for the fur trading posts scattered along the banks of the Upper Missouri and for merchants waiting at the head of navigation at Fort Benton. To this were added goods that JW and Larpenteur needed to trade with the Indians over the coming winter months.

The boat's manifest comprised around five thousand items including mining equipment, shovels, agricultural hardware, tableware, ammunition,

The stern-wheeler *Rosebud* on the dusty banks of a levee loading supplies. Courtesy of National Archives, photo no.111-SC-83751

clothing, wine, bedding, firearms, tools, and a limited amount of timber for the boiler. Most of the cargo was stored in the hold beneath removable decking and on the lower deck. Many passengers had already embarked in St. Louis, Kansas, and Omaha, and the decks were alive with over a hundred passengers who had paid up to $300 for the trip.

JW and Larpenteur were upper deck cabin passengers, a significant improvement on deck passengers, who were crammed into whatever space they could find among the bales, barrels, crates, and livestock and alongside the steam boilers that fired the engines. Miners heading for the goldfields of Montana, army officers and soldiers returning to their forts, fur trappers, and roustabouts of all hues endured a crowded, fetid, and sweaty journey. Everyone was on a mission; most were focused on making money.

High above them, the captain and the pilot, paid huge sums to guide the boat and its valuable cargo through the treacherous waters, stood in a wheelhouse clad with iron plates to ward off the bullets and arrows of raiding Indians. Those who learned to read the river—its snags, sandbars, currents, hostile Indians, and shallows—and could bring their boats home safely could make large profits for their owners. An experienced and seasoned master was paid as much as $1,200 per month plus a large bonus for a successfully completed round trip. It was a small price for owners to pay when a successful trip could net a profit of over $100,000, more than three times the cost of a new boat.

As the boat cautiously threaded its way upstream, it regularly stopped to buy timber from the woodhawks or friendly Indians who lined the banks. During the stopovers JW had the opportunity to view the landscape teeming with vast quantities of game: buffalo, elk, and deer gathered on the banks to drink and occasionally, grizzly bears, wolves, and coyotes. When the boat anchored for the night, the silence was broken only by the sounds of night birds and beavers with their young as they played and splashed alongside the boat.

This was JW's first exposure to the upper reaches of the Missouri River, and it was a relatively uneventful experience. They were not attacked by Indians, nor were they stranded on a sandbank. And they avoided being snagged by timber and rocks hidden below the surface of the river.

He arrived at Fort Buford in early August. It had taken thirty days for the sturdy, flat-bottomed, three-deck vessel to force its way seven hundred miles upriver to their destination at the confluence of the Yellowstone and Missouri Rivers. There, seventy yards from the riverbank, shimmering in the evening sun, surrounded by knee-high native grasses, stood the recently built Fort Buford. A few basic log cabins with turf roofs and a handful of adobe buildings stood outside the army stockade. Scattered along the riverbank were a few Indian lodges. Indians sat in small groups as children played and dogs barked. Behind the fort a dense forest of cottonwood and willow trees extended to the bluffs, half a mile distant. The surrounding prairie was the country of the Assiniboine Indians; farther west lay the traditional hunting grounds of Sitting Bull and the Hunkpapa Sioux, one of the most warlike and feared of all the Indian tribes. Everywhere there was an abundance of game.

The stern-wheeler strained against the current, steering carefully between the sandbars toward the riverbank, and Indians gathered on the bank to watch the drama of its arrival. As the steamship's engines reduced power, clouds of smoke rose from its twin stacks, and warps were thrown ashore as the ship's whistle announced her safe arrival. JW and Larpenteur disembarked and supervised the roustabouts as they transferred the goods supplied by Richards & Whitney to their warehouse. At sunrise the next morning the stern-wheeler pulled away from the fort and, with a last long blast of its whistle, headed farther west to its final destination upriver at Fort Benton.

CHAPTER 11

Fur Trader on the Upper Missouri: Winter of 1869–1870

DURING HIS FIRST THREE MONTHS AT FORT BUFORD, BEFORE THE MIS-
souri froze and became unnavigable, JW traveled along the river visiting
small trading posts and friendly Indian villages within a five- or six-day
journey from the fort. One destination was Fort Peck one hundred thirty
miles upriver, built in 1867 to trade with the Sioux and to exploit the
vast buffalo herds that still roamed the surrounding plains.[1] The fort was
set on a narrow ledge of shale about thirty-five feet above river level, its
rear wall abutting the hillside. It possessed a good wharf, so it served as
a convenient landing for the stern-wheelers bound for Fort Benton three
hundred miles upriver. The stockade was about three hundred feet square
with walls twelve feet high of cottonwood logs to give protection from
hostile Indians. Inside were log buildings, including quarters for men,
storehouses, a blacksmith shop, stables, and a corral.

It was a picturesque but isolated location, home to 160 residents
including a post trader and his 15 staff, 14 fur traders and trappers, and
110 woodcutters.[2] The woodcutters were there to satisfy the insatiable
demand for timber for fuel and buildings. They used the fort as a base
but spent many days away working in small groups cutting and selling
cords of logs to passing steamboats, which traveled with as little wood as
possible to maximize the space available for valuable freight.

During this time, JW met and befriended Frank Grouard, one of the
West's most colorful and enigmatic characters. He was a frontiersman

89

Fort Peck, as JW would have known it, located on the confluence of the Missouri and Milk Rivers one hundred thirty miles upriver from Fort Buford. Painted by Arthur H. Buckley. Public Domain

employed to carry mail between the forts and trading posts on the Upper Missouri. He was born in 1850 to a Mormon father and a French Polynesian mother. After coming to the United States, he left home in 1865 and moved north to the goldfields of Montana. There he led a precarious existence on the very edge of the Western frontier, earning a living as an express rider and stage driver. He was a quick learner, could read and write, and had a friendly way about him that made him easy to like. That and the fact he had inherited his mother's color and looks and could easily pass for a full-blooded Indian were probably the keys to his survival. His autobiography is full of extraordinary adventures, some undoubtedly true, others perhaps embroidered.

In the summer of 1868, eighteen-year-old Frank was employed to carry mail along the Upper Missouri to Fort Peck. It was a dangerous job, as it entailed traveling alone on horseback with a packhorse across hundreds of miles of inhospitable terrain through hostile Indian territory. He was often forced to sleep rough for two or three consecutive nights, and on one occasion he was hijacked by a group of Blackfeet Indians. They stripped him naked, stole his horses and belongings, and left him to walk seventy miles to the nearest trading post. The experience left him bedridden for three months, but he survived.

Despite this, a year later he was carrying mail to Fort Peck again.[3] It was there, in that remote outpost on the very edge of the Western

Frank Grouard, the enigmatic frontiersman, was a mail carrier on the Upper Missouri and regularly visited Fort Peck in 1869. MS 4605, James E. Taylor Scrapbook of the American West, National Anthropological Archives, Smithsonian Institution

frontier, that he met JW, and a lasting bond was established between these two young men. Four years later, when Frank was living with Crazy Horse's band, he and JW renewed their friendship under vastly different circumstances.

After Fort Peck the Upper Missouri flowed west and became increasingly treacherous. Depending on the state of the river, it could take up to thirty days to complete the final three-hundred-mile leg of the journey to the head of navigation at Fort Benton. Journeys could not start until spring when the snow melted, adding extra hazards: spring floods raised the water level and fast-running currents brought ice floes, trees, and other debris careering down the river. Currents changed the size and shape of sand and gravel banks, and many boats ran aground, becoming vulnerable to Indian attacks. Other boats were fatally damaged by boiler explosions or wrecked by submerged trees. The average life span of a steamboat on the Upper Missouri was two years.

When gold was discovered in Montana in 1862, Fort Benton became the main point of entry to the goldfields.[4] By 1869, despite over twenty boats a year completing the round trip to the fort, it still had the appearance of a crude frontier town with little to suggest its future potential. Small adobe buildings and log huts made up the main street. The mile-long levee was piled high with commercial goods, bordered with a row of disreputable saloons, gambling dens, and hurdy-gurdy houses where girls were paid to dance with men and ply them with high-priced drinks. Surrounding all this was a tented city where most of the transitory population lived. It had the reputation of being "a squaw town, a scalp market, the home of cutthroats and horse thieves, and an ammunition and whiskey trading post for hostile Indians."[5]

A young man on his travels west described the colorful scene that would have greeted JW as the boat nosed its way into the wharf:

Eastern pilgrims watched with mixed emotions the motley crowds that greeted them . . . for there stood merchants in high-collared broadcloth coats, French-Canadians and Creole rivermen wearing bright-colored sashes, tough trappers and traders heavily armed wearing buckskin, bullwhackers and muleskinners in coarse rough denim and in the background, Indians wearing leggings and blankets. Such a diverse collection of humanity was eloquent testimony that Fort Benton was the most cosmopolitan city on the plains. Through this inland port passed pious missionaries and hunted desperadoes, merchants and gamblers, hopeful land seekers, speculators, miners and fur traders.[6]

By mid-November the last boat of the season had left heading south. Temperatures dropped as winter set in, and JW was back at Fort Buford before the river froze. The next contact this isolated military outpost of four hundred fifty souls had with the outside world was six months later, in early May, with the arrival of the first steamboat of the season. Dakota winters were harsh, with short days and long nights and temperatures that often fell twenty degrees below freezing. During the long winter months JW's social life was restricted to mixing with officers stationed at the fort; Charles Larpenteur and his wife, Rebecca; and a handful of fellow traders and interpreters. He spent many hours reading, playing cards and backgammon, writing letters to family and friends, speculating on the outcome of the season's trading, enjoying a drink, and smoking his pipe.

By the late 1860s, the buffalo's last remaining stronghold in America was on the northern plains around the Upper Missouri, Yellowstone, and Milk Rivers. November and December were quiet months for the people at Fort Buford, but not for the Indians. The buffalo hunting season was the three-month window from November to February, after which buffalo started shedding their winter coats and their hides became worthless. During this period the Indians scoured the plains in search of the great herds. Buffalo were killed mainly with arrows, which were less expensive than bullets and could be retrieved and used again. The animals were skinned, and the native women then began the long and arduous job of tanning the hides. They were scraped and dried before being bundled onto poles and dragged, sometimes a hundred miles by Indian ponies to traders and trading posts along the Upper Missouri.[7] It was a scene that had changed little over hundreds of years.

In the new year a steadily increasing flow of Indians braved the inclement weather to visit Fort Buford with robes and furs to trade. JW benefited greatly from working alongside Larpenteur, and the two men had a very successful season.

In spring when the river thawed, Larpenteur and JW loaded their furs and robes onto the first available stern-wheeler heading downriver to Omaha where Richards & Whitney arranged for the skins to be transferred to the lucrative East Coast market. Robes exchanged for beads, trinkets, and sometimes whiskey could change hands in Omaha for $4 or $5, and it was not unusual for a steamer to offload twenty thousand robes with a market value of $100,000.

JW and Larpenteur made a handsome profit. Larpenteur recorded in his diary that "On 7 June 1870 went down to Omaha to settle with Richards & Whitney with whom I was concerned. I bought them out and returned to Buford."[8]

With their shares of the profit agreed, JW bade farewell to his companion of the last nine months and left for Virginia, where he was reunited with his family after an absence of more than two years.

CHAPTER 12

Red Cloud Meets the President: 1870

RED CLOUD SIGNED THE FORT LARAMIE TREATY IN NOVEMBER 1868 but agreeing to the terms of the treaty became a long, drawn-out process that took many years to resolve. The location of the new agency caused immediate controversy.

None of the local politicians and businessmen in the newly created State of Nebraska, nor the neighboring territories of Wyoming and Dakota, wanted the permanent home of the Indians on their land. They wanted it for themselves so homesteaders could be encouraged to settle and work their claims; railroads could open new areas for commercial exploitation; and any mineral deposits discovered, like gold, silver, or coal, would benefit their state or territory and not the Indians. They resented the federal government giving away what they considered to be their valuable lands. The army, supported by the OIA, wanted Red Cloud's agency to be located on the Missouri River in Dakota Territory, where Indians would be isolated from whites, they could be relatively easily controlled by the army, and their rations and annuities could be delivered to them cheaply and efficiently by river.

Red Cloud was adamantly opposed to moving four hundred miles to Fort Randall, the site the OIA had selected on the Missouri for the Indians to collect their rations, claiming it had not been part of the Fort Laramie Treaty. He wanted the agency to be located near the traditional hunting grounds of the Oglala either in Wyoming or Nebraska, and to trade and draw their rations at Fort Laramie. He viewed the Missouri as a place that was mosquito ridden and unhealthy, where "Bad Whites" would wreak havoc among his people by bringing diseases such as small-pox, making whiskey easily available, and encouraging his women into prostitution. He flatly refused to move.

Four months after he had signed the treaty, Red Cloud and more than a thousand Indians gathered outside Fort Laramie demanding to trade and receive their rations there. To avoid bloodshed the commander at the fort eventually relented and rations were issued.[1] To further ease the tension, local traders John Richard Jr. and his partner, Jules Ecoffey, were given a license by the OIA to trade with the Oglala in the Fort Fetterman area north of the Platte River, close to the Indian traditional hunting grounds.[2]

Twenty-five-year-old John Jr. was the eldest of the infamously wild Richard brothers. Born to a wealthy and successful French frontier man, John Richard Sr., and his half-Oglala wife, Mary, the mixed-race man was Red Cloud's first cousin once removed. John Jr. had been educated at an expensive school in St. Charles, Missouri.[3] He was fluent in several Indian dialects including Lakota and Crow, and he had an intimate understanding of the Oglala.[4] He was a slim, good-looking, and stylish young man, highly intelligent, but was wild, unpredictable, and impulsive. He had a reputation for liking women and whiskey, and these were to be his downfall.

On September 9, 1869, in a drunken dispute over a woman, John Jr. killed a soldier at Fort Fetterman. A grand jury in Cheyenne found him guilty of murder, so he fled custody and sought refuge with Red Cloud. John Jr. stayed with Red Cloud's band throughout the winter. Given his ability to straddle two cultures and having the ears of the powerful Indian chiefs Red Cloud and Spotted Tail, he was too useful to the government to hang. Several influential politicians and army officers therefore lobbied for his acquittal in recognition of his "service to the Government during the 1866 Powder River War."[5]

Before the Civil War, few whites had settled on the Great Plains, but after the war demand for space for white settlement increased greatly. The federal government wrestled with the question of how to handle the Northern Plains Indians. Should they attempt to assimilate, concentrate, or exterminate them? They were costing the nation too much. Despite some hawks proposing extermination, and the strident advocates of

Manifest Destiny who believed white Americans had a God-given right to develop and direct the country in a way they considered to be in their best interest, the consensus was for peace not war.[6] This sentiment was captured in Grant's election slogan during his 1868 presidential campaign: "Let us have peace."

President Grant's thinking had been shaped by the terrible bloodshed he had seen during the Civil War. He wanted to resolve the Indian problem and to treat them with dignity, and to end the corruption that existed in the OIA. He had become president at a critical junction of westward expansion, and there was enormous pressure from all quarters for the release of millions of acres of federal land to pioneers, settlers, and mining and railroad companies. Although his goal was peace, at the same time he needed to create room for white settlement—he was not planning to keep whites out of the vast tract of land the Indians used for hunting. Perhaps naively, he believed he could achieve peace and white settlement without conflict.

During their tour of the Indian tribes in the first half of 1869, peace commissioners had encountered Indian agents they felt needed "to be removed and replaced by honest, fair-dealing men who would be able to secure respect and confidence from the Indians."[7] In December, President Grant presented his Indian Peace Policy to Congress. In his address he said "the building of railroads . . . is rapidly bringing civilized settlements into contact with all the tribes of Indians. . . . I see no remedy except placing all the Indians on large reservations . . . and giving them absolute protection."[8]

Much to the War Department's annoyance, he declared the Indian reservations would be off limits to the army. And he ruffled the feathers of the OIA when he called for the replacement of politically appointed (and often corrupt) Indian agents on the nation's seventy reservations with civilians sponsored by various religious denominations. The key question was whether the churches could appoint honest and competent agents where politicians had failed.[9]

In the spring of 1870, four months after Grant's address to Congress, Red Cloud and the Oglala again camped close to Fort Laramie. They were desperate to trade and draw their rations. On the verge of starvation, they pleaded to be issued with ammunition to enable them to hunt small game. The tribe was seething with discontent, and to reduce tension Red Cloud proposed a delegation to visit Washington, DC, for talks with the OIA and President Grant.[10]

The commandant at Fort Fetterman supported his request, believing it would "stop, in a short time, all Indian depredations in this section of the country."[11] On May 3, the Cabinet agreed to grant Red Cloud his wish. It was a clear indication of how seriously the president and the government viewed the current unrest, and the importance they placed on enlisting Red Cloud's support. The invitation was also extended to Spotted Tail.[12] Once the decision was made the government did everything possible to ensure their visit was a success in the hope that further conflict would be avoided.

Five hundred Indians gathered at Fort Fetterman on May 16, to see Red Cloud leave for his historic meeting with the President of the United States.[13] Two days later at Fort Laramie he met Colonel John E. Smith, who had been sent from Washington to accompany the delegation to the capital. He had been given $2,500 to provide the Indians with "clothing or anything else they might need."[14] The Indians were equipped by the post trader at Fort Laramie, William Bullock, and entertained in style in the commanding officer's residence.

The twenty-one-strong delegation, which included John Richard Jr., William Bullock, and, at Red Cloud's request, the trader Jules Ecoffey, then traveled to the Union Pacific Depot at Pine Bluffs, forty miles east of Cheyenne, where they boarded a special coach on the "great iron horse" bound for Washington.

Hopes for Red Cloud's visit were high. The *New York Times* wrote: "The visit of Red Cloud to Washington cannot but do good. . . . Red Cloud is undoubtedly the most celebrated warrior now living on the American Continent . . . a man of brains, a good ruler, an eloquent speaker, an able and fair diplomat. The friendship of Red Cloud is of more importance to the whites than that of any other ten chiefs on the plains. Let every care be taken . . . to win his goodwill."[15]

The government's charm offensive started on Friday and continued throughout Saturday with sightseeing tours of the city. They visited the Capitol building, the Arsenal, and the Navy Yard, all selected to impress the Indians with the white man's power and accomplishments. The Indians were polite but reserved, and probably more than a little over-whelmed by their first visit to the capital.[16]

On Monday evening Red Cloud and his delegation visited the White House to meet the president, an occasion designed to impress them with the grandeur in which he lived. The Indians were led into the East Room, where Red Cloud was introduced to President and Mrs. Grant, members of the Cabinet, and officials from the OIA. After a reception they moved into the State Dining Room for a lavish banquet. The *New York Times* commented that "in every respect the entertainment was as elegant as that given to Prince Arthur [the third son of Queen Victoria] last summer."[17]

Red Cloud took his introduction to Washington in stride and was not overawed by the impressive display of pomp, ceremony, and power. When the meetings began the next day, various points from the Fort Laramie Treaty were discussed. Red Cloud acted as the lead negotiator and set out the Indian demands clearly and firmly: the government must honor its promise to provide the Indian annuities; they must be allowed to trade and draw their rations from their traditional hunting grounds in Wyoming, and not along the Missouri River; John Richard Jr. must be granted a pardon; and Fort Fetterman must close. The authorities refused this last request but granted Richard a pardon, and eventually conceded the Oglala would not have to move to the Missouri to receive their rations. However, agreeing on an alternative location that was acceptable to the Indians, the army, and the Wyoming authorities proved to be a challenge.

Red Cloud had shown himself to be a wise and competent negotia-tor, and consequently, his status rose. The warrior-turned-statesman and his entourage had taken the country by storm. Newspapers recounted his every word and deed, and large crowds of onlookers gathered at every public sighting of the celebrated group. The adulation continued in New York when the Indian delegation arrived there later in the month.

Thousands of people lined Fifth Avenue to catch a glimpse of the man who had beaten the US Army. A few days later the speech he delivered at the Cooper Institute in Manhattan received glowing reviews and enhanced his reputation still further.[18]

When the delegation passed through Omaha on its way home the media frenzy continued, and the local press covered its every move. The big wholesalers and trading houses opened their doors to welcome the Indians, and a contemporary account describes the scene:

> Large delegations of Sioux chiefs and warriors, on their way to and from seeing the Great White Father in Washington, generally stopped at Omaha, and while here, made the store of Stephens & Wilcox their headquarters, holding their councils on the second floor, sitting on rolls of carpet. Red Cloud, Spotted Tail, Red Dog, Blue Horse, Big Foot, Young Man Afraid of His Horses, and other well-known warriors were among them. On one of these occasions Red Cloud presided, as the great chief, sitting in an armchair and dressed in a black frock coat, trousers and a soft hat, furnished by Stephens & Wilcox. Red Dog, the second chief, a large fat chief, became jealous of Red Cloud's clothes and raised a disturbance which stopped all further proceedings until he had been similarly attired, when he looked upon himself with great complacency, though his limbs protruded through the garments in a manner that was amusing to see.[19]

The first visit of the Indians to Washington had been a success: Red Cloud had won his fight not to move to the Missouri; Spotted Tail had secured agreement to relocate the Whetstone Agency and the Brulé from the Missouri to Big White Clay Creek in Nebraska; the delegation had secured a pardon for John Richard Jr.; and, in the eyes of the government and the general public, Red Cloud had established himself as the most powerful Indian in America.

However, the army and the power brokers in Wyoming were extremely unhappy with the concessions Red Cloud had secured in Washington. They did not want the Oglala or their agency in Wyoming, and it would be another year before a compromise location for the first Red Cloud Agency was agreed upon.

CHAPTER 13

Virginia, Royal Oaks, and West Again

As Red Cloud was winning admirers in Washington, JW arrived home to a hero's welcome in Virginia. When he had gone West two years earlier, he had very little money, but the will and determination to make something of himself.

By the age of twenty-four JW had seen and achieved more than most men do in a lifetime, and his material success exceeded his wildest expectations. He had fought in the Civil War, started a newspaper, worked in the bustling city of Omaha and among frontiersmen and Indians on the open plains surrounding Fort Laramie, and had spent nine months in a remote fur trading post deep in Indian country on the Upper Missouri. He returned to his beloved Virginia with countless stories of the colorful and dangerous life he had led, but most importantly, with enough money from his Upper Missouri adventure to buy one of the finest houses in Fairfax County—Robert Whaley's four-hundred-acre estate, Royal Oaks, which he bought at auction for $4,746.[1]

His four brothers and sister, who still lived with their parents, were in awe of his achievements and saw him as the de facto head of the family, taking over from their unreliable father.

During the early days of the Civil War, Royal Oaks was the military headquarters for two Union generals. It was built on top of a low hill shaded by oaks, standing at the end of a hundred-yard, tree-lined drive, away from the bustle and dust of Braddock Road, one of the main roads into Centreville. It spoke of its owner's aspirations to status within the community, the quintessential home of a Virginia gentleman farmer. The house had two stories, a large attic, and a cellar. There were ten rooms with nine-foot ceilings.

The house was believed to have been built in the 1780s by General Daniel Roberdeau, George Washington's first chief of staff and a member of the Continental Congress.[2] In 1850 the estate was acquired by Robert Whaley, who lived there with his family until he was involved in an acrimonious dispute with his business partner and was forced by commissioners handling the dispute to sell Royal Oaks.[3] JW knew the estate well; he had boarded nearby and was a friend of Robert's son Walter.[4]

The sale was finalized on July 28, 1870, and in the space of a few weeks JW had arranged for his parents, George and Sarah, to move from their modest home in Mount Gilead, where George had spent the last ten years struggling as a tenant farmer, to a fine house on a country estate

Royal Oaks, at the center of a four-hundred-acre estate, bought at auction by JW from the Whaley family in July 1870. The porch was rebuilt by JW in 1872. Photographed in the 1920s. Royal Oaks Collection, MSS 04-06, Virginia Room, Fairfax County Public Library

where the family could now run their own four-hundred-acre farm. JW terminated George's tenancy at the farm in Mount Gilead; settled the rent due; and purchased George's livestock and agricultural equipment from him for $722, which he then assigned to his younger brother Richard for the "use and benefit" of their mother, Sarah.[5] Clearly, JW was still not confident his father could be trusted with money, so he arranged for the estate to be managed in such a way that his father could enjoy the benefit of the house but was legally excluded from any financial involvement. His mother and Richard were given authority to make important financial decisions.

After taking possession of Royal Oaks, JW spent the next three months with his father and brothers renovating the main house and repairing damage done during the war. It was a happy time for JW, back home in his beloved Virginia among family and friends, knowing that his decision to go West had been vindicated, seeing the fruits of his hard work and sacrifice being enjoyed by his family.

His affection for Fairfax County grew stronger during this period, and his relationships with the Cross, Whaley, DeBell, and Utterback families continued to strengthen. When he could, he visited Willow Cottage to see his friend Sam Rogers and Sam's sister, Mary Ann. Sam was managing the family estate for his mother, and Mary Ann was teaching school.

JW and Mary Ann spent as much time as they could together. They went for walks, and on one occasion when they visited the Leesburg Fair, JW introduced Mary Ann to Colonel Mosby. She was suitably impressed and often recalled the encounter in later life. However, JW did not take Mary Ann to see Royal Oaks, and the couple kept their growing friendship from their families and friends. Despite his success, JW still felt he wasn't worthy of someone from such a fine family and that he still had something to prove.

JW had used his hard-earned money to buy a home for his family's use, not for himself, and three months after the purchase, when he was satisfied his family was settled in their new home and could support themselves, he returned to his old job in Omaha.[6] A few days before his departure, on a cold and rainy day in early November, he spent the day with Mary Ann. She gave him a photograph of herself, and although they wrote to each other frequently and he sent photographs to her depicting his life out West, it would be almost three years before they would meet again.[7]

JW's younger brother Clay, now twenty-three, was excited and impressed by JW's success and his stories of the opportunities—and dangers—out West.[8] The two brothers were close; both had fought with Mosby in the Civil War, and both had a taste for adventure. So when JW returned to his old job with Richards & Whitney in Omaha, he took Clay with him. The two brothers arrived in the city on Saturday, November 5. JW moved into new lodgings at 538 13th Street, and Clay boarded a block away at the recently built Metropolitan Hotel.[9]

On Monday JW returned to work, the same day that Clay started work as a salesman for the wholesaler Stephens & Wilcox, a job that JW had arranged for him.[10]

JW had not lived in Omaha since July 1869 when he and Charles Larpenteur had left for Fort Buford, and he was surprised and impressed how the city had changed.[11] New commercial buildings and hotels had been built, and the Omaha Horse Railway Company had extended its service south from 9th and Farnam Streets to Jones Street, a block north of the Union Pacific depot.

Although many new buildings had appeared, the basic city infrastructure still left much to be desired. The bridge linking Omaha with Council Bluffs on the east bank remained in the planning stage, which meant travelers from the east had to cross the Missouri by ferry or, in winter when the river froze, by an ice bridge.

JW quickly settled back into the familiar routine he had established when he had lived in the city two years earlier. He managed the office and accounts for Richards & Whitney and traveled west to visit customers along the Platte River and at Fort Laramie. He introduced Clay to his friends and contacts, and for the next five months, over the winter of 1870–1871, the two young brothers worked hard. But life was not all work. The burgeoning city offered many diversions to its thousands of young bachelors. Masonic lodges, gentlemen's clubs, bars, and restaurants were some of the more reputable attractions on offer.

During this period JW forged an increasingly strong relationship with Clay's employer, Captain William Wilcox of Stephens & Wilcox. The company was an aggressive wholesaler that specialized in the fur and Indian trade, and to further its interests and strengthen ties with customers, it often invested in, or underwrote, both personal and commercial projects.[12] Stephens & Wilcox made a great deal of money trading furs on the Upper Missouri and for a number of years had been a major supplier to William Bullock's sutler store at Fort Laramie, regularly buying his furs and robes. It developed a solid trading relationship with the Indians, and particularly with Red Cloud and the Oglala. Business relationships between the major trading houses, traders, and sutlers were opportunistic, fluid, and often transitory. Everybody knew everybody, and where there was a common interest, partnerships were quickly formed. But if circumstances changed, they were equally quickly severed.

Encouraged by the success of JW and Larpenteur's fur trading venture a year earlier, Richards & Whitney were keen to return to Fort Buford to open a trading post. In the spring of 1871, they entered a partnership with the Wyoming-based traders, Jules Ecoffey and John Richard Jr.

After Richard had been pardoned for the murder of a soldier at Fort Fetterman, he had rejoined his partner, Jules Ecoffey, near Fort Laramie, and they had resumed their fur trading business. They owned two trading posts in Wyoming, one fifty miles south of Fort Laramie, the other near Fort Fetterman.[13] They bought goods the Indians wanted from Richards & Whitney and used them to barter with the Sioux and Cheyenne for furs and robes, which were then sold back to the firm. The arrangement worked well, and they agreed to form a partnership to manage their combined fur trading businesses: Ecoffey and Richard's two existing posts in Wyoming with the new post Richards & Whitney planned to open at Fort Buford.

Jules Ecoffey was one of the West's early pioneers. He was a Swiss citizen who had been educated at Freiburg University in southwestern Germany. He had moved to America in 1853 and the following year was living in the Fort Laramie area. He initially worked for the old American Fur Company and was soon trading with the Oglala, which was when he first met Red Cloud. He married an Oglala woman and as a natural linguist, added Lakota to the six languages he already spoke.

Ecoffey was a seasoned frontiersmen with an eye for personal gain and a reputation for getting things done. By the mid-1860s he and a partner owned a six-hundred-head cattle ranch, forty miles west of Fort Laramie. They were the largest operators in the area, supplying beef to Fort Laramie and freighting supplies from the railhead at Cheyenne to the army and Bullock's store at Fort Laramie. They also shipped hay and timber, did construction work, and transported buffalo robes and beef hides from Fort Laramie to the railhead at Cheyenne. In the late 1860s Ecoffey added another arm to his business when he and Richard opened two fur trading posts on the Wyoming hunting grounds of the Lakota.

JW had been an integral part of Richards & Whitney's successful Fort Buford venture with Charles Larpenteur; he was trusted by the partners and had known Ecoffey and Richard since 1868 when he first met them at Fort Laramie. He was the obvious choice to manage the new business venture. His first task was to open the trading post at Fort Buford, and on April 4, five months to the day after he and Clay had arrived in Omaha, JW left by train for Sioux City. The next day he boarded the *Ida Reese*, a 180-foot stern-wheeler owned by the trading company Durfee & Peck, laden with supplies for the forts and trading posts scattered along the Missouri.

JW was an upper deck passenger, with his own cabin, or "stateroom," with access to a dining room serving hotel fare prepared by a chef. On April 22, 1871, JW wrote to his friend James Cross in Centreville from his cabin on the *Ida Reese*:

> Today makes me seventeen days out of port. Am on my way to my old point Fort Buford for the purpose of setting up the old business for the [partners] at that distant point. I have left behind all signs of civilization, and [we] are now drifting towards the wilds of the far northwest. As I write the old steamer is gradually ploughing her way up the rugged Missouri. I am sitting alone in the old cabin, under the glare of the lamplight, as most of the passengers are on the deck. Thousands

of Indians swarm along the banks as we pass through the grounds of the different tribes. Droves of elk, antelope and deer dash startled over the prairie at the approach of the boat—and some of the finest scenery ere greeted the eye—passes before the beholder as we traverse through this wild and rugged portion of the country—a place where no human habitation exists, and where even the game that abounds has never been disturbed by the crack of a huntsman's rifle. Tho' I have passed over the same country before, I cannot but still appreciate it.[14]

After thirty days aboard the *Ida Reese*, JW disembarked at Fort Buford, where he discovered his plans to establish a fur trading post had been thwarted—a recently passed Army Bill decreed there could be only one military-appointed trader at any fort and that a wide exclusion zone applied to all civilian traders.[15] Opening a post at Fort Buford was therefore not possible.[16] JW was left with no alternative but to return empty-handed to Omaha on the next boat heading south, which fortunately for him was not the *Ida Reese*. Six weeks later, laden with two hundred tons of freight, $100,000 in furs and robes, and fifty-five passengers, she hit a sandbar, broke in two and sank.[17]

When JW arrived back in Omaha, he briefed the partners on developments at Fort Buford. He agreed to move six hundred miles west to manage their two Wyoming trading posts.[18] This was a dangerous but potentially lucrative assignment.

JW spent the next few hectic days closing his affairs in Omaha. He bade farewell to Clay and his many friends and on a warm May morning, left his lodgings for the last time and traveled by streetcar twelve hundred yards to the Union Pacific Railroad Depot, where he boarded the train to Cheyenne. It was a journey he had made several times before. He was familiar with Cheyenne and Fort Laramie, which were both raw and basic frontier communities, but Fort Fetterman and the surrounding plains where the two trading posts were located, were unknown to him. Nevertheless, by the end of May, he was in his new home, an isolated trading post on the north bank of the North Platte River, forty miles northwest of Fort Laramie.

CHAPTER 14

JW Meets Red Cloud: Summer of 1871

RED CLOUD ARRIVED BACK IN WYOMING FROM HIS FIRST VISIT TO
Washington, DC, on June 24, 1870.[1] His visit had been a success, and he
returned clearly pleased with the concessions he had wrung from President Grant. His good humor, however, was soon replaced by frustration
and then anger. No progress had been made on agreeing upon a location
for the first Red Cloud Agency, and the rations he had been promised,
when they materialized, proved to be woefully inadequate, leaving his
people on the verge of starvation. The OIA wanted the Indians to move
to Raw Hide Buttes, forty miles north of the Platte River, where there
were very few whites. Some Indians supported this, but others, particularly the young braves, wanted to remain on their traditional lands south
of the Platte River. Red Cloud had the difficult task of balancing these
two factions while maintaining his influence over the tribe.[2] As winter set
in, conditions worsened and the issue remained unresolved.

Under the terms of President Grant's Peace Policy, the Episcopal
Church had been given responsibility for the supervision of the Oglala.
Their first appointee as Indian agent, Major Joseph Wham, an ex-army
officer, arrived at Fort Laramie on February 5, 1871, where he had the
thankless task of selecting the site for the new agency.[3] The task was not
made any easier by the fact that by now the Indians were hungry, angry,
and uncooperative. To force the Oglala to cooperate, the authorities
refused to allow the Indians to trade or be issued with ammunition to
hunt small game until the site had been agreed. This infuriated them, and
Red Cloud warned the new agent that unless the stalemate was resolved

he would be unable to control his young braves. Violence would escalate, and he feared many would leave to join the northern non-reservation Indians under Crazy Horse and Sitting Bull.

The long and bad-tempered process of choosing the location of the agency continued, and by late May the relationship between the Indians and the authorities was tense and confrontational. At that critical point JW arrived to take responsibility for Ecoffey and Richard's two trading posts. His letter to James Cross records: "I am 120 miles due north of Cheyenne, in the heart almost of the hunting grounds of thirty thousand Indian warriors." He continues, "my year [contract] will expire next May [1872]."[4]

Fort Fetterman had been built four years earlier at the height of Red Cloud's War, to protect miners and settlers traveling along the Bozeman Trail. It was sited high on the bluffs on the south bank of the North Platte River, seventy miles upriver from Fort Laramie.[5] As it was located on the south bank, it had been excluded from the provisions of the Fort Laramie Treaty, which resulted in the abandonment of all forts farther to the north. It could accommodate up to three hundred men; had stabling for fifty horses; and consisted of a group of low, dirt-roofed log cabins surrounding the parade ground.[6] Buffalo grass flourished on the vast, flat plains surrounding the bluffs where the fort stood, green and lush in the spring, brown and dry during the rest of the year.

This unrelenting landscape was broken by a few tall cottonwood trees that grew along the river valley, and it was there, a few miles east of the fort on the north bank of the North Platte River that one of Ecoffey and Richard's trading posts was located. It consisted of a few log and adobe buildings, a trading house, a dry goods store, a simple residence, and a wooden horse corral.[7] Spread across the open plains as far as the eye could see were Indian villages teeming with dogs and ponies, and the general detritus of daily life scattered around them. Among them was Red Cloud and his band of more than thirty lodges.

It was a scene that epitomized the Western frontier and a way of life that had become second nature to Ecoffey and Richard. Much of their success had been due to their close relationship with Red Cloud and the Oglala, and after the government had made Fort Laramie and William

Bullock's post store off limits to the Indians, their trading store had benefited. The Oglala came to trade there and Red Cloud was a regular visitor.

JW was first introduced to Red Cloud during the summer of 1871, when Ecoffey and Richard paid a courtesy visit to Red Cloud's village. Three men, in the dark frock coats habitually worn by men of business in the West, cantered over the open plain heading for Red Cloud's village a few miles north of their trading post. Ecoffey was an old friend of Red Cloud, and Richard was part of his family.[8] Both men were fluent in Lakota, but the greenhorn riding with them, JW, spoke only English with a soft, slow, and melodious Southern drawl. The purpose of the visit was to introduce JW to Red Cloud and the other chiefs of his village. It was important the Indians would be comfortable with their new manager.

Receiving guests followed a time-honored ritual.[9] As the three men dismounted and entered Red Cloud's tepee, they were ushered to the folded bedding that formed raised seating around the inside walls. Indians sat on buffalo robes or stood by the entrance to watch the proceedings. The visitors presented gifts, a pipe to symbolize friendship and goodwill was passed around the circle, and Ecoffey and Richard introduced their new employee to Red Cloud and the assembled members of his band.

This was the first time JW had visited an Indian chief's village and seen the rituals associated with Indian hospitality. He had heard many stories about the legendary chief and was excited to meet him, but for Red Cloud it was very different. His first meeting with the twenty-five-year-old, slightly built, dark-haired white man who didn't speak his language barely registered. It was an unexceptional start to a relationship that over the years grew in trust and respect and lasted for the rest of JW's life.

A letter to James Cross written from JW's trading post that summer gives a vivid description of his new job and the strain he was under:

> Even as I write to you, I hear the prowling wolves howling in the distance, and the beating of the Indian drums and their war whoops as they gather round the war dance and feast telling of their former exploits. At night one cannot lay down without a thought of suspense of what might occur ere another sun rises. Belting on of pistols as each sun rises. Pistols under your pillow. Trusty rifle at all times at your bedside.

Red Cloud and JW met for the first time in the summer of 1871 on the Wyoming hunting grounds of the Oglala. Courtesy of the Library of Congress, LC-USZ62-91032

The parties [Ecoffey and Richard] for who I am working have large trading posts . . . all doing a large trade. Every month or so we ship overland with our own wagon train large lots of robes, hides, furs etc to the RR there [Cheyenne] to be sent over to the States. I have my hands full, as the whole business of the trading posts is under my supervision and frequently am compelled to travel from one to the other in order to keep matters running. The firm is mostly in the States but seldom see them, not once in three months. In fact, have everything on my shoulders—so you can imagine it keeps me moving.[10]

During these testing months, what little social life JW had was centered on Fort Laramie rather than Fort Fetterman, which during its brief existence was regarded as a hardship posting. The officers and men complained about the cold, isolation, and lack of women. This latter complaint was partially resolved with the establishment of a brothel, or "hog ranch" as it was colloquially called, on the north side of the river. But the men still had to cross the Platte to get their entertainment, and in winter that was no easy task.[11]

Thousands of buffalo hides at a railroad depot await shipment to "the States" in the East. JW's hides were packed and transported by ox-wagon train to depots like this at Cheyenne and Sidney. Courtesy of National Archives, photo no. 520093

In contrast Fort Laramie, a seventy-five-mile ride away, was a thriving multi-cultural community with hundreds of people coming and going all the time. Of the two hundred or more forts in the American West, many historians consider Fort Laramie the quintessential frontier army post and rank it the most historically significant of them all.[12] Here a complete cross section of the extraordinary characters that inhabited the West met and could purchase almost anything they could conceivably need. JW was a regular visitor to Fort Laramie that summer, and the carte de visite he gave to Bullock remains in the fort's archives.

Located next to Bullock's store was a saloon where "the whole fantastic social strata of the frontier assembled and tossed coins at the bartender, gurgled barrels of whiskey, engaged in occasional knifings and shooting scrapes, plotted robberies and assassinations, boasted of Indian scalps and gold nuggets; and dreamed of (or dreaded) a time when this vast, wild land would be tamed and civilized."[13] It was where JW; veteran mountain men; pale-faced Easterners; professional gamblers; desperadoes of all descriptions; and characters like Kit Carson, Wild Bill Hickok, William "Buffalo Bill" Cody, Mark Twain, Wyatt Earp, and a few years later, Calamity Jane, all came to drink and while away the long winter evenings.

JW befriended the officers and civilians stationed at the fort: mixed-race interpreters and army scouts like Louis Shangrau; John Richard Jr.'s brother, Louis; Big Bat Pourier and the Janis brothers; Oliver Unthank, the telegraph operator; Frank Yates, the justice of the peace; and young officers, Lieutenants James Buchanan, Josh Fowler, and William Carter—all these men played a part in JW's life, and many knew Red Cloud.

In early 1872, JW's new business partners, Ecoffey and Richard, together with Adolph Cuny, opened a road ranch on the north side of the Laramie River, three miles west of Fort Laramie. It was known as the Three Mile Hog Ranch.

At first it was run as a general road ranch. But after two years when business became slack, Ecoffey employed ten young women from Omaha and Kansas known as "sporting characters," and eight two-room cottages were built for their occupancy.

JW's carte de visite, left by him at Bullock's sutler store in 1871. Unthank Collection, Fort Laramie National Historic Site

Lieutenant James G. Bourke, aide-de-camp to the commander of the Army of the Platte, General Crook, wrote in his diary: "a nest of ranches on the road from Fort Laramie were tenanted by as hardened and depraved a set of wretches as could be found on the face of the globe. . . . In all my experience, I have never seen a lower, more beastly set of people of both sexes."[14]

The infamous Martha Jane Cannary, better known as Calamity Jane, worked briefly at the Hog Ranch before moving to Deadwood in 1876.

By midsummer 1871, agreement had still not been reached on the location of the agency. In an attempt to force a decision, the authorities once again withheld the Indians' rations on July 5.[15] They rapidly backed down, however, when it became clear Red Cloud could not control his angry young braves and violence would ensue. A few days later the issue was finally settled.[16] It was agreed the agency would be in Wyoming, thirty miles east of Fort Laramie and one mile north of the Platte River and would be known as the Red Cloud Agency.

The location pleased no one. The Indians knew it was a compromise. Many of the younger Indians wanted to be south of the Platte and were openly hostile to taking the "White Man's Road," as they believed they had received only broken promises in return. Their sympathies lay more with Crazy Horse and Sitting Bull than with Red Cloud, who was having great difficulty in managing an increasingly explosive situation. The whites wanted the Indians out of Wyoming and resented Red Cloud for persuading the authorities to allow the Indians to remain in "their" territory. The army feared the Indians would clash with the increasing number of cattlemen and white settlers in the area and that they would be called to restore order. They still wanted the Oglala on the Missouri River, where they would be easier to control and where their rations could be delivered efficiently.

It was against this background that JW had the challenging task of managing Ecoffey and Richard's fur trading posts, and Indian Agent Wham had the unenviable task of building and opening the first Red Cloud Agency as quickly as possible.

PART III

INDIAN TRADER AT THE RED CLOUD AGENCIES: 1871–1879

CHAPTER 15

The First Red Cloud Agency: 1871–1873

CONSTRUCTION OF THE NEW AGENCY STARTED IN AUGUST. AGENT Wham recruited his key staff, and William Bullock was appointed Indian trader. Bullock had left Fort Laramie in early August when Seth Ward's license as post trader to the army was not renewed. He took up his position at the new agency, but within two months he was a casualty of local politics—he was a Virginian, a Confederate, and a Democrat.[1] He was forced to resign and in October was replaced by Ecoffey and Richard. The financial backer who guaranteed their $5,000 bond to the OIA was Stephens & Wilcox.[2]

By this time JW had been working for Ecoffey and Richard for six months. He had met Red Cloud and had made a favorable impression on his employers. As a result, they gave him the additional responsibility of overseeing their fur trading activity at the new agency. JW now had three fur trading posts to manage. His salary was increased by $500 to $2,500 per annum, backdated to May 1871, and he was given a 50 percent share of one of the posts now under his control. JW estimated this would be worth $6,000 a year, a very considerable sum.[3] With this new responsibility, JW moved to the agency when it opened in early October, and it became his home for the next twenty-two turbulent months.

The 300- by 250-yard compound was located on a small creek a mile from the north bank of the North Platte River, and a mile west of the Nebraska border. It consisted of a sod-and-dirt-roof accommodation block of ten rooms and a council room, one timber and two sod store houses for storing and dispensing rations, a timber and sod horse corral,

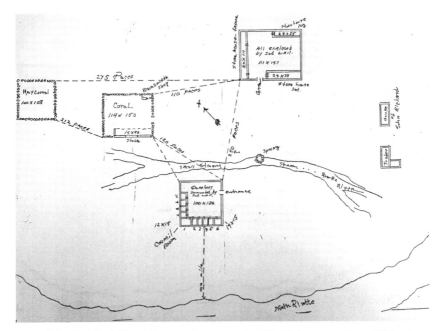

Plan of the first Red Cloud Agency, known as the "Sod" Agency, where JW lived from October 1871 to July 1873 in the accommodation shown as the "House of John Richard." Fort Laramie National Historic Site

a blacksmith shed, and a hay corral. The buildings to the west and south of the compound formed the perimeter wall, and a sod wall, loop-holed for riflemen, enclosed the northern and eastern sides.[4]

The agency soon became known as the "Sod Agency," as most of the walls were made of slabs of prairie sod cut from the ground and stacked like bricks. Living conditions were grim, and the interior walls had to be lined with domestic cotton sheeting to minimize the dirt, dust, and insects. The sod walls also tended to erode in heavy rain and made a convenient place for vermin to nest. Those employees not fortunate enough to be allocated a bunk bed slept in tents in the horse corral. Standing slightly apart to the east of the main buildings were the Indian traders' single-story log house and store, which is where JW lived.

The agency was located near the Oregon Trail, which meant that Indians were exposed to unscrupulous whites selling whiskey. The surrounding land was flat and arid, offering poor-quality grazing for Indian ponies, and there was no timber to be found within twenty-five miles. Almost as soon as the Indians moved to their new home, the authorities began searching for a more suitable location, ideally on the Great Sioux Reservation in Dakota Territory, well isolated from white settlers and with good transport access for the Indian rations.

Working at the Sod Agency was a challenge. Some years later George Colhoff, who was employed there as a clerk, recalled it was "a mighty tough place that served as a meeting place for Indians coming to trade, frontiersmen and outlaws, many sporting colorful names like Black Doc, Fly Speck Billy and many others who infested the Sidney Road and worked in western Wyoming. Some got killed; some ended up in the penitentiary; they all gambled and were just about as versatile in crime practices as it was possible to be."[5]

JW knew it would be a tough posting, but he saw it as a step toward becoming a licensed Indian trader and the opportunity to make a great deal of money. After three years in the West, he had a sound knowledge of the fur and Indian trade, had built a wide network of business contacts, and had been trading with the Sioux and Cheyenne in Wyoming and Nebraska for the previous six months: he was determined to put his hard-earned experience to good use.

Among those appointed to the agency at the same time as JW was Frank Yates, whom JW had first met at Fort Laramie.[6] Frank, who became a good friend, was a young man from a prosperous New York family. At the end of the Civil War, he had gone West and in 1870 moved to Fort Laramie, where he was appointed justice of the peace.[7] Agent Wham recruited Frank as his deputy. Frank worked at the Sod Agency for the next ten months before moving with Spotted Tail's Indians to the Whetstone Agency on the Missouri as their Indian trader.[8]

About this time JW met Billy Garnett, the sixteen-year-old illegitimate son of Brigadier General Richard Garnett, Thomas Dear's brigade commander at Gettysburg. Between 1852 and 1854, Captain Garnett had been the commanding officer at Fort Laramie. Thirty-seven-year-old Garnett had had an affair with a fifteen-year-old Oglala girl. She became pregnant, but shortly after their son Billy was born, Garnett was posted to California. Billy was brought up by his Oglala mother as an Indian and never saw his father again. But because he was an officer's son, he attended the army school at Fort Laramie, where he learned to read and write.[9]

Billy lived with his mother near the Sod Agency. He was a good-looking, intelligent, and likeable young man, equally at ease with both whites and Indians. He became a sought-after interpreter, who some years later worked for JW. He was described as "half savage and half aristocrat," and although he had been educated at an army school, his roots and loyalty lay with the Oglala, with whom he lived until his death in 1928.[10] It is likely that JW and Billy made the connection that Corporal Thomas Dear, JW's brother, and General Garnett, Billy's father, had died alongside each other on that terrible Friday afternoon at Gettysburg in 1863.

A month after JW arrived at the Sod Agency and when building work was nearing completion, Wham was fired for incompetence and suspected corruption.[11] With Frank Yates's help, the new commanding officer at Fort Laramie, Colonel John E. Smith, oversaw the management of the agency until Wham's replacement, Dr. Jared Daniels, arrived in February 1872. He was one of the most respected and experienced of the Episcopalian Church's Indian agents. He had served as a surgeon with the Union army in the Civil War and subsequently as an inspector of Indian agencies.[12]

Over the winter of 1871–1872, JW used the agency as his base for supervising the trading posts under his control. Early in the new year, his boss, John Richard Jr., decided he needed additional help running the day-to-day activities of the agency store. He recruited Hopkins Clark, who had previously worked in the sutler store at Fort Laramie. Clark's tenure was short lived. In April he was accidentally shot and killed by Richard. No charges were brought, and the whole affair was quickly forgotten. But the excitable and accident-prone Richard had now been directly involved in the deaths of at least two people.[13]

With the agency in turmoil, continuing Indian unrest, and constant traveling between trading posts, JW lived a dangerous and demanding life. He desperately missed the companionship of his family and friends in Virginia, as his letter of February 15 to James Cross reveals:

> My dear friend it really did my heart good. I felt ever so much better after reading [your letter], for you are surrounded by the social pleasures of home in the midst of friends and loved ones, who can lay down at night without a thought of suspense and what might occur ere another sun rises. [You] Can form no idea how much it cheers one here far away on the broad plains and rolling prairie of Northern Wyoming to receive a cheering line . . . from friends tho' they are three thousand miles away.

He asked James's advice about his brother Richard, whose education had suffered because of the Civil War. "Don't [you] think it best that the boy should go to school? I know from experience, that a little education, however small it may be, helps very much to smooth the rough spots along life's pathway. Is not this so? One-year schooling to Dick now, will be worth . . . in all probability thousands of dollars. What think you, besides this the boy deserves it, don't you think so?"[14]

The outcome was that JW paid for Richard to attend the Virginia Agricultural and Mechanical College in Blacksburg, two hundred miles south of Royal Oaks. In September he was one of forty-two students to enroll in the newly opened college.[15] It was run on strict military lines and had been established to provide "the best education and the best military training in Virginia."[16] Today it is known as Virginia Tech.

The new Indian agent's priorities were to bring stability and discipline and to obtain agreement on a new location for the agency that was acceptable to all parties.[17] Daniels's initial assessment of the Oglala was that they could be divided into three groups: those who were loyal, dependable, and helpful; those who were passive and did not want any trouble, were over thirty-five, past their prime, and would accept the consensus; and a third group made up of young braves who were anti-white, had little respect for their traditional chiefs, and were heavily influenced by the northern Indians. This group Daniels concluded would only respond to force: "Let them feel the full force of powder and the day of meek submission on the part of the Govt. will be at an end and their advancement will commence." As government rations were distributed, he observed that the tribes showed "as little gratitude as hogs."[18]

During his first few months in charge, Daniels's problems were exacerbated by an increase in violent clashes between whites and Indians. The incident that caused the most outrage involved a cattleman who was driving a thousand Texas longhorns from Texas to Montana. In early March he was ambushed, killed, and scalped near the Laramie River, reputedly by Oglala Indians "from Red Cloud's band."[19] This strengthened the resolve of the authorities to move the Indians from Wyoming as soon as possible, but getting agreement on a new site continued to be a problem.

Red Cloud was particularly difficult to pin down. He regularly changed his mind as he struggled to retain authority and balance the conflicting views within his tribe. He was finding the transition from warrior to statesman a challenge. Controlling the varying factions in peacetime was proving more difficult than leading the Oglala, Northern Cheyenne, and Arapaho in war. Red Cloud's negotiating style, described as "giving little by little and only after bedeviling his adversary through endless consultation with his fellow chiefs, irrelevant demands, bewildering changes of mind, qualified promises, theatrical bluster, and a host of niggling delaying tactics," was a major cause of tension between Red Cloud and Daniels.[20]

Red Cloud proposed a second meeting in Washington, DC, to find a solution. This was agreed, and on May 17, Agent Daniels left for Washington with Red Cloud and twenty-six subchiefs, including Red Dog.[21] Red Dog often acted as Red Cloud's right-hand man and spokesperson, and was seen by whites as being a wise and mature individual who helped bridge the gap between the two cultures. The party also included Jules Ecoffey and Red Cloud's favorite interpreter, Louis Richard, John Richard Jr.'s younger brother.[22]

The day the Indian delegation left for Washington an incident took place that had far-reaching repercussions for JW. John Richard Jr., Billy Garnett, Louis Shangrau, and Peter Janis left the Three Mile Ranch to visit Yellow Bear's lodge five miles west of the Sod Agency. Yellow Bear was chief of the Spleen Band of the Oglala, and Richard had been

Red Dog, Red Cloud's close confidant and trusted lieutenant. Photo Lot 90-1, George V. Allen Collection of Photographs of Native Americans and the American Frontier, National Anthropological Archives, Smithsonian Institution

married to one of his sisters. He had left her but now wanted her back. He was drunk and things got out of hand. After a short argument Richard shot and killed Yellow Bear, and he was then hacked to death by Yellow Bear's enraged supporters. Billy Garnett, who witnessed the event, fled to the Sod Agency, where he stayed in hiding for a week.[23]

Over fifteen hundred miles away in Washington the Indian delegation attended a series of meetings, and on May 30, in the presence of President Grant, Red Cloud finally agreed the Oglala would move to the White River in Nebraska, ninety miles north of the Sod Agency. When news of Richard's death reached the Indian delegation a few days later, Ecoffey immediately realized he would need someone to supervise the move and to manage his trading store at the new agency.

In early June the delegation left Washington, and Red Cloud, Jules Ecoffey, and Louis Richard stayed a few days in Omaha before heading farther west. They had ample time to discuss and agree who the new manager should be. With both John Richard Jr. and Hopkins Clark dead, JW was the obvious choice. When they returned to the Sod Agency JW was offered the post, and although he had planned to leave Ecoffey when his contract expired at the end of May, he agreed to stay.

Agent Daniels and Red Dog did not return directly to the agency but went north to Fort Peck on the Upper Missouri where they briefed the northern Indians on the outcome of the meeting in Washington, and once again tried to persuade them to give up their nomadic lifestyle and accept reservation life. They were unsuccessful. Very few Indians attended the meeting, and those who did continued to reject reservation life. The round trip of eighteen hundred miles by steamboat took two months to complete, and Daniels and Red Dog did not arrive back at the Sod Agency until September 1.

During Daniels's absence, a small group of trusted Indians, agency personnel, and OIA officials traveled north to select the location for the new agency. JW was a member of this group, which chose a remote site on the White River, ninety miles northeast of Fort Laramie. But Red Cloud was once again finding his young braves difficult to manage and struggled to get his tribe to support the move. When some of them defied his instructions by grazing their ponies south of the Platte River on grassland being used by contractors to grow hay for the army, a stand-off ensued. On August 20, with Red Cloud's full support, the army forced the braves to move their ponies back north of the Platte. Having lost face, they made it clear to Red Cloud they had no intention of moving to the White River.[24]

In a council meeting on September 11, 1872, Red Cloud, under tremendous pressure, spoke for the first time about the possibility of aborting the planned move. Over the coming days Indian hostility and aggressive behavior escalated, and staff at the agency began to fear for their lives.

The strain JW was under was reflected in the letter he wrote on September 15 to Mary Ann: "I have your picture now before me on the desk, and the face looks so natural, that it carries memory back to the last time I saw you, now nearly two long years ago. Do you remember that cold rainy eve?"[25]

He then continued to describe his life at the agency:

> Have been expecting to move for some time, as the Agency will be located and rebuilt some ninety miles still further north but am now waiting for remainder of Indian Annuities. They will be here in day or so, when will take up our line of march—for a more northern point. We have now about nine thousand Indians here at the Agency, waiting for their goods and the Agency to move. The broad plains are dotted for miles with lodges. All night long you hear their war dance, keeping time with their miserable war drum, and then a war whoop as one tells of feats done and scalps taken. This is a terrible life to lead . . . 15 Whites, a mere handful, to about 9,000 Indians . . . and alarms here sometimes to make every man grasp his gun, and the stoutest heart to quail . . . but I am getting pretty used to it. I never allow thoughts of our true position to trouble me.[26]

A week later, when the wagons were loaded and ready to roll, Red Cloud, realizing he had no mandate from his tribe, reneged on the agreement he had made in the presence of the president just three months earlier. He informed Daniels that "they should not go to the White River for thirty years."[27] Daniels, with the backing of the army, advocated withholding the rations to starve the Indians into submission. But the OIA backed down, and the Indians remained on the Platte.[28]

This was a major setback for JW, as he now faced the prospect of spending months, perhaps years, in an extremely stressful and inhospitable environment, forced to trade with the volatile and increasingly dangerous and unpredictable Oglala. In the midst of this unfolding drama, JW still found time to have a magnificent ring made for Mary Ann. He had found a large agate and arranged for Clay to have it cut and mounted by a jeweler in Omaha. JW described his gift to her as a "trinket" and sent it to her together with a fine buffalo robe via Fort Laramie. Ten days later an excited Mary Ann collected both gifts from Leesburg station.[29]

The politicians, failing to understand the complexities of tribal decision-making, made the mistake of believing a chief could speak for all his people and expected the tribe to follow his lead once an agreement with him had been made. While Red Cloud was clearly prepared to take the white man's road, bringing his people with him was another matter. As head chief Red Cloud had considerable influence but still only acted as the spokesperson for the decisions of the subchiefs, which often took considerable time and diplomatic skills to obtain. He was unable to keep his promise to the president because he could not enforce it and retain authority over his warriors.

A few weeks later young braves, drunk on whiskey, threatened to kill the agent and all white men at the agency. JW and the rest of the staff barricaded themselves in. And eventually, with Red Cloud's support, the army was summoned, and bloodshed avoided.[30] One of the officers involved in the rescue operation, whom JW was to get to know well, was Captain James "Teddy" Egan, the Irish-born commander of Company K of the 2nd "White Horse" Cavalry. His command had been posted to Fort Laramie in May 1872 and remained in the area, involved in the Sioux troubles for the next five years.[31]

Threatening and potentially dangerous incidents occurred intermittently over the next few months, making it impossible for JW to travel across the plains without an armed escort, but by the spring of 1873 the danger had passed, as many of the more violent Indians had drifted north away from the Platte.

Life for JW gradually became less stressful, and a regular pattern to his day began to emerge. His trade with the Indians at his store was steady, but not spectacular. He was gaining acceptance, as he had an easy manner and got on well with the mix of people who frequented the agency. His freestanding log house, set slightly apart from the main compound, gave him a degree of privacy and a reasonable level of comfort. Salesmen from Omaha wholesalers regularly visited the area, sometimes coming to see him at his store, but more often he met them at Fort Laramie. One of these salesmen was Clay, who was still working for Stephens & Wilcox.

Discussions over the location of the agency dominated the first half of 1873. In June the Commissioner of Indian Affairs, appointed yet another commission to break the deadlock. A frustrated and exhausted Daniels had resigned just before the commission met but agreed to stay until his replacement arrived. On June 22, after two days of wrangling, Red Cloud finally agreed to move to the White River, providing he received the arms and ammunition he needed to hunt small game.[32] Five weeks later the first contractor's wagons left the Sod Agency heading north, and on August 2 Daniels wired the Indian commissioner triumphantly announcing: "Agency gone to place selected."[33]

A month earlier, JW had made a brief visit to Virginia to attend Richard's college diploma ceremony, where his guests included James Cross and his family.[34] Now that JW had helped Richard with his education, finding a job for him out West was his next challenge, as there were few prospects in Virginia. He visited Royal Oaks to check on the welfare of his parents and younger siblings, and he also saw Mary Ann at Willow Cottage, the first time they had been together for nearly three years. At some point he broke the news to her and his parents that he planned to remain out West and had agreed with Ecoffey to move with the Oglala to the White River in northwest Nebraska.

A few weeks later JW arrived at the site of the second Red Cloud Agency for what was to be the most exacting six months of his life.

CHAPTER 16

Camp Robinson and the Second Red Cloud Agency

THE NEW INDIAN AGENT, DR. JOHN J. SAVILLE, ARRIVED ON AUGUST 13, 1873, to take up his appointment. Saville had received his medical training at Michigan University and served during the Civil War as a surgeon with the Union infantry. He had then worked as a government contract surgeon before returning to his home in Sioux City as a general practitioner. On July 7 he had been nominated for an Indian agent's position, but there was little in his background to indicate his suitability or experience to manage one of the largest and most difficult agencies in the country. Despite the good intentions of President Grant's 1869 Peace Policy, the selection of competent Indian agents was still a major problem. The appointment of well-intentioned but often inept men proved disastrous and continued to plague the Indian service.[1]

Saville later admitted that he was ill prepared for the task ahead: "Inexperienced in this business myself, and having no one familiar with the forms of business, and without papers, books, or instructions for guides, I was left in a sufficiently embarrassing position to undertake so complicated a business."[2] He was described as small in stature, but willful and waspish by nature with an agitated, nervous, and abrasive disposition. It was perhaps not surprising that he and Red Cloud would clash.[3]

The new agency site was enthusiastically described by the retiring Agent Daniels as being "in a pretty valley with good water and farming land, standing high on a bluff overlooking the verdant valley of the White

River, handsomely located and indeed it could be described as the finest fruit of the peace policy."[4] In reality the farming potential was modest, and the site was one hundred thirty miles from the nearest railhead and eighty-five miles from the protection of Fort Laramie.

John Saville's troubles started the day he arrived, when on the banks of the White River he met Dr. Daniels and eight thousand Indians, most of whom had also just arrived from the Sod Agency. Commissary stores and building materials were piled on the ground covered with tarpaulins, and the agents' quarters were a tent. As soon as the formal transfer of property was completed, Daniels and his clerk left, leaving Saville and twenty agency employees, whom he barely knew, to fend for themselves.

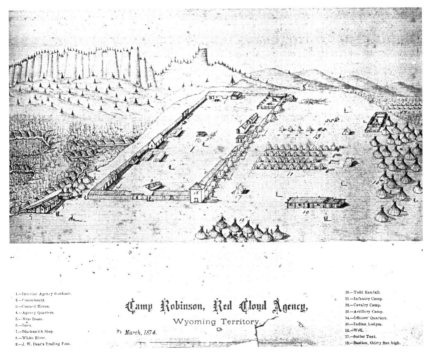

1.—Interior Agency Stockade.
2.—Commissary.
3.—Council House.
4.—Agency Quarters.
5.—Mess Room.
6.—Barn.
7.—Blacksmith Shop.
8.—White River.
9.—J. W. Dear's Trading Post.

Camp Robinson, Red Cloud Agency,
Wyoming Territory.
March, 1874.

10.—Todd Randall.
11.—Infantry Camp.
12.—Cavalry Camp.
13.—Artillery Camp.
14.—Officers' Quarters.
15.—Indian Lodges.
16.—Well.
17.—Sutler Tent.
18.—Bastion, thirty feet high.

This drawing of the second Red Cloud Agency dated March 1874 shows JW's trading store on the far left, west of the stockade. It was found in the attic of the New York home of the author's aunt. Its discovery marked the start of this story. Dear Family Collection

The guns, ammunition, and horses promised to the Indians for moving to the new site had not materialized, and Saville's charges were in a foul mood.[5] This was also JW's introduction to the place he would be closely associated with for the next ten years.

Ecoffey, with JW's help, moved his stock and equipment from the Sod Agency to the White River and started to build his trading store and accommodation fifty yards west of the new agency. He had also won the tender to supply logs to build the agency stockade.[6] Red Cloud had not traveled to the new location with the main body of Indians, and some took advantage of his absence. They conspired to have Ecoffey, whom they did not like, removed as their trader. They told the new agent that Ecoffey had brought whiskey onto the site.

Saville saw this as a violation of the department's rules and destroyed the whiskey in front of Ecoffey's quarters and revoked his trading license. When Red Cloud arrived at the agency and heard the news, he was furious. Both he and Colonel John Smith, the commanding officer at Fort Laramie, liked and respected Ecoffey, and his dismissal soured their relationship with Saville.[7] To further add to Saville's woes, Ecoffey then defaulted on the log contract, which severely delayed completion of the stockade.[8]

With Ecoffey gone, JW was left to manage the business and finish building the trading store. It is likely that he was appointed Indian trader immediately after Ecoffey's departure, although his license was not formally issued by the OIA until two months later, on October 11.[9] He then employed Louis Shangrau as his clerk and interpreter. At some point JW negotiated with Ecoffey the transfer of ownership of both the stock and trading store. No details of the deal survive, but Stephens & Wilcox underwrote JW's $5,000 bond to the OIA. At the age of twenty-seven JW had become the licensed Indian trader at one of the largest, but most troublesome, Indian agencies in the country. It was a position that had the potential to make him a great deal of money.

Despite the chaos and upheaval of building a large complex with its associated buildings on a bare-earth site, the main warehouse was completed by mid-September. Construction of the other buildings, including JW's trading store and accommodation, was by then also well underway.

By the end of the month JW and Todd Randall, the second trader at the agency, started trading with the Indians. However, everyone was concerned that the stockade, which was being built to protect the agency, was still far from finished.

The first annuity goods for Red Cloud's reservation Indians arrived in early October. This attracted bands of non-reservation Indians, which more than doubled the number Saville had rations for, and the mood once again turned ugly. Saville later wrote: "Many of these people had never been to an agency before, and were exceedingly vicious and insolent. They made unreasonable demands for food, and supplemented their demands with threats. They resisted every effort to count them, and as their statements of their numbers were frequently exaggerated, it became necessary to arbitrarily reduce their rations. . . . This caused a constant contention with them."[10]

At one point in October northern Indians surrounded Saville and tried to kidnap him when he was attempting to count the lodges north of the White River. A disaster was averted when he was rescued by Red Cloud and a group of his armed followers, who escorted Saville back to the agency.[11] Shortly after this the OIA inexplicably ordered Saville to attend a series of meetings in Washington, DC, to discuss the future of the Cheyenne and Arapaho Indians. Consequently, Saville was away throughout November, a critical time in the agency's development.

JW's store and accommodation were completed by mid-November, and, in spite of the unrest and continual threat of violence, he was keeping his head above water commercially. He was trading with the Indians and buying their robes, furs, and beef hides, and a check of his inventory showed that he offered more than two hundred fifty items ranging from saddle blankets to glass beads and from calico shirts to candles.[12]

His life was not all work. In early December he traveled to Fort Laramie to attend a party held in honor of Lieutenant Buchanan. He spent the evening reminiscing with friends and discussing the challenges he faced.[13]

When Saville returned from Washington on December 15, he found conditions had deteriorated. Bad weather with heavy snow meant that provisions from Cheyenne for the Indians had difficulty getting through, forcing Saville to ration supplies once again. Recognizing the difficulty of his position surrounded by thousands of irate and hungry Indians, and fearing for the safety of his staff, he requested protection from the army. This, however, was politically unacceptable to the Interior Department and the OIA, which were keen to demonstrate they could handle Indians without help from the War Department.[14]

On Christmas Day, to ease tension and find a resolution to his problems, Saville called the chiefs and head men together for a feast and used the occasion to again raise the question of holding a census to determine how many Indians needed to be fed. Red Cloud rejected the idea out of hand and demanded the promised arms, ammunition, and horses, which had still not been delivered. The gathering ended in disarray.[15] The relationship between Saville and Red Cloud was going from bad to worse, and Red Cloud started scheming to have Saville replaced.

With the shortage of food, the breakdown in communication between Saville and Red Cloud, and the aggressive stance of the northern Indians, the threat of physical violence to agency staff became an increasing concern. On January 7, 1874, Frank Appleton, Saville's nephew and chief clerk, wrote home to his family putting a brave face on events: "We are getting along very well with the work. By next Saturday we will have this enclosed [the stockade around the agency buildings] so on Sunday we can open our door and not be afraid. . . . It will be a relief, I assure you, to know that we are perfectly safe."[16]

Saville was not so sanguine, and on January 14, this time backed by the OIA, he requested that a military post be established to protect his staff. This was refused by General Sherman on the grounds that intervention by the army ran the risk of triggering an all-out Indian war, and he recommended the decision be postponed until the spring.[17] Sherman had opposed the Oglala move to the White River on the grounds it was in Nebraska and not on the Sioux Reservation, it would be hard to control the Indians if there was trouble, and it was a difficult and expensive site to supply. Events had proved him right.[18]

The threat of violence grew as January progressed. Several of Saville's staff felt they were poorly protected by only a pine board stockade and, fearing for their lives, resigned and left the agency. JW's friends became increasingly worried about his safety, and on February 2, JW wrote a letter to Oliver Unthank at Fort Laramie, which confirms the enormous strain he was under:

> Shipped 370 buffalo robes, hides, skins, furs, etc., last night. My stock is running low, but let her run. I cannot venture out of my room after night. Indians all the time with guns loaded and bows strung. Agent has concentrated every man in stockade with him. Cheyenne held a council yesterday. Told him the Sioux were constantly coming into their camp saying these houses here would soon be covered with blood. Times my dear boy, are here indeed dangerous. What is Agent telegraphing for, troops or what? He should have gone up, if anyone, instead of poor Frank Appleton. Am striving to keep up a brave heart, but this constant strain on the nerves is wearing me out. Again, good bye.[19]

On February 8, Saville left Appleton in charge of the agency and traveled forty miles to discuss the worsening security situation with the agent at the Spotted Tail Agency.[20] In the early hours of the following morning a Miniconjou warrior climbed into the stockade at the Red Cloud Agency and shot Frank Appleton, killing him instantly.[21] JW was in bed in his trading complex seventy yards from where the attack took place. Later that same day, twelve miles east of Laramie Peak, Lieutenant Levi Robinson and Corporal Coleman were ambushed and killed by Indians after they were separated from a Fort Laramie wood-collecting patrol.[22]

The morning of Appleton's murder, Bill Rowland, the Cheyenne interpreter, rode eighty-five miles to Fort Laramie to alert the army of the explosive situation.[23] Three days later JW traveled with two Indian guards to Fort Laramie, presumably to give a firsthand account of events that had unfolded at the agency.[24] The next day Unthank wrote to his wife telling her about the three murders and that he didn't know when he would get home for his leave. Apart from Unthank, the quartermaster's employees at Fort Laramie had been discharged, the passenger stage had been suspended, and mail was only carried between Fort Laramie and Cheyenne. Unthank was desperate to leave the fort at the very first opportunity: "This place is just like a grave yard, and has been so for a week. . . . There is no doubt but there will be a general Sioux war."[25]

When JW arrived back at the agency, he immediately wrote to Unthank:

> Times here very unsafe—cannot venture out to my meals after dark. Two pistols around me while writing you. . . . Don't know how matters may terminate. Am risking more probably than I should. Yet old boy, will ever try to keep up the nerve. Would to Heaven I could now leave the Country, but I cannot. My heart feels Sick & Sore from this Constant, constant strain and here tonight, All alone, my Soul longs for something better than this life. Good bye my dear, dear, old boy. I hope we may meet again.[26]

A few days later, underlying tensions between JW and Saville surfaced, and JW openly criticized Saville's conciliatory approach toward the Indians. On February 19, in a confidential four-page letter to Colonel Smith at Fort Laramie, JW gave an updated account of the situation at the agency and complained that Saville vacillated, was weak, and should take a far harder line with the Indians.

He also asked for Smith's advice about his future and whether he should cut his losses and leave:

> Tell me candidly what you think I had better do, you know my position, and you know what the probable movements will be soon. There is danger in remaining here but the question is, how will the future be, whether quiet or rough and whether I should try and get away with what I can, and break up my business here, or remain? Please advise me if you can by return of bearer.[27]

Because of the deaths and the escalating threat of further violence General Sherman was forced to act, and on February 19 he ordered Colonel Smith to take troops to protect the Red Cloud and Spotted Tail agencies. This worried JW, as he feared that when the northern Indians learned of the army's intervention, they would burn the agency buildings before the troops arrived and "every man be compelled to fight for his life. God help us if we are caught this way for we can do but little with thousands before us."

By this time accounts of the turmoil had reached JW's mother in Virginia, who wrote to Clay in Omaha asking for further news. She was desperately worried and had every right to be. JW wrote again to Unthank on February 23. "I am so lonely and worn out. A long letter from Clay came with yours. He implores me for Ma's sake to come back, thinks should anything happen to me 'twould cause her death, as she is now delicate. This touched me to the hearts core and has decided me to leave tomorrow night. My dear old boy we may yet live to meet again. Should any thing befall me ere that time, God bless you."[28] For whatever reason, JW did not leave.

Colonel Smith, who estimated he would face two thousand angry Indians, had requested a large contingent of reinforcements and ammunition to augment his small force at Fort Laramie. His request was granted, and a "Sioux Expedition" of approximately one thousand men assembled at Fort Laramie. From there the infantry and cavalry struggled through freezing weather and deep snow to Red Cloud Agency where they arrived on March 4.[29]

The northern Indians, who had learned of Bill Rowland's role in alerting Fort Laramie of the troubles at the agency, held him responsible for the arrival of the troops, and a Cheyenne warrior tried to shoot him. Rowland fled to the new military camp for protection. Agency staff rescued his Cheyenne wife and children, but their home was burned to the ground.[30] The Indians then fled north, and without their unsettling influence a degree of normality returned to agency life. The worst fears of JW and many others had proved to be unfounded.

The Board of Indian Commissioners acted quickly to investigate the cause of the troubles and recommended, much to the annoyance of the army, that in the future all agencies should have the protection of a nearby military force.[31]

The army initially believed the tented camp, which had been named Camp Robinson in honor of Lieutenant Robinson, would be a temporary cantonment and was confident that both Red Cloud and Spotted Tail agencies would be moved to permanent sites on the Missouri. The OIA, however, decided the Indians should remain in Nebraska. As a result, Camp Robinson was relocated to a permanent site one and a half miles west of the agency in June.[32]

The army camp had moved, but the squalor around the agency and JW's trading store remained. The Indians never cleared away their refuse. Rubbish, bones, and offal from the slaughter of cattle and residue from food preparation were left for dogs and coyotes, and as the weather grew warmer the smell, coupled with the stench of urine and feces, was overwhelming. As nomadic people on the plains this had not been a problem, for when conditions around their camp deteriorated and grass and firewood had been depleted, they simply moved. Now forced to live within three miles of the agency as the Fort Laramie Treaty dictated, the detritus of daily life became a growing health problem.[33]

The army's presence stabilized the situation, and whites and Indians settled into an uneasy daily routine. JW's business began to prosper.[34] Not only was he the Indian trader, but now he became a supplier to the army, and the hundreds of troops billeted a mile and a half away at Camp Robinson. The first contract he secured with the army was in May to supply five hundred tons of hay to the cavalry.[35] To help him grow his burgeoning business he needed people he could rely on and trust—who better than his brother Richard?

CHAPTER 17

Richard Goes West: 1874

FOR RICHARD, JW'S INVITATION TO COME TO WORK FOR HIM OUT WEST was a lifeline. There were few employment prospects for him in Virginia. The one impediment was their mother, Sarah, who was against his going. She had already lost her eldest son at Gettysburg; Clay was twelve hundred miles away in Omaha; and JW was living deep in Indian territory, where two months earlier, he had been in fear for his life surrounded by angry Indians.

Richard was occupied helping their father manage the Royal Oaks estate and was also courting Ridie Jamesson, the attractive daughter of their neighbor, Malcolm Jamesson. Old man Jamesson clearly had reservations about young Richard. When the twenty-four-year-old asked for Ridie's hand in marriage Malcolm refused, saying that he should return when he had made something of his life. Jamesson's response probably gave Richard the impetus he needed to head west. He arrived at the agency in late April 1874 and worked for JW for the next seven years.[1]

One of the first things JW did on Richard's arrival was to introduce him to Red Cloud and other senior chiefs. To show their respect, they visited Red Cloud's village, a short ride past the buttes northeast of JW's trading store.[2]

The village, located on the bank of the White River, was made up of more than thirty lodges. Tall conical tepees were arranged in an irregular circle, around which many ponies of every color were feeding. Nearby was a medicine pole, crowned with a bundle of colored rags and red and blue streamers to ward off evil spirits. A few buggies stood in seemingly random confusion where their owners had left them, and smooth-skinned dogs played and scavenged, unaware that they were destined for the pot. Dog was a much-prized delicacy in Indian cuisine. Outside each tepee was a soup kettle, some bubbling over campfires.

Red Cloud's tepee was over twenty feet in diameter and by some margin the largest in the village. A covered wagon, known as an ambulance, used to visit the agency stood outside. Red Cloud, dressed in his usual attire—a blue flannel shirt and trousers, blue blanket, and a black felt hat with an eagle feather—welcomed them and ushered them into his tepee.[3] Around the inside edge of his tepee was arranged his family's wardrobe, neatly folded, and laid out in handsomely painted bags of dressed skins. JW and Richard sat on skins and blankets that had been spread on the ground, and Red Cloud introduced his family and the other chiefs who had gathered to meet them. Conversation was conducted through Louis Shangrau, JW's clerk and Red Cloud's friend.

Two months after Richard arrived, a French artist, Jules Tavernier, visited Camp Robinson and the agency. He had been commissioned by the national journal *Harper's Weekly* to sketch scenes from across America. Before he arrived, he wrote to his mother in Paris, "I am going to see Red Cloud, one of the biggest Indian chiefs. . . . I will really see the wilds."[4] He was particularly interested in witnessing the secretive, three-day annual Sun Dance of the Lakota, which was to be held at the agency while he was there.[5] In the past, agency staff and officers from Fort Robinson had been allowed to attend the ceremony, and on this occasion JW and his friend Lieutenant William Carter, through their relationship with Red Cloud, arranged for Tavernier to sketch the proceedings.[6]

The Sun Dance was an annual ritual at which young braves were initiated into manhood to become members of the warrior body. Holy men pierced children's ears to ensure the next generation heard the "voices and spirits of the grandfathers," thus perpetuating the Lakota way of life.[7] The scenes Tavernier captured were probably the earliest "from life" illustrations of the Sun Dance ever made. It was a ceremony the authorities were determined to ban. They believed it perpetuated the most primitive of all tribal traditions and underlined how ingrained cruelty was in the Oglala culture.

The ceremony took place in a round enclosure of high poles interlaced with branches covered with buffalo robes. In the center of the arena stood a twenty-foot pole, adorned with flags of white and red cloth, from which hung several deerskin thongs. The young men to be inducted, wearing nothing but loincloths and moccasins, sat in a circle around the pole. When a brave was ready for the ceremony he stepped before one of the chiefs, who cut two slits on either side of each breast with a sharp knife. A piece of wood was inserted through the cuts and under the skin, extending three or four inches on each side of the cut. Each end was then fastened to the thongs attached to the top of the pole.

The old warriors encouraged the young initiates to dance to tom-toms and sing traditional songs. As the young men danced, they pulled backward on the ropes in an effort to tear the pieces of wood through their breasts. The longer a brave took to do this, the more courage he was considered to have. If, with a sudden jerk, he quickly tore them out, he was considered a coward. For several initiates the ordeal lasted more than two hours. At the ceremony watched by Tavernier, one particularly zealous brave was strung up by both breasts, and by two incisions in his back. He danced until he was exhausted and as he collapsed, tore out the thongs from all four wounds at once.

On the final day of the ceremony a violent storm broke and lightning struck the dance pole. The Indians saw this as a bad omen and a sign of displeasure at the white man's presence. JW, Jules Tavernier, and the other whites quickly left and returned to JW's trading complex. JW, Tavernier, Lieutenants Carter and Buchanan, Billy Garnett, and the Indian chief Red Leaf were later photographed in JW's complex by Lieutenant Thomas Wilhelm, who was a keen and accomplished amateur photographer.[8]

Throughout the summer groups of northern Indians visited the Red Cloud Agency to meet reservation Indians and to buy and trade items at the two trading stores. Indians were coming and going all the time, and it was impossible for Saville and his staff to differentiate between

Lieutenant William Carter (1), Jules Tavernier (2), JW (3), Lieutenant James Buchanan (4), Red Leaf (5), and Billy Garnett (6) in JW's trading complex, Red Cloud Agency, June 1874. Courtesy of National Archives, photo no. 111-SC-83148

thousands of reservation Indians and small groups of visiting Indians. The Sun Dance was the most important event in the Lakota calendar, and Indians from Crazy Horse's band attended. Among them was Frank Grouard, JW's old friend, whom he had last seen on the Upper Missouri four years before.

JW learned that since their last meeting in January 1870, Frank had been captured by Sitting Bull's Hunkpapa tribe while carrying mail on the Upper Missouri. Fortunately, Sitting Bull had taken a liking to him and allowed him to live with his tribe for almost three years until a disagreement between the two men forced Frank to leave. Crazy Horse's uncle, Little Hawk, who had befriended Frank, urged him to join their band. He did and gradually gained Crazy Horse's confidence.

Frank looked like an Indian and learned to think and behave like one. He became conversant in several Lakota dialects and sign language and gradually became integrated into their society. Crazy Horse allowed him more freedom than Sitting Bull, and occasionally, he visited the Red Cloud Agency. It was on such a visit in the summer of 1874 that he renewed his friendship with JW.[9] A photograph taken outside JW's trading post captured the reunion of these two old friends.[10]

Todd Randall, the second trader at the agency, was finding it impossible to work with Saville and sold his business to B. F. Walters.[11]

Richard Dear's first few months in the American West had been a baptism of fire. He had begun to learn about JW's business and had developed a respect for the Oglala and their traditions. He had met many colorful characters but had also witnessed how quickly violence could erupt in this raw and unforgiving environment.

Red Cloud Agency, June 1874. From left to right, Red Dog, JW, Frank Grouard, Richard Dear, and Red Leaf. Red Dog and Red Leaf feature in a number of photographs with JW. Red Dog was a band chief of the Oglala, and Red Leaf was a band chief of the Brulé. Dear Family Collection

CHAPTER 18

The Black Hills and the Badlands of Dakota

THE NEWS THAT COLONEL CUSTER WAS LEADING AN EXPEDITION OF A thousand men into the Black Hills reached Red Cloud Agency in July 1874. Ostensibly, his mission was to find and survey a site for a new army post, but most understood this was a convenient cover to ascertain if gold was present in viable commercial quantities.[1] Rumors circulated, and speculation was rife.

This was a clear breach of the 1868 Fort Laramie Treaty, which prevented whites from entering the Great Sioux Reservation. A member of Custer's expedition commented, "The United States Government . . . forgot its honor, forgot the sacred treaty, forgot its integrity, and ordered an expedition for the invasion of the Black Hills."[2]

Custer's large, well-equipped expedition, which included botanists; geologists; and significantly, two mining experts, did not encounter any opposition from non-reservation Indians. On July 27 his miners started work, and five days later they struck gold in a place they named French Creek. Journalists who accompanied the expedition filed their reports, and the American public, still reeling from the economic panic of the previous year and desperate for good news, dreamed of another gold rush. Within weeks prospecting expeditions were being planned, and businessmen, local politicians, and organizations such as the Union Pacific Railroad Company, began to plan and lobby.[3]

Custer's 1874 Black Hills Expedition: 1,000 soldiers, 110 supply wagons, 70 Indian scouts, and two gold miners line up with Custer (on white horse on left) for the photographer, William H. Illingworth. Courtesy of PaulHorsted.com Collection

Red Cloud's reaction to Custer's violation of the Fort Laramie Treaty was, surprisingly, one of ambivalence. He was too preoccupied with his fight with Agent Saville and the shortage of rations to give the matter the consideration it deserved. This was a mistake. The Black Hills became a major factor in both Red Cloud's and JW's lives.

A few weeks after the news of Custer's expedition broke, there was a further distraction. On July 26 the War Department approved plans for the construction of quarters and barracks for a permanent army post to replace the tented Camp Robinson. Construction started on August 6, and for the next twelve months building contractors brought welcome business to JW's store. The first troops moved into their new barracks in November, but the camp was not completed until July 1875 and was eventually home to approximately three hundred officers and men.

Within days of the troops moving into their new accommodation, trouble again flared at the agency. Agent Saville decided to erect a flagpole in the agency stockade for what appeared to be perfectly sensible reasons. Indians came to the agency every day of the week. They did not observe Sunday as a day of rest, and Saville believed that by raising the flag on Sundays it would signal that no business would be conducted. It was also intended to be used to alert the soldiers at Camp Robinson in case of trouble. To the fiercely patriotic Saville it had the additional benefit of displaying the American flag on a public institution.

To make the flagpole, Saville sent his staff to cut several tall pines, which were hauled into the stockade.[4] News of Saville's plan had spread, and the Indians objected strongly. For them the agency was there to administer to their needs, and flags were only flown over army encampments. The following day, on October 23, more than two hundred enraged, mostly non-agency Indians dressed in war costume, their faces covered in war paint, entered the stockade and first tried to remove the logs, but finding them too heavy, instead hacked them to pieces with their hatchets.

As this was happening both Red Cloud and Red Dog were talking to Saville, but they could not, or would not, stop the actions of their angry northern cousins. Saville, after ordering the Indians to stop, sent a runner to Camp Robinson for help. At about one o'clock the camp commander received Saville's request, and Lieutenant Emmet Crawford and twenty-six men on horseback were dispatched to the agency. The Indians were incensed that the soldiers had been called, and by the time Crawford arrived at the stockade, more than five hundred mounted warriors had gathered with more arriving all the time. The situation was rapidly deteriorating.

At that critical moment a group of Oglala led by Young Man Afraid of His Horses arrived and forced a corridor through the angry mob, which allowed Crawford and his men to reach the safety of the stockade. Agency staff immediately closed the gates and outside, directly in front of JW's store, fighting broke out between the two rival groups of Indians. Frank Appleton's father, Amos, watched events as they unfolded from his upstairs window, rifle by his side, and later wrote that the incensed reservation Indians "at it they went—first with whips, and such as would leave for that went, and such as would not they used clubs, guns and more clubs . . . and they were in dead earnest. They knocked men from their horses and in one instance an Indian's scalp was laid open so that after the affray was over with, he came to the surgeon and had it dressed."[5]

The melee lasted for more than two hours before breaking up. The agency Indians told their defiant northern cousins they would not tolerate any more trouble. The northern warriors expressed their disgust at the lack of support from the agency bands and by the next morning, had moved away from the area to north of the White River.

Saville, understandably shaken, decided not to erect the flagpole. This did not go down well with the army; Saville had placed Crawford and his men in grave danger, and his yielding showed weakness, in their view.[6]

During the summer and fall of 1874, Red Cloud spent much of his time in and around the agency. For those whites living and working there, Indians were an integral part of daily life. Dressed in their ubiquitous leggings, blankets, and soft felt hats, they collected their rations from the agency warehouse and, tethering their ponies and travois outside, regularly visited JW's store, sometimes carrying armfuls of fossils inside for his approval.

The remote and unexplored Badlands north of the agency were a vast depository of prehistoric fossils, and JW, fascinated by the world of paleontology, had encouraged the Indians to bring their finds to him. The bones would be laid out on his trading counter, his clerk, Louis Shangrau, summoned to act as interpreter, and the haggling would begin. Perhaps a large jawbone would change hands for a blanket or a giant molar for a packet of glass beads or a plug of tobacco. Very quickly JW had amassed a creditable collection, which he was happy to display to anyone interested and which he reviewed and catalogued with the help of Colonel Thaddeus Stanton, the army paymaster at Fort Laramie, who was an enthusiastic and knowledgeable amateur paleontologist.

In early October, Stanton wrote to one of the world's leading paleontologists, Professor Othniel Charles Marsh of Yale College in Connecticut, telling him about JW's fossil collection:

Mr. JW Dear, Trader at Red Cloud Agency, Nebraska, has a very nice collection, and he promised me he would hold it until I could inform you. I go into that country again on 1st of November. Cannot you come with me. . . . [There are] one three horned head (rhinoceros or elephant) . . . immense serpents heads, turtles and bones of all sorts, jaws, vertebrae, teeth are scattered over the country [10 miles north of Red Cloud and covering an area of six square miles], making it look like a vast bone yard.[7]

Marsh was no stranger to the fossil fields of Nebraska and Wyoming, as he had led expeditions there on four previous occasions. He was intrigued by Stanton's letter and the promise of a new fossil field in the Badlands and decided to travel west to investigate. Leaving the railroad at Cheyenne, Marsh and his party reached Fort Laramie in early November and from there proceeded to Red Cloud Agency, accompanied by Colonel Luther Bradley, the commanding officer at Fort Laramie, and Colonel Stanton.

When the party arrived, the atmosphere was tense. Memories of the flagpole incident were still fresh in everyone's mind. Northern Indians were still in the area, and many believed the expedition's real purpose was to search for gold, not fossils. At a dinner at which JW and Red Cloud were guests, Marsh spoke about his plans, and the Indians agreed the expedition should go ahead under the protection of the army with a group of reservation Indians acting as guides.

The next day four inches of snow fell, which delayed the start of the expedition. At the same time, annuities were issued and the atmosphere changed. Having received their rations many Indians were no longer on their best behavior, and those who were to accompany the expedition were reluctant to do so for fear of clashing with the northern Indians.

Marsh's party was staying at Camp Robinson and was unaware of this change of sentiment. As the expedition left the camp to travel to the agency a mile and a half away, it had to pass several Indian villages. The sight of soldiers and the expedition's wagons excited the Indians, guns were pointed at the party, and women and children fled from harm's way. Runners were seen galloping to villages to recruit more warriors. Faced with such a hostile reaction Marsh's party quickly withdrew and returned to the safety of Camp Robinson.

The rest of the day was spent in consultation. An eyewitness who wrote about a "perilous fossil hunt" in his memoirs recorded that it was JW who broke the deadlock and advised Marsh how to proceed. He suggested the professor host a feast for the leading chiefs; the main dish should be dog and appropriate presents should be given. This was agreed. The feast was held in one of the largest lodges; only twenty of the more eminent chiefs were invited and every detail of Indian etiquette was strictly observed.

Several dogs were selected from the many scavenging around the Indian village. They were killed, then put into large kettles to boil. After two hours the dogs were pronounced done, and the feast was ready.

JW, Marsh, and his expedition members were each seated on a buffalo robe between two Indians. Each man was furnished with a pan, and two Indians were detailed to dish out the dogmeat. In accordance with Indian etiquette the guest of honor received a dog's head. At the end of the feast, presents were given to the Indians, and the professor again assured them he was interested in bones, not gold. Reluctant consent was given, and a band of scouts promised to escort his expedition. Marsh was warned, however, that the northern Indians might attack the party if they crossed the White River.

Very early in the morning of November 5, the expedition threaded its way as quickly and quietly as possible across the plains, which were alive with reservation Indians, their families, dogs, and ponies, and crossed the White River at the only fordable spot for many miles. It was a bitterly cold day, and as they ascended the highlands, the cold was so intense that those on horseback were forced to walk to keep from freezing.[8] They eventually arrived at the fossil fields and worked there for several days, braving extreme conditions. Bearded members of the party were festooned with icicles, and many were severely frostbitten. Eventually the cold moderated, but then came the snow and a warning that the Miniconjou were planning to attack. Marsh and his party quickly and carefully packed the two tons of fossils they had collected onto their wagons and beat a hasty retreat to the agency.

On arrival, Marsh allowed Red Cloud and his fellow chiefs to examine the wagons of rocks and fossils, and, seeing that no gold had been secreted and that Marsh had kept his promise, Red Cloud invited him to the nearby Oglala encampment. There was a good rapport between the two men, and Red Cloud used the opportunity to complain about the quality of rations the Indians were receiving and about general corruption among US government officials and agency personnel. Marsh was persuaded by Red Cloud's arguments and promised to raise the issue with influential friends in Washington, DC.[9]

JW did not accompany the expedition to the fossil fields, but given their shared interest in old bones, he remained in contact with Marsh for several years.

The expedition was deemed a success, and Marsh returned to Yale in early December, with several previously unknown specimens, including the jawbone and teeth of a *brontothere*, an odd-toed ungulate that was fifteen feet long and like a rhinoceros. The specimens came from JW's collection and are still at the Yale Peabody Museum of Natural History.[10]

A few days after his return, Marsh arranged for details of corruption at Red Cloud Agency to be published. He accused Saville of being guilty of fraud and unfit for the job. He claimed the Indian census was too high, that systemic fraud by the agent and contractors had resulted in inferior beef being issued, and that the freight contract had paid for 212 miles of transport when the actual distance was 145 miles.[11] The *New York Herald* and *New York Tribune* were particularly vigorous in their efforts to expose conditions at the agency.[12]

Marsh, a friend of President Grant, was a powerful and well-connected man, and the authorities had to take his intervention seriously.[13]

As 1874 ended, JW had a chance to reflect on his first full year as an Indian trader. His trading license had been renewed in November for another twelve months, a permanent army encampment had been set up to protect the agency and control the Indians, and the violence had almost disappeared. JW was gaining the trust of Red Cloud and his fellow chiefs and was seen by many as someone who could bridge the cultural gap between whites and Indians and whose advice was valued. He was on good terms with army officers at Fort Laramie and Camp Robinson, and he knew many leading businessmen in Omaha, Sidney, and Cheyenne. His younger brother, who had worked for him since April, had proved to be a great asset to the business.

Although he could look forward to 1875 with confidence, JW sent a reflective letter to Oliver Unthank in late November, which gives a sense of his inner turmoil:

> these [trying and dangerous] days are now past and gone—gone I hope ne'er to return. We are now under the protection of the Stars and Stripes. Our red friends are rather more docile than they formerly were, and everything is running quietly. My business is first rate, and hope to clear a few thousand this year. If 'tis, my dear friend, the kind will of Providence to spare me and give me health, I am determined to some day, tho' it may be in the distant future, win success for myself.
>
> My life is indeed lonely at times. At night when sitting alone, far away from home and friends, can you wonder that I feel the deep heart yearnings and soul longings for a brighter and better life, to once more mingle among friends—to enjoy again some of the congenial associations of life. Yet it cannot, cannot be. A moment's reflection, and my future came before me, long years of toil, long years in which I must bind my nerve with every energy to the one task to build up fortune and success. For a time, I must work and hope, and be comforted by the words of the old song:
> Be Still, Sad heart! And cease repining,
> Behind the clouds is the sun still shining
> Thy fate is the common fate of all,
> Into each life some rain must fall,
> Some days must be dark and dreary.[14]

There was, however, one worrying cloud on the horizon that could wreck his plans. In December reports appeared in the press that the first illegal, but well-funded and managed, expedition had left Sioux City to prospect for gold in the Black Hills.[15] Whites pouring into the sacred grounds of the Lakota would almost certainly reignite violence and bring instability.

CHAPTER 19

Gold, Betrayal, and Corruption: 1875

AFTER THE TURMOIL AND UPHEAVAL OF THE PREVIOUS YEAR AND WITH the departure of the northern Indians, 1875 started quietly. Relations with the Indians had stabilized, and more people visited Camp Robinson and the agency. To take advantage of this, JW opened a small hotel in February, which complemented his expanding business interests.[1]

He increasingly left the running of his trading operation in Richard's capable hands. Most of his time was concentrated on seeking business opportunities in Cheyenne and Sidney. In this more relaxed environment, he felt confident enough to travel alone. To do this at speed and in comfort he bought, at considerable expense, a phaeton, a carriage for gentlemen drivers. It was built to his own design and was a fashionable and stylish addition to the transport options available at the agency. A few months after taking delivery, he sent a picture to Mary Ann proudly recording, "This is my team which I have driven many thousands of miles over the plains and they have made 132 miles in 26 hours including stoppages."[2]

JW's old friend, Frank Yates, the former justice of the peace at Fort Laramie, married sixteen-year-old Hattie Brown at Dyer's Hotel in Cheyenne on January 20. JW was among the guests.[3] Shortly after the wedding he made the long journey back to Virginia, where he spent time with his family at Royal Oaks, saw Mary Ann in Hamilton, visited the Geology Department of the University of Virginia in Charlottesville, where he donated a "fossilized turtle and an immense molar" from his

JW on his phaeton outside his trading post in early 1875. He sent this photograph to Mary Ann. Dear Family Collection

personal collection, and spent time with friends he had not seen for two years.[4]

While he was in Virginia news broke that an illegal expedition of miners had returned from the Black Hills to Sioux City with reports that they had found paying quantities of gold. The *New York Times* announced to the world there was money to be made in the Black Hills, and a new wave of gold fever gripped the nation. The consequences of this announcement were to overshadow everything else that happened at the agency that year. Rumors were rife that for the right price the Indians would sell the Hills. If that happened commercial opportunities would open for JW and many others.[5]

On hearing the news, JW left Virginia and returned to the agency, where he could better monitor developments and make plans. It must have been a difficult decision, as it meant missing the wedding of his friend Sam Rogers to Elizabeth "Lizzie" Megeath. The couple were due to be married on April 26 at the Baltimore home of Burr Richards, who was married to Lizzie's sister, Sarah. Many of JW's friends from his days as a Mosby Ranger would be there—his former commander; Burr's younger brother, Dolly; Mary Ann with her family; and others. Mary Ann's cousin, the Reverend Arthur Rogers, was to officiate.[6]

When JW arrived back at the agency in early April, he learned that Frank Yates, backed by his father-in-law, Major Brown, had bought out the other Indian trader, B. F. Walters. Frank was now the second Indian trader at the Red Cloud Agency and, as a result, had become JW's competitor.[7] However, this doesn't appear to have affected their friendship. JW spent a few days sorting out his affairs; then he and Richard traveled to Cheyenne, where they met Clay and Captain Wilcox of Stephens & Wilcox.[8]

Sixteen hundred miles away in Washington, DC, Professor Marsh's charges of fraud and corruption at the Red Cloud Agency, which he had first raised the previous December, were being discussed. On April 28, Marsh presented his detailed allegations to the Board of Indian Commissioners, which led to a commission being appointed to investigate the "State of Affairs at the Red Cloud Agency." The terms of reference of the commissioners involved gathering evidence from a wide cross section of people, and the hearings started in Washington on July 20.[9]

As Professor Marsh's charges were gaining traction in the capital, developments in the Black Hills were moving quickly.

The Black Hills occupy an oval-shaped area approximately one hundred twenty miles long and sixty miles wide, one hundred miles north of Red Cloud Agency and more than two hundred miles north of Cheyenne and Sidney. They are surrounded by hundreds of miles of open, arid plains. The white, gravelly soil sustains little but millions of prickly pears and is dotted with prairie dog holes often occupied by rattlesnakes. Devoid of trees or bushes, the desolate wasteland is a soul-destroying spectacle in the searing heat of summer.

In stark contrast, the Black Hills rise majestically above the flat landscape, shaded, cool, and lush. The high terrain attracts rain clouds with occasional thunderstorms and the high rainfall encourages forests of pine, oak, and elm to flourish. This makes the Hills appear as a black strip on the horizon to the approaching traveler, which gave them the white man's name.

During hot summer months, the valleys and gulches running through the Hills are carpeted with grass and flowers. Crystal clear water flows through the many streams and gullies that feed lakes full of fish. The whole area teems with wildlife: the tree-lined hillsides are a haven for birds, and animals large and small roam freely, providing both food and fur.

The Hills were a sacred sanctuary for the Indians in the very heart of the plains. To them, "Paha Sapa" was "the heart of everything that is." They believed it was the place where spirits of their ancestors came when they died and that these spirits could inflict dreadful punishment on anyone who disturbed the solitude of this sacred area. The thunder and lightning the Hills attracted added to the Indian belief that this was a powerful and special place. Even though the Hills had an abundance of game, timber, and water, and in summer a climate more favorable than that of the open plains, the Indians visited only for short periods and treated the area with reverence and respect.[10]

The Fort Laramie Treaty had confirmed the Indians were the legal owners of the Black Hills and required that the US Army keep whites from entering the Great Sioux Reservation, which surrounded the Hills. Soon after the treaty was signed, unsubstantiated stories of gold deposits in the Hills began to circulate. However, the remoteness of the place, the threat of attack by Indians, and the army's undertaking to keep whites out meant that these rumors were never tested. But in July 1874, partly driven by the financial panic of the previous year, which began a long period of economic depression and high unemployment, the military authorized an expedition to survey the Hills for gold.[11]

Colonel Custer's expedition confirmed gold was present, which triggered an immediate response, many acting as if the treaty had not been signed. From early 1875, Omaha, Sidney, Cheyenne, and other frontier towns embarked on a frenzied rush to become "the gateway to the Black Hills" and seize the largest share of this potentially lucrative trade. Public opinion, encouraged by the press, believed it would only be a matter of time before the government regained ownership of the valuable land from the Indians.

The rationale was that although the Indians held title to the land, they did nothing with it; fifty thousand "savages" had no right to impede progress. White Americans should be free to lay railroads to connect the East and West Coasts to help build their great nation, cattlemen should be allowed to raise cattle efficiently on the Great Northern Plains, settlers should be free to farm there, and Americans should benefit from the rich mineral deposits found in places like the Black Hills. The only solution was to accept the government had made a mistake in ceding the Hills to the Indians and to negotiate another treaty whereby the Indians relinquished the land for a fair price.

Cheyenne was already a boom town and was rapidly establishing itself as the "Cattle Capital" of Wyoming. Banks were lending huge sums of money for the purchase of Texas cattle to stock the ranges, and the arrival of the railroad meant that the longhorn cattle could now be moved on the long drive from Texas in the south to the rich grasslands of Nebraska and Wyoming. There they were fattened on the open plains before being sold to feed the Indians or shipped from railroad towns like Cheyenne to the canning factories in Omaha and Chicago and then on to the vast consumer markets of the Eastern Seaboard.

The emergence of open-range ranching heralded the slaughter of the buffalo, and between 1868 and 1874 more than six million were killed to free the plains for cattle. Buffalo provided meat for the Eastern markets, skins for drive belts in industry, and bones for fertilizer. The railroad also brought recreational sportsmen who came for the thrill of slaughtering tens of thousands of buffalo, which further contributed to their demise.[12]

Thousands of tons of bleached buffalo bones littered the plains, and by 1874 the buffalo were in danger of extinction. The Democrat-controlled

Congress was so concerned that a bill was introduced to protect them.[13] On the advice of the Secretary of the Interior this was vetoed by President Grant on the grounds that the elimination of the primary food source of the Indians and their way of life would make it easier for the government to force them onto reservations.

This was supported by General Sheridan, who said, "These men [buffalo-hunters] have done in the last two years . . . more to settle the vexed Indian question than the entire regular army has done in the last thirty. They are destroying the Indians' commissary . . . for the sake of lasting peace, let them kill, skin and sell until the buffaloes are exterminated. Then your prairies can be covered with speckled cattle and the festive cowboy."[14] The slaughter of buffalo was now government policy. Unsurprisingly, the effect was to make non-reservation Indians feel threatened and more hostile and aggressive as they struggled to survive on the diminishing game.

The new cattle barons, many passionate advocates of Manifest Destiny, wielded great influence and had quickly consolidated their growing power. The Stock Association of Laramie County was established in 1872. It was based in Cheyenne and organized roundups and cattle shipments and registered and tracked cattle brands. It also employed agents, and sometimes gunslingers, to deter and catch rustlers and to discourage settlers from erecting fences on the open plains. The Association was often accused of secrecy and heavy-handedness, but it was instrumental in shaping Wyoming's early political, economic, and social infrastructure. It was also alive to any commercial opportunity offered by the opening of the Black Hills.

By the spring of 1875, the government had realized the flood of miners entering the Black Hills could not be controlled, and a way had to be found to wrest the Hills from the Indians. Given that under the Fort Laramie Treaty three-quarters of all adult male Indians had to agree, the administration adopted a course of persuasion to the point of coercion.[15]

The government's new hard line with the Indians convinced Union Pacific Railroad bosses that the Black Hills would soon open for business, and they entered into an agreement with George Homan, the proprietor of the Omaha City Omnibus Company. He planned to offer rail and stagecoach packages to the Black Hills via Sidney or Cheyenne to the thousands of miners and their followers expected to make the journey.[16]

Clay, together with his boss Captain William Wilcox, visited the Hills in March to survey potential stage and wagon routes. On their return to Cheyenne, they met JW and Richard to discuss how they could take advantage of the opportunities that were likely to emerge. During the visit Captain Wilcox told the press he believed that Cheyenne, and not Sidney, would become "the base for supplies for the new mining country in Northern Wyoming."[17] George Homan agreed; in May, he decided to back the Cheyenne route to the Hills and announced that all his plans were now in place.

Clearly, Homan had decided the route his stagecoaches would take, who would build and manage the required stage stations, and how the project would be financed.[18] It was estimated a stagecoach from Cheyenne would take between two and three days to reach the Hills: horses would need to be watered, fed, and changed at regular intervals, and it was likely that up to twelve paying passengers would need overnight accommodation. This required a series of stage stations to be built along the route.

JW was in regular contact with Homan, and the fact that Stephens & Wilcox had surveyed the trail in April suggests they were considering taking a financial stake in the project. It seems likely therefore that it was with their financial backing that JW agreed to build and manage a number of stations along the dangerous one-hundred-fifty-mile section of the trail from Fort Laramie to the Black Hills.

This was a big undertaking. The trail crossed uninhabited and uncharted territory known to the Indians, but only to a handful of army scouts and the miners who illegally ventured into the Hills. JW and his business partners had to survey the route and identify locations suitable for stage stations. Each station needed to be close to fresh water and timber and ideally, have good grazing. When the sites were selected, JW needed to approve the layout and design of the stations and arrange for them to be built, staffed, and stocked—a complex, dangerous, and costly exercise, but one he embraced enthusiastically.

To reach an agreement to buy back the Hills from the Indians, the government had to be seen to be keeping whites out of the area until a new treaty had been negotiated. It also needed to confirm beyond reasonable doubt that gold was present in commercial quantities, and on May 15 a government-sponsored scientific expedition led by Professor Walter P. Jenney left Fort Laramie for the Black Hills. Four hundred troops provided military protection for the expedition and its sixty supply wagons.[19] A young man who was to play a major role in JW's life, Valentine McGillycuddy, was one of the surveyors who accompanied the expedition.[20]

As the Jenney Expedition set out, the government invited a delegation of Indian chiefs to Washington, which included Red Cloud and Spotted Tail, to resolve the Black Hills problem. They also wanted to discuss two other issues: the Sioux hunting rights on the Republican River, which local politicians claimed they had never agreed to and argued the federal government had "no legal right to impose," and the removal of the Red Cloud and Spotted Tail agencies from Nebraska.[21]

The meeting was not a success. Red Cloud was obsessed with his feud with Saville, to the point he was blind to the larger and more important issues being discussed. He and his fellow chiefs flatly refused to talk about the question of the Black Hills and the unceded territories. Red Cloud did, however, present his case against Saville, but his testimony was contradictory and unimpressive. Despite this, preparation to investigate affairs at the agency, which had been initiated by Professor Marsh, continued.

The government offered the Indians $25,000 for the termination of Sioux hunting rights on the Republican River, which they agreed to consider and subsequently accepted.[22] Finally, the relocation of the Oglala and Brulé agencies from Nebraska to Indian Territory in present-day Oklahoma was discussed. Spotted Tail spoke for his fellow chiefs saying this required the negotiation of a new treaty, which they were not authorized to do.

President Grant then lectured the Indians on the potential consequences of not ceding the Hills: white people outnumbered the Indians two hundred to one, and nothing could prevent swarms of miners invading the Hills. They must cede them, and any resort to hostilities "would necessarily lead to withholding of rations." Neither the Indians nor the government were happy with the outcome of the talks.[23] The chiefs were shocked by the president's threats. Weeks of discussion in Washington produced only an agreement to return to their people to ask them to accept $25,000 for the hunting rights on the Republican River. The Indians returned home disappointed, and the favorable impression Red Cloud had made during his two earlier visits to the capital was, for the moment, badly damaged.

Despite the lack of progress, pressure was mounting, and newspapers were quick to reflect the mood. The Washington, DC, weekly newspaper *The Commonwealth* commented, "If any number of white men wish to go to the Black Hills, they will go there, treaty or no treaty. The rule has always worked that way, and it always will. Treaties are a thing of a day, made to be annulled."[24]

Following the failure to even begin negotiations for the Black Hills, the Secretary of the Interior appointed a commission to convene a "Grand Council" meeting with the Lakota Sioux chiefs at a place of their choosing on the Great Sioux Reservation in September. Senator William Allison of Iowa was appointed chairman. His brief was to negotiate a settlement to buy the mining rights of the Black Hills. Faced with this level of uncertainty, businessmen, including George Homan, were forced to put their plans on hold until the future of the Hills was decided.[25]

JW, however, was confident that a compromise would be found, and although plans for the Cheyenne stage were on hold, he started planning his own stage line in the fall. His vision was for a daily service from Sidney to the Black Hills via his trading post at Red Cloud Agency.

In preparation for the Allison Commission's visit and the planned Grand Council meeting, a subcommission was appointed to make the necessary arrangements and to encourage as many northern Lakota tribes as possible to attend. The government was keen to ensure that any changes to the terms of the Fort Laramie Treaty had the agreement of the required 75 percent of adult male Indians.

Congressman Abram Comingo of Independence, Missouri, was appointed chairman of the four-member subcommission.[26] Their first

stop was Red Cloud Agency, where they arrived on July 4, 1875, accompanied by a group of journalists from leading national newspapers. The
commissioners stayed in the agent's house and held their meetings with
Red Cloud and the subchiefs in a large warehouse at the back of the
agency stockade. Several journalists stayed at JW's hotel, others were
billeted in tents along the stockade wall, and most took their meals in
JW's restaurant.[27] Members of the subcommission had separate mess
arrangements.

On the evening of July 6, Congressman Comingo and his fellow
commissioners were relaxing with JW in his billiard room when, at ten
o'clock at night, there was a knock on the door and ten Kiyuksa Lakota
Sioux presented themselves, wanting to talk. JW cleared the room and
provided a table for the secretary and reporters. The commissioners
assumed a proper air of solemnity, and when the interpreter appeared,
a council with the Indians began. Despite the dramatic, late-night start,
the meeting itself was an anticlimax—the Indians requested that the
commissioners stay longer at the agency. This was not possible, and a few
days later they left for Spotted Tail's agency.[28]

A major topic of discussion was where the Grand Council should be
held. The commissioners favored a location on the Missouri River, but
although this was firmly vetoed by both Red Cloud and Spotted Tail,
the two old rivals could not agree on an alternative. Spotted Tail favored
Chadron Creek, which was midway between their two agencies, but Red
Cloud wanted a location nearer Red Cloud Agency to underline his status as the leader of the reservation Sioux. The issue was still unresolved
when the subcommission left Spotted Tail's agency on July 16 escorted by
the 2nd Cavalry for their five-hundred-mile journey to the three Lakota
agencies on the Missouri River: Standing Rock, Cheyenne River, and
Crow Creek.

The day after the late-night meeting in JW's billiard room with
the Kiyuksa, another delegation left the agency. It was considered too
dangerous for the commissioners to venture into hostile Indian territory,
so they negotiated with Red Cloud that, in return for a payment of one
hundred ponies, a delegation of Oglala led by Young Man Afraid of His
Horses would travel north to meet Sitting Bull, Crazy Horse, and the

northern Indians. The authorities, knowing Frank Grouard was spending more and more time at Red Cloud Agency and aware of his understanding of the Indians and his friendship with Crazy Horse, recruited him to help gauge the reaction of the northerners to the government's proposals. He was paid $500, a considerable sum at that time.[29] Louis Richard was appointed the delegation's official interpreter.

The delegation traveled three hundred miles to the Tongue River, where they met Sitting Bull and Crazy Horse on July 20. It was the first time Grouard had seen Sitting Bull since their disagreement two years earlier, and relations between the two men were still strained. Both Sitting Bull and Crazy Horse rejected the government's proposal to purchase the Hills and refused to attend the Grand Council. They did, however, agree that their representative, Little Big Man, would lead a party of northern Indians to monitor the proceedings and disrupt the council if necessary.[30] Grouard and Richard arrived back at the agency on August 16, after a month of arduous travel.

CHAPTER 20

The Black Hills Become a Problem

SHORTLY AFTER CONGRESSMAN COMINGO'S SUBCOMMISSION LEFT FOR the Missouri River agencies and Young Man Afraid of His Horses's delegation departed to meet the northern Indians, the special commission initiated by Professor Marsh to investigate the "State of Affairs at Red Cloud Agency," started its work. In total they interviewed eighty-seven people. After collecting evidence in Washington, DC, Cheyenne, and Fort Laramie, the five-man commission arrived at the agency on August 6. Over the following twelve days they interviewed army officers from Camp Robinson, several Indian chiefs, agency personnel, and a disparate collection of contractors, frontiersmen, scouts, interpreters—and JW.[1]

Throughout the whole of this period the agency was a hive of activity with dozens of people coming and going. Some of those called to give evidence stayed at Camp Robinson, but many others took accommodation in JW's hotel. Every evening his restaurant, bar, and billiard room were full of people discussing, speculating, and arguing about the day's proceedings and the likely outcome of the hearings. Would Saville or any of his suppliers be found guilty of corruption?

JW was interviewed for over an hour by the commissioners. They were keen to hear how the fur trade worked and how he made money buying and selling beef hides. They also sought his thoughts on the relative costs and advantages of hauling freight along the Cheyenne and Sidney roads to the agency. When asked for his views on Saville, JW replied he felt the agent was doing his job to the best of his ability, but if the OIA only paid their agents $1,500 a year they would struggle to

JW's trading post at Red Cloud Agency, where commissioners, frontiersmen, journalists, scouts, and interpreters congregated to discuss the day's events over a drink and perhaps a meal and while away the hours playing billiards and cards. Dear Family Collection

recruit and retain top-quality operators.[2] The commissioners went on to ask, "Do you observe any change in dress on their [Indians'] part that would indicate an approach to civilization?"

JW replied, "There are quite a number . . . who take pride in dressing in white man's clothing. Red Dog, for one, never feels so proud as when he has got on a white man's suit. I fitted him out several times."

Jules Ecoffey, JW's former boss, was questioned by the commission about his dismissal as Indian trader by Agent Saville in August 1873, how beef contracts were awarded, and whether he thought corruption was involved. The evidence he gave, like that of many witnesses, was of a general nature and inconclusive. His views about Saville were uncomplimentary.[3]

Saville himself was asked to explain why he employed his two nephews, Frank and Oliver Appleton; how he came to award a major contract to build the agency to his brother-in-law, Amos Appleton; and how he checked deliveries from his suppliers for quality and quantity. His relationship with the Bosler brothers, his major beef contractor, was also discussed in detail, but again, nothing new or conclusive emerged.[4]

One of Professor Marsh's main charges involved corruption in awarding and monitoring beef contracts. The commission spent many hours
interrogating the Bosler brothers, who were by far the biggest suppliers
of beef. George Bosler was stationed in Cheyenne; J. H. Bosler, in Pennsylvania; and the third brother, in Washington, DC, where his job was to
maintain close ties with the OIA officials responsible for awarding beef
contracts. The brothers bought longhorn cattle in Texas and employed
teams of cowboys to move them to Nebraska. The eleven-hundred-mile
drive took three to four months to complete. The cattle were then fattened on the open plains around Cheyenne before being sold to the OIA
for consumption by the Indians. This was big business, and the Boslers
regularly delivered lots of two thousand cattle or more to the agency.
Rumors about the brothers and their dubious practices had circulated for
years, but proof of their corruption was never established.[5]

The commissioners, however, insisted on watching the issuing of cattle, which normally took place on a Saturday. Issue Day was known to the
Sioux as *wanasapi*, their word for a communal buffalo hunt, and that is
what they tried to replicate with the domestic cattle. The commissioners
gathered at the corral outside the agency stockade as five hundred Bosler
cattle awaited their fate. The head man from each band received between
one to twenty animals, according to the number of lodges he represented.
About three thousand mounted Indians surrounded the corral where the
cattle were confined and where, for the previous hour or so, Indian boys
had shot arrows into them and cut off their tails to ensure they were in
an active and aggressive state when they were released.

As the names of Indians were called, the gate of the corral swung
open, and the requisite number of animals released. Indians mounted on
horses and armed with breech-loading rifles immediately began to chase
and fire at the animals, replicating a buffalo hunt. Some had as many as
a dozen rifle balls emptied into them before the tortured beasts fell. The
butchering process was crude and basic. The hides were stripped from the
carcass, the meat cut from the bones, and the entrails and stomach carried
away as choice delicacies. Bones and congealed blood were left strewn on
the plains for dogs and coyotes. At the Missouri River agencies, the beef

hunt had been abolished, but Agent Saville had neither the strength nor the will to ban it at his agency.[6]

Red Cloud's favorite interpreter, Louis Richard, was also quizzed about his views of Saville, how the Indians were treated, and whether their rations were sufficient and of acceptable quality. The evidence he gave was again inconclusive, but he did express his dislike of the agent, which was not surprising, as Saville had failed to support his application to become a trader.[7]

Bishop William Hare of the Episcopal Church, who had pastoral care for the Lakota and whose church had nominated Saville as agent, was defensive and initially noncommittal with his answers. When the commissioners pressed him, he conceded that after the meetings with the OIA in Washington in May and June, at which he and Saville were present, he had changed his mind about the agent. He now considered Saville did not have the skills necessary to do the job and that, as there were questions about his integrity, he should be replaced.[8]

The hearings were spread over four weeks. Much of the evidence given was repetitive, and in late August, its work complete, the commissioners returned to Washington to finalize their report.

One week later, on September 4, Senator William Allison's Commission arrived at Red Cloud Agency to begin negotiations on the vexing question of the Black Hills.[9]

The immediate task of Senator Allison and the six commissioners was to obtain agreement on the location for the Grand Council, which Congressman Comingo's earlier subcommission had been unable to resolve. After two weeks of tense and acrimonious negotiation, and much debate and petty squabbling between Red Cloud and Spotted Tail, a compromise location near Little White Clay Creek, seven miles east of Red Cloud Agency, was finally agreed upon.[10]

The Grand Council was expected to be the largest gathering of its kind in American history, with the potential to shape the future of white America's relationship with the Northern Plains Indians. The discovery of gold in the Black Hills had already received widespread publicity, and the public was concerned by the threat of an Indian war if a satisfactory solution could not be found. The outcome of the Grand Council was of national importance, so many journalists from the nation's leading newspapers were sent to cover the story. Once again, several stayed with JW, either sleeping on a bed in his hotel or on buffalo robes covered with blankets in his billiard room, and all ate in his restaurant.

The Grand Council meeting also attracted international interest, and some wealthy overseas visitors with the necessary connections arranged to watch the once-in-a-lifetime spectacle. Viscount Lewisham, a young English army officer soon to be elected to the British Parliament, was the guest of the army and the Wyoming Legislature. He and the command-ing officer at Fort Laramie arrived at Camp Robinson on September 14 and over the next two weeks, observed the remarkable events as they unfolded.[11]

JW was ideally placed to keep abreast of the latest developments. He was on good terms with the journalists who frequented his bar and restaurant. He had a close relationship with Red Cloud and Red Dog, and his friend Frank Grouard, who understood the northern Indians, was boarding with him. Despite Red Cloud's behavior in Washington in May, where his refusal to discuss the future of the Black Hills had infuriated the authorities, both he and Spotted Tail were prepared to sell the Hills in the long-term interests of their people, for the right price. JW was aware of this, and it is believed that he was the author, under the byline "D," of a number of leading articles about the Grand Council that appeared in the *Cheyenne Daily Leader* during September.[12] His name also appeared as a source of information in newspapers published in many different states.

On Sunday, September 12, one of the members of the commission, Reverend Samuel Hinman, held a service in the stockade warehouse. This was a rare occurrence, as no regular services were held at the agency. An eyewitness description of the proceedings has survived:

Mr Will Dear, the popular trader at this agency, assumed leadership of the singing exercises with a reckless confidence characteristic of western men. He got along finely with the first line of the opening hymn, and would have closed the hymn with victory perched upon his banners, had not the discovery been made—as it was upon his tackling the second line—that he was endeavoring to dovetail a short metre hymn into a long metre time, and also that he had pitched the latter upon so high a key that no one not possessing ability to wrestle with "high C" could carry it. Then he wilted, and with his face the color of the red, red rose, backed out, whereupon the ladies . . . quietly stepped in . . . and filled the long building in which the services were being held, with sounds of sweetest melody.[13]

JW's trading post, with its saloon, cardroom, billiard room, and restaurant, was where soldiers, interpreters, scouts, frontiersmen, and journalists gathered to discuss the day's proceedings, drinking and arguing late into the night. On September 13 the *Omaha Daily Bee* commented: "Mr. JW Dear . . . an old resident of Omaha . . . is universally esteemed . . . meals are served that are not surpassed . . . by any hotel . . . west of the Missouri."[14] A week later, the paper continued, "He is a gentleman of sterling worth, has a heart as big as an ox, a sense of humor as sharp and keen as a Damascus blade, and business qualities rarely vouchsafed to one of his years. He is justly rolling up wealth here, but that does not interfere with his unbounded hospitality."[15]

Prior to the first council meeting, the commissioners had had informal discussions with the Indians and were exposed to some colorful aspects of their lives. One such occasion occurred on September 15 when a grand Omaha Dance was performed by the Oglala in their honor. This was one of the most important of the Sioux dances, which depicted stories of battles won and great feats achieved. Chanting in time with the rhythm of a drum, several hundred Indians dressed in their magnificent ceremonial robes rode slowly past JW's trading store as they approached the gates of the agency stockade. A graphic account of the proceedings appeared in the *New York Herald*:

> The great drum, heard afar off, gave early warning of their approach . . .
> with the big medicine man and head warrior of the Society of Omahas
> at their head, with the banner of feathers held aloft and lances with
> human scalps attached; the sight was imposing. A great throng of
> braves all mounted followed . . . joining in the guttural music, keeping

time to the heavy stroke of the huge drum. [They] . . . halted in front of the stockade and the gates were thrown open. A circle was formed in the center of the stockade . . . [in front of the agent's house where the commissioners were seated] . . . near which the medicine man sat upon his horse. He wore a huge war bonnet decorated with eagle feathers. . . . His body was nearly naked and painted a dull yellow. Opposite . . . was a small inner ring, formed by the musicians sitting around the drum. Red Cloud sat on the left of the musicians . . . with his head on his hand, his long heavy hair drooping over his cheeks and his face peculiarly sad.

One by one the braves rose from the circle and began a slow dance to the stroke of the drum and the chanting of a chorus by all those still seated. Parts . . . were rendered quite beautiful by the sudden accession of female voices. The deep, guttural base also produced melody.[16]

Slowly, the tempo of the music and dancing increased until it reached a crescendo. This dramatic, almost spiritual, performance was watched by JW and a large crowd of whites and Indians who filled every square inch of the stockade. When the commissioners were wearied of the spectacle, they gave the medicine man an order that could be exchanged for goods at JW's trading store. The Indians crowded into the store to claim their bounty, then marched home to their villages where festivities continued late into the night.

On Monday, September 20, the commissioners were escorted seven miles to the council site by two companies of the 2nd Cavalry led by Captain Egan and Lieutenant Crawford together with fifteen infantrymen. The commissioners arranged themselves on chairs in a large open-fronted tent; Indian chiefs and subchiefs, decked out in their finery, sat on the ground facing them. Several hundred delegates attended that first council, but between twenty and thirty thousand Indians from the many tribes that had traveled there were camped around the agency. Senator Allison gave the opening address, with Louis Richard acting as official interpreter. The Indians were at first shocked and then amused to learn of the government's proposal to lease the Hills. Red Cloud, the most senior and influential chief, had decided not to attend the meeting, but Red Dog, who often spoke on Red Cloud's behalf, told the commissioners: "There are many tribes here and it will take us several days to make up our minds." After a quick discussion the commissioners closed the meeting.[17]

The Council met on the following two days. But many chiefs failed to appear, and little progress was made. Although many reservation chiefs and some northern Indians were prepared to relinquish the Hills for the right price, most were reluctant to openly state this, as they feared the reaction of Sitting Bull's representative, Little Big Man. He had threatened to kill anyone who supported the sale. The atmosphere of intimidation and lethal reprisal meant that by Wednesday evening rumors of impending trouble had begun circulating. The prospect of violence was not far from anyone's mind.

The pivotal meeting of the Grand Council took place on Thursday, when at last all the key players deigned to attend. The commissioners were escorted by the cavalry to their tent, arriving by midmorning, and over the next few hours two thousand five hundred Indians dressed in their ceremonial robes, with feathers in their hair and rifles and guns glistening in the sun, arranged themselves around the tent of the commissioners. It was a truly magnificent sight and was to be the last Grand Council gathering ever held in America. But the atmosphere was tense. The first sign of danger came when friendly Indians from the Standing Rock Agency refused to dismount. When asked why, their reply was, "We are afraid there will be trouble, and we want to be with our horses."[18]

At around two o'clock an Indian crier with a powerful voice heralded the opening of the meeting, and nearly a hundred chiefs came forward to shake hands with the commissioners. A silence then fell over the conclave, and the two old adversaries, Red Cloud and Spotted Tail, both magnificently dressed in their ceremonial robes, advanced from opposite sides of the great circle and greeted each other before taking their positions on an inner circle. Other chiefs quickly followed their example, and once the inner circle of around two hundred chiefs was formed, the council began.

Red Dog arose and started to speak, but he was interrupted by Sitting Bull's representative, Little Big Man, who had come to make trouble. Sitting astride a powerful charger, he began to circle the outskirts of the crowd accompanied by a group of heavily armed, mounted warriors who alternately circled and charged the delegates. Young Man Afraid of His Horses sensed the danger to the commissioners and ordered a group of Oglala braves to form a line in support of the troops. His quick and decisive action avoided bloodshed. Little Big Man shouted abuse at the commissioners and at those Indians who favored selling the Hills, but then withdrew. The council broke up, and the commissioners scrambled into an artillery ambulance and were safely escorted back to the agency.[19]

Over the following two days the commissioners regrouped, trying to find a way forward after Thursday's debacle. On Sunday they invited a group of twenty chiefs to dine in JW's restaurant.[20] They met at midday and JW served a meal calculated to please the Indians. At two o'clock the party retired to their room, where discussions on how to solve the impasse continued. The Indians were pressed for a decision on whether they were prepared to sell the Hills. Once again, they said they needed more time.

At the Council gatherings on Monday and Tuesday, many speeches were given, but no progress was made. On Wednesday, September 29, Senator Allison detailed the government's final offer for the Hills—$6 million paid in fifteen annual instalments. By this time many Indians had left, and Red Cloud had not bothered to attend. The council petered out, and the next day the commissioners left for home empty-handed.[21]

The general feeling was that the commission had handled the negotiations badly and did not read or respond to the reaction of the Indians correctly. If the Indians had been given more time, a successful outcome could have been achieved. After the commission left, the atmosphere at the agency was unsettled, but most felt a solution would still be found that would suit the whites and not cause too much discontent among the Indians.

Shortly afterward, JW secured a lucrative contract to supply the hundred horses promised to the Indians for their part in trying to persuade Sitting Bull and Crazy Horse to attend the Grand Council.[22]

A few weeks later, on October 16, the final report into the "Affairs at the Red Cloud Agency" was published. It was over a thousand pages long but found no proof of corruption or malpractice by Agent Saville. It did, however, find him an incompetent and weak leader and recommended he be dismissed. But Saville, anticipating the report's findings, had already resigned.[23] This meant the agency was without an agent for two months until Saville's successor, James Hastings, arrived in early December.

Shortly after Saville's departure, Frank Grouard made an important decision. Throughout the summer he had considered leaving Crazy Horse and his band. He had lived with the Indians for five years and was ready for change. He claimed he finally made the decision to leave on October 22 when he was having his hair cut in JW's store. It was a day he remembered, as it was the day the interpreter Bill Rowland shot and killed his Cheyenne brother-in-law. His decision made, Frank continued to board with JW, paying for his keep doing odd jobs around the store.[24]

The failure of the Allison Commission presented President Grant with a major problem. The Jenney Expedition had confirmed gold was present in the Hills in paying quantities, and public opinion would not allow Grant to prevent Americans from entering the Black Hills. But nor could he legally allow them to go there.

At a little-publicized meeting on November 3 between Grant, army commanders, and the OIA, a series of measures were agreed to that allowed the government to force the Indians to relinquish ownership of the Hills. The army would abandon policing the Hills and would not prevent miners entering the area, nor would they evict them. A civilian invasion of the Hills could then begin.[25]

At the same time non-reservation Lakota were given an impossible ultimatum. On the pretext, real or imaginary, that they were committing atrocities on settlers outside the reservation, they were ordered to report to their designated agencies by January 31, 1876, or be considered hostile and hunted down. The demand was not made until December 5, which made it impossible for thousands of non-reservation Indians, who were spread over the plains in their winter quarters, to travel hundreds of miles through deep snow and freezing temperatures to meet the deadline.[26]

Grant's strategy quickly became public knowledge, which triggered a cascade of events that defined the fate of the Lakota. This was the green light George Homan and the Cheyenne city authorities had long been waiting for, and they immediately pressed ahead with their plans to make travel to the Black Hills possible. The Union Pacific Railroad Company, major wholesalers like Stephens & Wilcox, and consortiums of business-men from Omaha and Cheyenne with money and connections all set out to take advantage of the opportunities this offered. The race between Cheyenne and Sidney to become the major supplier to the Black Hills was on.

JW and many like him were uncomfortable with the way the Indians were being treated, but the outcome was inevitable—the United States would regain ownership of the Hills. JW was a man of his time, and like many others, set out to use his knowledge, experience, and contacts to his advantage.

As businessmen implemented their plans and miners flooded into the Hills, General Sheridan and his commanders systematically put into effect their plans to bring in the northern Indians when they failed to meet the January 31 deadline. The Great Sioux War was about to begin.

CHAPTER 21

The West Becomes Wild: 1876

PRESIDENT GRANT'S DECISION NOT TO STOP MINERS ENTERING THE Hills quickly became public knowledge, and by Christmas 1875 hundreds of miners had flooded into the area. Construction teams were soon hard at work building the facilities that were needed—accommodation, trading posts, hardware stores, and bars. The first town was built on an open plain in the center of the Hills, near to where gold had first been discovered. It became known as Custer City and for a few chaotic months, served as the main point of entry to the goldfields.

The sense of urgency in both Cheyenne and Sidney was palpable as the two towns vied with each other to secure the lion's share of the new business and establish stage services to Custer City. JW was heavily involved in both routes. On the Cheyenne route he built a series of stage stations for George Homan's planned stage line, stopover points where passengers could be fed and horse or mule teams changed. But on the Sidney route he not only built stage stations but was also the driving force behind the stage line itself.

Although the Hills were still legally owned by the Lakota, *The Sidney Telegraph* reported in January 1876 that Custer City had already spread over a square mile and had four stores, four saloons, a sawmill, and around a thousand miners, all frantically prospecting for gold.[1] JW's friend, Jack Crawford, the Black Hills correspondent of the *Omaha Daily Bee*, wrote to him on February 7 from Custer City praising its potential and recommending he open a store there: "We are progressing splendidly. Nearly 100 houses are completed and 100 more commenced and under

Custer City was the miners' initial destination in the Black Hills. JW's stage from Sidney completed its first through journey to Custer City on April 3, 1876. This photograph was taken two days later. Courtesy of PaulHorsted.com Collection

way. I believe if you had a branch store here you could do well. There are now nine places of business here and they are all doing well. New discoveries are being made north of here, which I think will be a good thing, as the diggings are shallow and easily worked. I think you will have a great deal of travel via Red Cloud."[2]

Throughout 1875 many businessmen had speculated about the potential offered by the Hills and planned accordingly, but the start of the new year was marked by a degree of caution, as the prospect of hostilities between the army and Indians made some investors nervous. In February JW met George Homan in Cheyenne to discuss the stage stations he was building for him. The meeting did not go well, as Homan advised JW he had decided to withdraw from the venture.[3] This was a setback for JW and his backers. But it did not deter them, and they pressed ahead with their plans for both the Cheyenne and Sidney routes.

Many considered the eastern route, Sidney, to have distinct advantages over the Cheyenne route. It was nearer to Omaha and closer to the Black Hills, and there was already an established and well-traveled trail from Sidney to the agency. Furthermore, it had the protection of two army posts, one at Fort Sidney and the other at Camp Robinson. A major

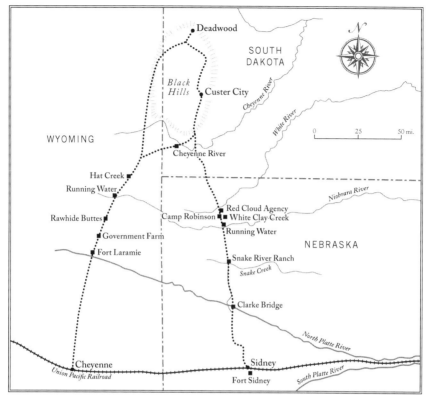

Map 4. Stage Routes: JW established nine stage stations on the two rival routes to the Black Hills. The one-hundred-fifty-mile sector from Fort Laramie to Custer City, where he built five stations, had the reputation of being the most dangerous road in America.

disadvantage was that, unlike the Cheyenne route, there was no bridge over the North Platte River. When the water was low the river could be crossed by ford, but when this was not possible a ninety-mile detour had to be made to the bridge at Fort Laramie. In late January, to overcome the problem, a group of businessmen, including Captain Wilcox of Stephens & Wilcox and the Union Pacific Railroad, underwrote a local builder, Henry Clarke, to build a toll bridge across the Platte.[4] When it opened in May it dramatically increased the competitiveness of the Sidney–Black Hills route. Travelers were now no longer dependent on fording the river and being subjected to the vagaries of changing river levels and unpredictable flows.[5]

JW had completed his plans for the Sidney stage route by mid-February. He had purchased three Concord coaches from the Abbot and Downing Company of New Hampshire and was building four stations along the Sidney trail: one at his existing trading post at Red Cloud Agency and a second at his general store at Little White Clay Creek, seven miles southeast of the agency.[6] These were supplemented by two new stage stations, one nineteen miles from the agency at Running Water on the Niobrara River, where he built a ranch and general store.[7] JW's fourth station was sixty-four miles from Sidney at Snake River, where he built a ranch, corral, hotel, and general store.[8]

On February 19, *The Sidney Telegraph* trumpeted the headline "All Aboard . . . A Stage Line Is to be Opened to the Black Hills!" The paper continued, "Mr JW Dear, the proprietor of the Sidney and Black Hills Stage line is now east purchasing the necessary stock for his stage line. He will return tomorrow. . . . He has established road ranches at suitable distances, . . . Sidney is to be congratulated in securing such a live go-ahead business man as Mr JW Dear, the proprietor of the stage line. He will leave nothing undone."

The same day, the paper reported many of Sidney's citizens had petitioned the postmaster general in Washington, DC, for a mail route "now that there is a regular stage line." The mail would be carried by Dear's Sidney & Black Hills company. A few days earlier JW had been awarded the contract to carry the quartermaster's mail from Sidney to Camp Robinson.[9] The US Mail route from Sidney was approved six weeks later.

JW's first stagecoach left Sidney for Red Cloud Agency on February 23. He advertised the service heavily, and local press gave the event wide coverage. When the stage reached the agency two days and one hundred thirty miles later, JW's bar and restaurant were open late into the night, full of friends congratulating him on his new business venture.

The Sidney Telegraph reported:

> On Wednesday last at 4 o'clock pm the first regular stage that ever left Sidney for the Black Hills took its departure. . . . On this first trip out,

Mr Dear had nine passengers and was forced to put on two coaches. . . . Mr Dear will leave for Denver next Tuesday where he expects to procure additional Concord coaches and will, in the course of a few weeks, establish a semi-weekly line. . . . In establishing this means of travel and communication between Sidney and the gold fields, Mr Dear has acted with his usual promptness.[10]

However, it was not until April 3 that his stage completed the through journey to Custer City.

Running a stage line was an expensive business. Robust stagecoaches suitable for the rough roads forged by the ox-wagon freight trains on the two-hundred-thirty-mile route had to be purchased. Teams of horses and mules, at least four and sometimes six, depending on the conditions between the stops where the teams were changed, had to be in place at regular intervals along the way. There had to be a corral and sufficient water and fodder to sustain them at each change stop, with blacksmiths on hand to cope with the inevitable problems with shoes and coach repairs.[11] And passengers also had to be catered for, with overnight

JW's Sidney to Deadwood stage made its inaugural journey from Sidney to Red Cloud Agency on February 23, 1876. Courtesy of PaulHorsted.com Collection

accommodation and regular meals provided at the road ranches. Reliable drivers, usually three to each journey, had to be distributed evenly along the road to allow for rest periods, and staff had to be hired to manage; cook; look after the horses and mules; and, crucially, defend each road ranch.

All this required considerable drive and capital. JW clearly had the drive, and Stevens & Wilcox provided much of the capital. *The Sidney Telegraph* on June 24 published an article about the "energetic men, who are doing, and will do all in their power to further the interests of Sidney . . . the enterprising gentlemen who are running the transportation lines, the heaviest of whom we might mention, JW Dear . . . will make any town prosperous."

"Mr Dear, the stage man," as the newspapers began calling him, already had a good working knowledge of the Sidney–Black Hills route, as he owned and managed a freighting company running multiple ox-wagon teams.[12] Nonetheless the planning and labor required to run a successful stage line did not just depend on the drive of the proprietor but on many factors outside his control.

The opening of Clarke's bridge across the North Platte River in May gave the Sidney route a distinct advantage and removed a major hazard, but passengers on those early stage journeys were still subjected to very uncomfortable and testing conditions. Soft sand was a significant problem on the Sidney trail, and passengers were often forced to walk, and sometimes to even push the coaches across difficult terrain. A writer describing the harsh conditions commented: "I would never advise any one to come that way without they want to pull a rope or lift a wheel, and walk considerably."

As a result of the Black Hills trade, Sidney grew in leaps and bounds. In 1874 it had a population of around seven hundred; three years later it had risen to more than four thousand. This tremendous growth attracted many rough characters. It was a gathering place for cowboys and hard men from all over the territory, and many fights, killings, and lynchings took place. The main strip in town boasted eighty-seven licensed premises, which included hotels, brothels, saloons, billiard halls, and gambling parlors. By 1880 over two hundred people had been buried on Boot Hill. Few had died of natural causes.

Large freighting outfits and wholesalers established their headquarters in the town running ox-wagon trains to the Black Hills, and it was not uncommon for five hundred tons of freight to leave Sidney daily for the twelve-day lumbering trek to Deadwood. The largest freight company operating out of Sidney was Pratt & Ferris.[13] The company's trains usually consisted of twenty-five ox wagons each carrying up to five tons of freight. The wagons normally returned to Sidney empty or with a handful of miners who paid $10 for the very bumpy ride. Miners, gamblers, outlaws, and ladies of the night flocked from Sidney to the goldfields. At its peak up to $2 million in gold a week (in today's money) came down the trails by stagecoach to Cheyenne and Sidney for onward shipping to Omaha via the Union Pacific Railroad. Stagecoaches suffered as many attacks from outlaws, known popularly as "road agents," as they did from Indians. These were dangerous, high-risk journeys.

In tandem with his Sidney venture and despite George Homan's withdrawal, JW continued with his plans to build five stage stations along the Cheyenne Trail.

Building stations north of Fort Laramie was the most audacious investment yet undertaken by anyone, as the proposed stage trail crossed the traditional hunting grounds of the Lakota and many were followers of Crazy Horse and Sitting Bull and hostile to all whites. At that time there was not a single dwelling between Fort Laramie and the mining camps.[14] The *Cheyenne Daily Leader* commented: "Mr Dear, the wide-awake trader at Red Cloud, is establishing way-stations along the line north of Fort Laramie, with the purpose of affording accommodations to the people going and coming."[15]

Situated about a day's walk apart, facilities were soon established at Government Farm, Raw Hide Buttes, Running Water, Hat Creek, and on the Cheyenne River.[16] JW's reputation in Cheyenne was that he was a "man with a nerve of iron, most enterprising and honorable . . . familiar with the Indian character . . . [and] knew what he was about."[17] Even though this was still only a roughly blazed trail, JW anticipated "the day when a regular stage service would travel an improved road using . . . his stops."[18]

Miners and their followers flooded into Cheyenne. On January 21 the *Cheyenne Daily Leader* commented, "Every day's arrival of people at this point is greater than that of the day before, until now they begin to come by hundreds, bound for the new Eldorado. . . . Already the crowd is such that three or four stages could be sent out daily."[19] Cheyenne's hotels were full, and wholesalers did a booming business, equipping miners with everything they needed. The town swarmed with newspapermen and reporters all eager to dispatch their stories to editors in Washington, New York, and Chicago. The excitement increased still further in mid-February when General Crook stayed overnight at the Inter-Ocean Hotel en route to Fort Laramie, where he was to prepare for his anticipated campaign against Crazy Horse, Sitting Bull, and the northern Indians.

JW and his backers were relieved when Homan's fledgling Cheyenne stage line was taken over in late February by a rival consortium of Omaha and Salt Lake City businessmen. They appointed an experienced stage operator, Luke Voorhees, as their general manager.[20] By March 10, Voorhees had completed negotiations with the Union Pacific Railroad to sell tickets from Omaha to the Black Hills via Cheyenne, and he appointed "Stuttering" H. E. Brown to manage the dangerous section of the trail between Fort Laramie and Custer City. Voorhees and Brown immediately entered into negotiations with JW to use his five stage stations. On March 19, a stagecoach on a trial run from Cheyenne took five days to reach Custer City, killing two horses in the process.[21] Despite this setback a regular service started two weeks later. The first stagecoach from Cheyenne arrived in Custer City on April 3, the same day that JW's stage from Sidney completed its first through journey.[22]

As winter gave way to spring and the weather became warmer, Indian depredations escalated. Traveling on the plains became extremely dangerous, and the West became truly wild.

When JW visited Sidney or Cheyenne he was forced to travel in a large group or with a military or Indian escort—to venture onto the plains with his treasured phaeton was completely out of the question.

For many Indians, any white man was a target. Small groups of Indians indiscriminately attacked vulnerable whites wherever they encountered them. Settlers, lone travelers, or a passing stagecoach were all fair game. And the threat was not just from Indians, but also from road agents attracted by the promise of easy pickings, whether it was money, gold, or horses. Sometimes it was difficult to know who had committed the crime, whites or Indians.

Being able to trust people was also a problem. In April 1876, Frank Grouard was surprised to find Bill Bevins, a notorious outlaw, working at Red Cloud Agency.[23] Grouard had first met him in Helena, Montana, almost a decade earlier, shortly after Bevins had made his fortune from a gold strike. He soon lost all his money at poker and eked out a precarious existence as a horse thief and serial escaper from the law before working at the agency as a coach and wagon driver, probably for JW. His fellow drivers were Herman Leslie, who later received ninety-nine years imprisonment for murder and robbery, and George Hastings, nephew of the new Indian agent, James Hastings, who had replaced Saville.

Bevins worked at the agency for some months before leaving and forming a gang, which preyed on the Deadwood stage. He and his gang were eventually arrested and imprisoned. He had the well-deserved reputation for being one of the original iron men of the West, once attempting to escape from Buffalo Bill Cody by running eighteen miles through deep snow, a prickly pear patch, and sharp stones wearing only one shoe.[24] When he was eventually apprehended, bloody but unbowed, Cody admiringly called him a "tough one" and his run "the most remarkable feat of the kind ever known, either of a white man, or an Indian."[25]

Throughout the spring and early summer months horrific incidents continued to dominate the headlines. On April 16, the Metz family and a handful of emigrants were traveling south along the Custer City to Sidney trail when, at Red Canyon three miles north of JW's Cheyenne River station, they were attacked by Indians. Three of the group were badly injured but managed to escape and sought refuge at JW's station. The Metz family's black cook was taken prisoner and never seen again, and the rest were killed, their bodies mutilated and dismembered. Luke Voorhees was in the party that discovered the carnage later that day.[26] A teamster named

Simpson, whom Voorhees knew well, was "carved beyond anyone that I ever saw. Every toe, finger, nose and ears were cut off, and he was scalped much more than the usual scalp lock. They had peeled off his entire face. . . . [I recognized him] by a mark on one of his [severed] ears."[27] He continued, "with some of my men we gathered up the fragments as best we could . . . under the circumstances and excitement to bury them, as we were looking for Indians to pick us up any moment."[28]

A week later Voorhees's colleague, "Stuttering" Brown was murdered, maybe by Indians, but the press speculated, more probably by the outlaw Persimmon Bill Chambers, on the trail midway between JW's Hat Creek and Cheyenne River stations. The violence triggered an immediate response from the army, and Captain Egan and his command were given the task of escorting wagon trains from Cheyenne to the Hills, a route Egan considered to be far more dangerous than the Sidney trail and one that soon gained the reputation of being one of the most dangerous roads in America.[29]

After the Metz and Brown murders the violence continued. In early May Indians attacked an ox-wagon train on the Sidney to Red Cloud trail carrying supplies for Frank Yates's store at Red Cloud Agency.[30] Three of JW's stage stations on the Cheyenne route were burned to the ground by Indians shortly after they opened—Raw Hide Buttes, Running Water, and Hat Creek each survived for less than three months.

On May 16, the mail carrier from Fort Laramie to Red Cloud Agency, Charles Clark, was killed by Indians. JW and Richard, together with fifteen Indians, recovered his bullet-riddled body.[31] A week later JW had a narrow escape. The *Cheyenne Daily Leader* reported:

> Mr Dear was accompanied on this trip by John Farnham, a very faithful and reliable man who had been in his employ for several years. Arrived in safety at Sidney, Mr Dear directed Farnham to make the return trip with the quartermaster's mail and the regular stage. Farnham reached Sage Creek station on the following day, but here he met his fate. The Indians attacked the stage, killed Farnham and captured his four horses.[32]

The Sidney Telegraph printed a labored joke at JW's expense. It reported that "Mr JW Dear, the proprietor of the stage line . . . will leave here next Tuesday on the stage for the Indian Agency. He will have his hair cut and head sandpapered before leaving here for the north."[33] A bald head, of course, was of no interest to marauding Indians looking for scalps.

Regular attacks by Indians and road agents forced both the Cheyenne and Sidney stage lines to suspend their operations in June.[34] Freight trains taking essential supplies to the Black Hills continued to operate, but had to have military escorts, and JW could only leave the agency with armed guards. On June 17, as the threat of violence increased, Agent James Hastings ordered Frank Yates's wife to move to Camp Robinson, where she could be protected by the army.[35]

Throughout these traumatic months JW encountered the many issues that bedeviled the proprietor of a stage line operating in a hostile environment. The crippling costs of running the line became apparent, and Indian attacks came thick and fast. With the burning of three of his stage stations, and regular attacks by Indians and gangs of road agents on anyone they found on the road, JW found it was impossible to make money. After seven torrid months as the trailblazing proprietor of the Sidney–Black Hills stage line, he threw in the towel and sought a buyer for the business.

In early September Marsh and Stephenson from Omaha became the new owners, and JW became their agent at Red Cloud Agency.[36] *The Sidney Telegraph* noted: "Our new line a settled fact . . . on Tuesday next [September 19] . . . starts its first trip with ten passengers." However, the new owners fared no better, and seven months later they also sold to the owners of the Cheyenne Stage Company.[37]

Although JW had sold his stage line, he retained his four stations on the Sidney route. He did, however, sell his Government Farm station to the Cheyenne Stage Company for $1,200, leaving him with only his Cheyenne River Ranch on the Cheyenne route.[38]

Perhaps JW's drive to succeed overcame his judgment of the risks and the likely financial return from his fledgling enterprises. But the sheer volume of newspaper articles lauding the limitless prospect of wealth from this new El Dorado drove thousands of miners along the railroad to Sidney and Cheyenne. The financial prospect of transporting this press of humanity those last few hundred miles to the Hills, as well as feeding them and selling them merchandise along the road, was difficult to resist.

The presence of the army and the escalating violence had little impact on the miners, who were prepared to risk everything in their search for gold. In May gold was discovered in large quantities fifty-five miles north of Custer City in Deadwood Gulch. Thousands flooded into the area, and within weeks Custer City was relegated to becoming just a transport and communications hub on the Sidney to Black Hills trail. By June Deadwood was home to ten thousand miners and their followers, and bars, banks, brothels, gambling dens, and hotels sprung up overnight. Deadwood became the gold capital of the Black Hills, and a local marshal was appointed to enforce the law to help keep the peace. His name was "Wild Bill" Hickok.

Main Street Deadwood in August 1876. By then Deadwood had taken over from Custer City as the gold mining center of the Hills. Courtesy of National Archives, photo no. 533172

CHAPTER 22

The Great Sioux War and the Battle of Little Bighorn

JANUARY 1876 FOUND SOLDIERS IN THEIR BARRACKS, MINERS IN THEIR shanty towns in the Black Hills, and Indians in their winter camps, all huddled against the extreme weather. Heavy snow and temperatures well below freezing restricted movement, and the army's first faltering campaign against the non-reservation Indians was delayed until March.

The OIA banned traders from selling ammunition to reservation Indians from January 18.[1] This made it difficult for them to hunt and supplement their meager winter rations with small game. It created anger and discontent, particularly among the young braves. Red Cloud's own son Jack was one of this band of malcontents who, disillusioned with agency life and the continual shortage of rations and feeling betrayed by the government, left their agencies to join the northern Indians. On their journey north they vented their feelings on miners and any white men they encountered.

When, as expected, it became clear the Indians would fail to meet the January 31 deadline to report to their agencies, responsibility for non-reservation Indians passed from the OIA to the War Department.[2] General Sheridan and his troops, which included General Crook and Custer's 7th Cavalry, planned to systematically scour the vast territory for the winter camps of Sitting Bull and Crazy Horse.

General Crook arrived at Fort Laramie in mid-February to prepare for his campaign. JW, who was on good terms with Crook, recommended

General George Crook, Commander of the Army of the Department of the Platte, 1875–1885. Brady-Handy Photograph Collection, Library of Congress, Prints and Photographs Division

to him and to Chief of Scouts Major Stanton (JW's fellow paleontologist) that they consider employing Frank Grouard as a scout, which they did.[3] Crook and his command then moved to Fort Fetterman.

Crook, nine hundred soldiers, and thirty scouts, including Frank, Big Bat Pourier, and Louis Richard, left the fort on March 1 for the Big Horn Expedition against the northern Indians.[4] This effectively marked the start of the Great Sioux War.

Crook's strategy was simple. His scouts would systematically cover the plains looking for large Indian villages. They were not interested in skirmishes with small bands of Indians. Crook's main force would then move quickly and quietly to the outskirts of the village to mount a surprise attack at dawn. Their objective was to destroy the village and food supplies, capture or stampede the Indian ponies, and destroy as many of their weapons as possible, leaving the Indians, including women, children, the old and infirm, exposed to the elements with little or no resources, forcing them into submission and back to their agencies.

On March 16, after days of traveling in bitterly cold weather across inhospitable terrain near the Montana border, they came across what they believed to be Crazy Horse's village. It was, however, a peaceful Cheyenne encampment. Crook's attack on the village resulted in the previously friendly Cheyenne joining the northern Indians and over a hundred Cheyenne lodges put themselves under the protection of Sitting Bull. The whole Powder River Affair, as it became known, was viewed as a strategic disaster.

Crook returned to Fort Fetterman, with none of his objectives met. The battle did, however, have a positive outcome for Frank Grouard. General Crook was impressed by his skills and by the way his new scout handled himself during the campaign. He rapidly became Crook's favorite scout partly because of his ability as a tracker, but also because of his instinctive understanding of the Lakota. Crook wrote to the War Department that "I would rather lose a third of my command than be deprived of Frank Grouard."[5] This favoritism created tension between Frank and the other scouts, particularly Louis Richard.

Two weeks after the battle the animosity between the two men bubbled over. Except for Frank, Big Bat, and Louis Richard, the other scouts were discharged. These three made their way to Red Cloud Agency for a few weeks of rest before rejoining Crook for his next campaign.

JW organized dances, which were eagerly anticipated and always well patronized by scouts, interpreters, and civilian staff from both the agency and Camp Robinson. Frank and Bat regularly attended, but when they returned to the agency, Bat heard rumors that trouble was brewing and that Louis Richard planned to have Frank killed at the dance. Frank described what happened in his autobiography:

> Bat said I will watch and you dance.... In the room ... I was dancing so I could face Bat, when he gave me the signal. Four half-breeds were standing against the wall. I heard Bat calling to me to watch out. As I looked, he had got after these men, and before I could get my partner out of the room Bat had all four half-breeds piled up in the corner, going at it right and left. He never used his revolver, only his fist, but he was a powerful man anyway. The dance broke up. Bat told me two of the men were Louis Richard's brothers, the other two were Richard's boys, and that Louis was the instigator.... Captain Egan got to hear about it and asked me to tell him the story. Soon after that Louis Richard was discharged from the service.[6]

A few weeks later Crook began to plan his second expedition and visited Red Cloud Agency with his aide-de-camp, Lieutenant James Bourke, to recruit Oglala scouts to help track down Crazy Horse and Sitting Bull. He was unsuccessful; Red Cloud refused to see him, and Agent James Hastings made it clear he was opposed to Crook's plan to recruit Indians from his agency.[7] An irritated Crook left empty-handed and returned to Fort Fetterman before moving north with more than one thousand troops on the next phase of his campaign.

The campaign, which became known as the Big Horn and Yellowstone Expedition, ran from May until late October, a time when the Indians were again fully mobile after the long hard winter—and a far deadlier foe.

On the morning of June 17 Crook's overnight camp on Rosebud Creek was attacked by Crazy Horse's band.[8] The ensuing battle between two equally matched forces continued for over seven hours before the

Indians withdrew. Despite the ferocity of the battle fatalities were light, and less than fifty out of the two thousand who had fought lost their lives. Instead of pressing forward and continuing the battle, Crook returned to base camp, and although he claimed a tactical victory, most historians consider the battle a strategic defeat.[9]

A week later, Colonel Custer located an Indian village on the Little Bighorn River, fifty miles northwest of the Rosebud battlefield. The initial plan was to mount a surprise attack at dawn on June 26. But the regiment was spotted by Indian scouts, and Custer decided to attack on June 25. What he had not appreciated was the size of the Indian encampment, which contained more than two thousand Sioux and Cheyenne warriors.

Custer attacked at around five o'clock in the afternoon, and an hour later the Battle of Little Bighorn was over. Custer and two hundred sixty-five men from the 7th Cavalry lay dead surrounded by their slaughtered horses. The final onslaught on the beleaguered troops was led by Crazy Horse, and the official report on the battle stated: "This fight brought Crazy Horse more prominently before all the Indians than anyone else. . . . he went at once to [Colonel] Custer's front and there became the leading spirit. Before this he had a great reputation; in it he gained a greater prestige than any other Indian in the camp."[10] Around thirty Indians lost their lives.

After the battle Indians swarmed over the hill where the soldiers lay. Warriors put final arrows and bullets into the dying, and women and children from the village emptied the pockets of the soldiers and stripped their clothes. Many bodies were mutilated. It took ten days for news of the disaster to filter to the outside world. On July 6, two days after the nationwide Centennial Fourth of July festivities, Crook received a telegram from General Sheridan informing him of the disaster, and the *Cheyenne Daily Leader* announced: "The terrible tale of the slaughter of Custer and his command will be found on our first page. We dress that page in mourning for the brave men who perished at the hands of Sitting Bull's fiends incarnate on the 25th of June."[11]

The tragic events at Little Bighorn shocked the nation and had a profound effect on the morale at Camp Robinson and Red Cloud Agency. Many of those killed were well known to the officers, soldiers, and agency staff. Frank Yates, whose elder brother, George, was killed leading one of the companies during the battle, was just one of many who lost a relative or a friend on that dreadful June day.[12] Public opinion turned against the Indians, but it was also critical of the OIA and the army for presiding over such a disaster.

During the first half of 1876 the full might of the US Army had searched the northern plains but failed to engage the northern Indians to force them to report to their agencies to surrender. By June all they had achieved was a handful of inconclusive skirmishes, and yet the first decisive battle of the Great Sioux War at Little Bighorn resulted in a crushing and humiliating defeat. This was politically unacceptable, and President Grant ordered an immediate response that left no room for failure.

The War Department assumed responsibility for agency Indians on July 22, and army officers replaced the civilian OIA-appointed Indian agents. The army suspected that reservation Indians supplied food, ammunition, and ponies to their northern cousins. In the past they had been powerless to act. But now that they were able to, the atmosphere at the agency changed, and there was more wariness and distrust on both sides.

It was at this time that one of the most famous showmen in America, William Frederick Cody, better known as "Buffalo Bill," seized the moment for self-promotion. The thirty-year-old had already found fame as a pony-express rider, buffalo hunter, and showman. On June 10, he signed up as a scout for his old regiment, the 5th Cavalry.

Cody and the cavalry left Fort Laramie on June 22 heading for the Powder River Country. On July 14 they heard reports that more than three hundred Cheyenne planned to leave Red Cloud Agency to move north to join the northern Indians. The news of Custer's massacre was still fresh in everyone's mind, and when, on the evening of July 17, Cody and Company K stumbled across seven Cheyenne braves acting suspiciously, Cody led a small group that galloped toward the Indians. His horse stumbled, and he was thrown to the ground in the path of the advancing Cheyenne. He picked himself up; took careful aim at the leading warrior, Yellow Hair; and shot him dead. He ran forward and scalped the Indian with his bowie knife. He later claimed he had swung the bloody scalp above his head and cried out, "the first scalp for Custer!" And perhaps he did, although no one else on the field that day ever recalled his dramatic outburst.[13]

The story became increasingly embellished as the weeks passed. Newspaper accounts declared Cody had single-handedly seen off an Indian war party and killed Yellow Hair in hand-to-hand combat. Whatever the truth, Yellow Hair's scalp toured the country, featuring prominently in Cody's Wild West show before eventually ending up in the Cody Museum. A fellow 5th Cavalry scout that day confirmed that Cody had taken the scalp and saw him the next day playing billiards in JW's bar at Red Cloud Agency with the scalp attached to his belt.[14]

JW had first met Cody some months earlier when he visited the agency to recruit young braves for his Buffalo Bill Combination Show (the forerunner of his Wild West show, which first toured the country in 1883). It would have been fascinating to eavesdrop on their conversation in the bar that evening and hear Buffalo Bill's version of Yellow Hair's demise.

For three months following the massacre at Little Bighorn, General Crook continued to unsuccessfully search the northern plains for Crazy Horse and Sitting Bull. In late August the weather worsened dramatically, and the troops struggled through blizzards and freezing temperatures and were forced to eat their horses to survive. The nightmare journey became known as the "Horsemeat March," and eventually, on September 18, the exhausted and demoralized men reached what later became known as Crook City in the Black Hills. Crook then left his troops to return to Fort Laramie, leaving them to make their way to Camp Robinson, where they were officially disbanded on October 24.

CHAPTER 23

General Crook Deposes Red Cloud

DURING AUGUST AND SEPTEMBER OF 1876, TWO THOUSAND TROOPS were drafted into Camp Robinson to strengthen the army's planned winter campaign against the northern Indians. For a few days in early October more than three thousand troops, approximately 25 percent of the entire US Army, were stationed in and around Camp Robinson. To accommodate the additional numbers two temporary camps were established, each capable of housing one thousand men. They were named Camps Canby and Custer, and the army allocated $20,000 to build temporary barracks, stables, and post stores.[1] Despite this investment many troops still had to be billeted under canvas.

JW arranged for both Clay and Richard to be interviewed for the positions of post traders at the camps, and in early October both were appointed. Clay left his job in Omaha to become post trader at Camp Canby, and Richard left JW's employment to become post trader at Camp Custer.[2] Richard's replacement was their younger brother, twenty-year-old Luther, who left his parents and their youngest brother, Frank, at Royal Oaks, to work for JW.

This was the first time Luther had left Virginia. He was twelve when JW had gone West in 1868. Over the following eight years he had heard stories about life on the Western frontier from the letters of his elder brothers and their intermittent visits home. However, nothing could have prepared him for the reality of what he found when he arrived at the agency after a seventeen-hundred-mile journey, culminating in a cramped and uncomfortable two-day, one-hundred-mile stage ride from Sidney.

Teams of contractors were working day and night to build the temporary facilities needed for the additional troops. Hundreds of soldiers swarmed around the area, settling into their new quarters and preparing for the army's winter campaign against Crazy Horse, Sitting Bull, and Dull Knife. Sullen and morose reservation Indians gathered in small groups, worried by the uncertainty of what the authorities had planned for them. And a steady stream of miners, freighters with their massive wagon trains, and stagecoaches on their way to the Black Hills, all broke the journey at JW's trading post. A sense of urgency pervaded the area, and there was a feeling that the conflict with the Indians was about to enter its final phase.

Luther's arrival was emotional, as it was the first time the four brothers had been together for six years. Despite the sense of uncertainty and worry that was in the air, there were celebrations in JW's bar that night—a night that marked the start of the brothers working together for the next five years.

During this period, in stark contrast to his stagecoach ventures, JW's trading and freighting businesses thrived, and he and his brothers enjoyed many months of profitable business.

Clay's store at Camp Canby was located half a mile northeast of JW's trading complex. Camp Custer, where Richard was based, was half a mile south. Stephens & Wilcox had the concession to supply Clay's store, where he employed five staff.[3] There was a similar arrangement at Camp Custer. Clay's store was built for the army by JW and his contractors, which explains the carefully staged photograph taken shortly after Luther's arrival, showing the four brothers standing outside the recently completed store.

Throughout August Red Cloud and his fellow chiefs waited with growing apprehension to learn how the government planned to deal with them. They did not have long to wait. Even though Red Cloud and the reservation Indians had played no part in the violence perpetrated by their northern cousins, the authorities decided to impose draconian new conditions on them.

An orderly line forms, posed for the photographer at Clay's army post store, Camp Canby, in October 1876. Standing foreground left to right, Richard, Clay, JW by his phaeton, and Luther. Eugenia Newberg

A six-man special commission chaired by sixty-eight-year-old George Manypenny, an experienced Indian administrator who had negotiated more than fifty Indian treaties, was given the task of delivering the unwelcome news to the Indians.[4] The commission arrived at the agency on September 6 and, acting under strict instructions from Washington, demanded Red Cloud and the reservation Indians sign away their rights to the Black Hills; give up hunting rights in the Powder River Country; and move to a location away from the Black Hills, Wyoming, and Nebraska. They were threatened that if they refused to accept these demands their food supplies would be withdrawn, and they would be starved into submission. This became known as the "Sign or Starve Treaty."[5]

The Indians were given time to consider their response. While waiting for their decision, the commissioners stayed at the agency, where they ate in JW's restaurant. One commissioner commented, "an excellent bill of fare was served though in that country mackerel was called fish and dried apples were respectfully referred to as fruit."[6]

Red Cloud and his fellow chiefs had no option but to accept the terms and sign, which they did in the agency stockade on September 20. All the commissioners were ashamed by the way the Indians had been treated. When Young Man Afraid of His Horses touched the pen held by the commission's secretary, he said, "I touch this pen hoping the Great

Father in Washington will let me stay in this country where I was born and where my people are buried."

This pathetic appeal from a representative of a proud tribe was greeted with silence; every white man present knew that his appeal was in vain, that the relentless purpose of government was to have all Indians finally settled in Indian Territory. Many Indians, as they touched the pen, did so in the full realization of the helplessness of their situation, faced with the overwhelming power of the white man.

George Manypenny wrote in his official report:

> many of our people think that the only solution of the Indian problem is in their extermination. . . . The Indian is a savage, but he is also a man. . . . He has a passionate love for his children. He loves his country. He will gladly die for his tribe. . . . He is capable of civilization. . . . A great crisis has arisen in Indian affairs. The wrongs of the Indians are admitted by all. Thousands of the best men in the land feel keenly the nation's shame. They look to Congress for redress. Unless immediate and appropriate legislation is made for the protection and government of the Indians, they must perish. Our country must forever bear the disgrace and suffer the retribution of its wrong-doing.[7]

Another member of the commission, Bishop Henry B. Whipple, wrote in a similar vein, "I know of no other instance in history where a great nation has so shamefully violated its oath."[8]

The next day, in protest at their treatment, Red Cloud and Red Leaf moved their bands twenty miles away to Chadron Creek. The authorities, fearful that they might join Sitting Bull, Crazy Horse, and the northern Indians, ordered them to return or their rations would be cut. They refused, and General Crook instructed Colonel Ranald Mackenzie together with two cavalry companies, forty Pawnee scouts, and Billy Garnett as the interpreter, to force them back to the agency. The Indians, finding themselves surrounded, surrendered, and being deemed disloyal, were immediately disarmed and dismounted. Fifty rifles and more than seven hundred ponies, including one hundred belonging to Red Cloud, were confiscated.[9]

Two weeks later, the ponies were sold at public auction at Fort Laramie.[10] Red Cloud and Red Leaf were told they would receive cows and not money as recompense for their ponies, but Red Cloud wanted money. Despite numerous heated discussions, the issue remained unresolved for thirteen years.[11]

Despite Red Cloud's humiliation at being forced to concede the Black Hills and hunting rights in the Powder River Country and having had his ponies confiscated for his meager show of defiance, General Crook decided a further public reprimand was required.

At a meeting in the agency stockade on October 24, 1876, Crook assembled the chiefs of the Oglala, Brulé, and Cheyenne and lectured them that any disloyalty would be punished by withholding their rations and any future violence or dissent would be severely punished. Then General Crook deposed Red Cloud as leader of the Oglala and Brulé as punishment for his disloyalty and appointed Spotted Tail in his place.[12] Most of those present viewed this as a petulant and empty gesture by Crook. JW was present at this historic meeting and witnessed Red Cloud's public humiliation.

A month later Crook's official campaign photographer, Stanley Morrow, visited the agency. He graphically captured the Indian chief's feelings—the anger, frustration, humiliation, and hopelessness of his situation. It is believed to be the first portrait photograph of Red Cloud taken at his agency. Morrow wrote to his wife that "through the kindness of the Indian trader, Mr Dear, I was enabled to procure some good negatives of Red Cloud, today, it being the first time he ever gave a sitting to a photographer. . . . He seems to take his disposition rather hard, but claims it will make no difference to his people."[13]

During the same photographic session, in gratitude for JW's help, Morrow also took a photograph of Red Cloud with JW and his brothers and gave it to JW.[14]

Over the following weeks the atmosphere remained tense as the reservation Indians struggled to come to terms with the reality of their situation. The army prepared for a revitalized winter campaign against the northern Indians, and in early November troops left Camp Robinson for Fort Fetterman. On November 14, General Crook with a force

Outside the agent's house, General Crook (in the light coat) humiliates Red Cloud by appointing Spotted Tail as the head chief of the Oglala and Brulé. October 24, 1876. Beinecke Rare Book and Manuscript Library, Yale University

of fifteen hundred men and four hundred thirty followers, including Frank Grouard and Billy Garnett, headed north. This marked the start of Crook's Winter Campaign and the final push to find the Sioux and Cheyenne to bring them in.

Ten days later, at the base of the Bighorn Mountains in northern Wyoming, Colonel Mackenzie found and attacked Dull Knife's Cheyenne village. More than forty Indians were killed, their ponies taken, and the remainder, including women, children, the young, old, and infirm,

Stanley Morrow's celebrated image of a reflective Red Cloud sitting outside JW's store shortly after his deposition as head of the Oglala. National Anthropological Archives, Smithsonian Institution, NAA INV.09851600

were left to survive the increasingly harsh winter conditions. This caused widespread hardship, and many Indians suffered severe frostbite and froze to death. Dull Knife and the survivors were forced to seek refuge in Crazy Horses's camp, barely managing to survive the winter.[15]

JW is sitting next to a clearly morose Red Cloud, who has hardly moved from his position in the previous image. Standing behind them left to right are his three brothers, Richard, Luther, Clay, and an army officer. Eugenia Newberg

By this time, it had become clear to everyone at the Red Cloud Agency that their lives were about to change. JW, agency staff, Red Cloud, and his fellow chiefs spent hours discussing the uncertainty over their futures. There were so many unanswered questions. When and where would Red Cloud be relocated? Would JW be reappointed Indian trader and move with Red Cloud? What would happen to his burgeoning businesses? What would happen to Camps Robinson, Custer, and Canby once the Indians had left?

CHAPTER 24

The End of Indian Resistance: 1877

AFTER THE CONFRONTATIONAL MEETING BETWEEN GENERAL CROOK and Red Cloud and the realization that the army was determined to force the northern Indians onto reservations whatever the cost, Red Cloud and Spotted Tail became preoccupied with the question of where they would be relocated. They knew many politicians were in favor of moving them to Indian Territory in present-day Oklahoma, but they did not want to go south, nor did they want to move to the Missouri. However, they recognized their negotiating position was weak, and in mid-December Spotted Tail and Red Dog led a delegation of ninety-four Indians to inspect the Indian Territory. They did not like what they found and spoke strongly against moving there, and the army and the OIA abandoned the idea.[1] Where the Indians would eventually be sent was still unclear, and they became increasingly apprehensive about their future.

After the sale of his stage line to Stevenson and Marsh in August, JW focused on his trading complex at the agency and his stage stations on the Sidney to Red Cloud trail.[2] To cater for the increase in his business he upgraded his bar and restaurant, and many commented on the improvements and how his facilities had been transformed beyond all recognition.[3] As JW was making improvements at Red Cloud, Clay and Richard, as post traders to the army, were building and stocking their new premises at Camps Canby and Custer. Both brothers opened their stores in mid-October.

A firsthand account of life in the trading stores of the brothers has survived in the memoirs of Fred Bruning, a young man Clay employed at

Camp Canby. His German parents moved to Omaha in 1861, and from the age of fourteen Fred worked for several Omaha retailers. In 1875 he was employed by a druggist whose shop was next to Stephens & Wilcox on Farnam Street, and this was where he first met Clay, who persuaded the eighteen-year-old to join him at Camp Canby. Fred paid $50 for his combined rail and stage ticket, and he arrived at the camp on October 20, 1876. His observations over the following months provide a fascinating insight into agency life.

"I got well acquainted with Frank Gerrard [Grouard] . . . he had a ugly face, but [was] a verry polite [man, and] liked to dance, play cards and have a good time. . . . [The Indians] spent their money freely, when they had any. They amused themselves evenings by dancing & singing, for I could hear their Tom Toms pounding soon after dark, and keep it up to early in the morning. Then it would be quiet all day."

Occasionally, there was an ugly incident at Clay's post store:

One Sunday evening while [officers from the 4th Cavalry] were playing billiards, a drunken bullwacker . . . came into the room and wanted to go into the store. I told him it was closed but he insisted on staying so I and [a lieutenant] got hold of his arm . . . and put him out. Short time later he came back with a six shooter . . . and wanted revenge . . . the Leiutenant hit him over the head with a billiard que and layed him out and called of the Sargent of the Guard [who] put him in the caliboose for the night.

JW's trading complex was the center of social life:

At the Agency was a large log cabin hall and once in a while . . . [JW] would give a public dance. Admission [was] 5 dol for men. Women free. Good many half breeds. Girls would attend, all dressed up to date. Music was a fiddell, guitar & banjo. Every one seems to injoy themselves [and] always they served a plenty of good things to eat and a gambling room attached, with plenty of money in sight. And it was well patronized. I wondered were all the people came from.

Bruning commented that Red Cloud was a friendly Indian but didn't have much to say. He "liked a drink of whiskey, but [I] never seen any of the Indians drunk. . . . Sundays we would spend going up to the Chalk Bluffs, which was about a mile back of our store. Sometimes [we] would try target shooting. We were good shots, but an Indian came along, and we let him in. He beat us all."

However, the stress of the frontier took its toll on many officers and men:

> It was the first day of January 1877 when the 4th Caverly troops left on their campaghn, General Mackenzie in command. . . . Lieutenant McKinney . . . [a fine-looking man, over six foot tall] . . . came to offi-cer's bar and was enjoying himself by drinking cock tails and wanted a few bottle to take along. He was feeling good, didn't care weather he was with the Company or not. He said he had a presentiment that he would never come back alive. It was about 8 am. General McKinzie came back after him, and reprimanding for not being with his Company . . . but his presentiment came true, for he was killed in the first battle they had.[4]

Several weeks after General Crook left Camp Robinson for his win-ter campaign, JW learned that Jules Ecoffey had died from a beating he had received in a brawl in a Cheyenne bar. On November 28, the *Chey-enne Daily Leader* reported that it "was a worthless bummer known as 'Stonewall,' who . . . administered a terrible castigation . . . but there was a woman at the bottom of the trouble."[5] Life was cheap on the frontier: JW and his brothers led dangerous lives.

On December 7, 1876, a new employee, Dr. Valentine McGillycuddy and his wife, Fanny, arrived at Camp Robinson. McGillycuddy had been a junior surveyor with the 1875 Jenney Expedition to the Black Hills. A year later, shortly after the Battle of Little Bighorn, he had joined Gen-eral Crook's ill-fated Big Horn and Yellowstone Expedition as a contract surgeon. After three harrowing months Crook's exhausted troops arrived at Camp Robinson, where they were disbanded.[6] During both assign-ments McGillycuddy had acquitted himself well, and as a result he was appointed the army's assistant surgeon at Camp Robinson.

Shortly after McGillycuddy's arrival, the authorities received complaints about Clay and Richard's stores. Frank Yates, JW's friend and fellow Indian trader at the agency, and Major Joseph Paddock, the newly appointed army post trader at Camp Robinson, complained that the two brothers, as post traders to the army, were able to trade with Indians without posting a bond and were also allowed to sell alcohol to soldiers from the two camps.[7] They claimed that some alcohol found its way into Indian hands. As Camps Canby and Custer were not on the Camp Robinson Military Reserve, the commanding officer had no jurisdiction over them, but nor did the OIA, as Clay and Richard were civilians contracted to provide a service to the army.

Paddock's and Yates's complaints were driven by commercial considerations. They wanted as many people as possible to use their stores and not Clay's or Richard's, so they used the "alcohol sales to Indians" argument to strengthen their case. The army's response was, "The post traders are there for the accommodation of the military, but if the Indians . . . [and others] . . . prefer to trade with them, there is nothing we can do about it."[8] However, after much correspondence, the War Department confirmed the brothers did not need to post a bond, but alcohol could only be sold through Paddock's post store at Camp Robinson, stopping the sale of alcohol from Camps Canby and Custer.

Despite the setback, the vast increase in activity at Red Cloud Agency meant that the Dear businesses were doing well. JW imported fresh oysters to sell to officers and their wives and purchased a croquet set to entertain guests. *The Sidney Telegraph* commented: "He expects to play with the 'friendly' Indians."[9] His stagecoach venture may not have been a success, but his other business interests had surpassed his expectations.

While JW's business boomed, General Crook's campaign against the northern Indians, helped by appalling weather, began to have its desired effect. Over the long, hard winter months many small bands of Indians succumbed to the army's relentless campaign and came to the agency to "surrender, disarm and dismount." By January, Sitting Bull, the most difficult of all the Indian chiefs, had been forced to move north to the Fort Peck area near the Canadian border.

JW was now seen as someone of standing and influence, and his opinions were sought after and valued. He mixed with many powerful people—senior army officers; Indian chiefs and subchiefs; and the business elite of Cheyenne, Sidney, and Omaha. In mid-January Crook returned to Camp Robinson, where his winter expedition was officially disbanded. On February 3 JW hosted a reception for him and fellow officers in his rooms at his trading post—fine wine, cigars, and music were offered, and the occasion was reported in the *Cheyenne Daily Sun*:

> One of the most enjoyable affairs it has ever been my lot to participate in on the frontier occurred over at the agency a few days ago. It was an informal dinner and reception tendered to General Crook and other officers now here, by Mr J W Dear, the agency trader. A dozen or more, among them the most accomplished and genial spirits of the camp, gathered at Mr Dear's pleasant rooms and spent the afternoon and evening in a most delightful and social reunion. There was a magnificent dinner, choice wines, fragrant Havanas and excellent music, interspersed with gossip crisp and fascinating enough for any circle. Mr Dear is a prince of entertainers and is noted the west over for his generous hospitality.[10]

Congress confirmed the Manypenny Agreement on February 27, 1877, unilaterally rescinding the 1868 Fort Laramie Treaty, and thus completed the forced sale of the Black Hills. It confiscated large tracts of Lakota lands and in their place, established reservations in Dakota Territory, where the land was of poor quality and of little interest to whites. It also forced the Lakota to relinquish hunting rights in the Powder River Country. This had the effect of freeing parts of Nebraska, Wyoming, and the Black Hills for exploitation by private investors. The government had tried and failed to obtain the required agreement of 75 percent of adult male Indians. Instead, they tore up the treaty.[11] It was one of the last acts of Grant's administration. Four days later Rutherford B. Hayes was sworn in as the nineteenth President of the United States.

As winter gave way to spring Indian resistance was now confined to a few local skirmishes. Sitting Bull was finding it increasingly difficult to survive in the harsh conditions near the Canadian border, and a steady stream of bands from his tribe left to seek sanctuary in Canada. On May 6 Sitting Bull, with less than ten lodges remaining, accepted the inevitable and crossed the border into exile.[12]

Both Crazy Horse and Dull Knife also considered surrendering. The first to make the decision was Dull Knife. In April he and Little Wolf, together with nearly a thousand starving and demoralized Northern Cheyenne left Crazy Horse's village, where they had shared meager winter rations following the destruction of their village the previous November.

As they approached Red Cloud Agency on April 21, they were met by Lieutenant William P. Clark and his interpreter, Bill Rowland. Clark had made it his mission to befriend and help the Indians, and guided by his reassuring presence the party moved peacefully to the agency to surrender to General Crook.[13] JW, together with groups of soldiers, agency staff, and reservation Indians watched the sad spectacle as it unfolded.[14] The *Omaha Daily Bee* of April 25 reported:

> The irregular cavalcade of over a mile in length, came into sight of the bluffs north of the Agency. Camp equipages, papooses and dogs were ludicrously mingled with the long train of a hundred travois, while many squaws and children were on foot. When the savages reached the broad bottoms of the White River, near the Agency, the non-combatants left to put up their tepees, and ninety young warriors rode forward to the position occupied by General Crook and his staff. The warriors formed into four companies, each company in single line, with skirmishers on either flank. The latter saluted by discharging their firearms, uttering terrific war whoops, and dashing at headlong speed on fresh war ponies. The main body then rode up to the General in perfect order, chanting the surrender song. Dull Knife and three other chiefs dismounted and gave their rifles to General Crook. The warriors then rode back to their camp by the river. Here they sat around in a dozen or more circles and disdained to move until the squaws had raised their tepees and prepared them something to eat.

Sitting Bull, the intractable medicine man and leader of the Hunkpapa Lakota, who refused to have any contact with the whites and sought sanctuary in Canada on May 6, 1877. Courtesy of the Library of Congress, LC-DIG-ppmsca-39879

Many of the Cheyenne were known to JW. The *Cheyenne Daily Leader* reported that he was soon "shaking hands with his many Cheyenne friends."[15]

When General Crook learned that Crazy Horse was considering surrendering, he persuaded Red Cloud to lead a delegation of eighty reservation Indians to meet Crazy Horse to discuss the terms of his surrender and to allay any fears he might have. The two chiefs met on April 20, within sight of Pumpkin Buttes, near Hat Creek Station, the isolated log stage station built originally by JW, but rebuilt by its new owners after it had been burned by Indians the previous year. Reassured by what Red Cloud told him, and with ten wagons of much needed food and supplies for his undernourished people, Crazy Horse agreed to lead his band to Red Cloud Agency to surrender.[16]

On May 6, as Crazy Horse and nine hundred northern Indians approached the agency, Lieutenant Clark and Red Cloud rode out to

No known image of Crazy Horse exists. This wood engraving gives a sense of the cavalcade as Crazy Horse and his band approach Red Cloud Agency to surrender to General Crook on May 6, 1877. Courtesy of the Library of Congress, LC-USZCN4-37

meet them. Once the terms of their surrender were confirmed, they smoked a peace pipe and exchanged gifts as a token of goodwill. The procession then moved onto the agency with Lieutenant Clark and Red Cloud in the lead; next came Crazy Horse, Little Big Man, and He Dog. They were followed by the various warrior societies, with each man dressed in his best. The rest of the band followed: old men, women, and children and more than three thousand ponies. The train stretched for two miles, and their arrival was watched by a large gathering of military personnel, reservation Indians, and agency staff. This was a highly symbolic moment that effectively marked the end of the Great Sioux War and Indian resistance.[17]

That evening Crazy Horse invited Frank Grouard to join him for supper, and he, together with Crook's aide-de-camp, Lieutenant Bourke, dined with the famous chief in his tepee. Even though Frank was Crook's favorite scout, Crazy Horse was delighted to see his old friend and gave him a warm welcome.

Two weeks later, on a blustery Friday evening, Frank led a small group, which included JW and the *Cheyenne Daily Leader* journalist "Rapherty," to meet Crazy Horse. They rode to his village three miles northeast of the agency, tethered their horses near the center of the camp, and entered Crazy Horse's tepee. He was seated on the ground, together with Little Big Man and several other chiefs of "lesser note." Crazy Horse was lithe and sinewy and in his mid-thirties, but he looked younger.[18] He had a light complexion and, unusual for an Indian, sandy colored hair.[19] After Frank had introduced JW and the rest of their party, "there was a general hand-shaking, and all sat down to smoke. The pipe was handed from mouth to mouth . . . and after all his guests and family had been served, when the pipe was emptied, a parting shake all around was given, and we left the palatial abode of the sullen chief who has made name and fame for himself during the past few years."[20]

This was the first time JW had met Crazy Horse, who, true to his reputation, was taciturn and barely spoke during their visit. For many Indians, particularly young braves, Crazy Horse was someone they greatly admired. For many whites he was someone they feared but grudgingly respected. The group left Crazy Horse's tepee accompanied by Little Big

Man, and, to show him respect, they visited his lodge before riding on to the Oglala encampment, where they visited Red Cloud before returning to JW's trading complex.[21]

The northern Indians had been subdued, and Crazy Horse's surrender had effectively marked the end of Indian resistance. Peace at the agency led to a troop reduction at Camp Robinson, and on May 26, Colonel Mackenzie and the 4th Cavalry departed. The next day Lieutenant Colonel Bradley, former commanding officer of Fort Laramie, arrived to take command of Camp Robinson, and Camps Canby and Custer were closed. Richard returned to work with JW, but Clay remained as temporary post trader to the army.

On May 29, Dull Knife and the Northern Cheyenne were moved, against their will, seven hundred fifty miles to the Darlington Reservation in Indian Territory in present-day Oklahoma.[22]

CHAPTER 25

The Death of Crazy Horse and the Move to the Missouri

FOLLOWING THE DEPARTURE OF THE NORTHERN CHEYENNE, THE authorities wrestled with how to handle Crazy Horse and where to resettle Red Cloud and Spotted Tail. The Tongue River in Wyoming, the Missouri River, and locations on the Great Sioux Reservation were all considered. The OIA and senior army officers, except for General Crook and Colonel Bradley, wanted the Oglala to move to the Missouri.[1] In June 1877, without making the decision public, the OIA committed to build a new agency at Medicine Creek on the Missouri for the Oglala and to move Spotted Tail and the Brulé to the recently vacated Ponca Agency near Fort Randall, Dakota. The Indian Superintendent of Dakota, Colonel John Henry Hammond, took charge of building the permanent agency at Medicine Creek and arranged for the Oglala winter rations to be warehoused there.

Dr. James Irwin replaced Lieutenant Charles Johnson as the civilian Indian agent at Red Cloud Agency on July 1.[2] Irwin was an experienced Indian hand who had spent most of his life on the Western frontier. Until recently he had been Indian agent at the Shoshone Agency in Wyoming, and he quickly established a positive working relationship with both Red Cloud and JW. His deft handling of his charges helped ease the tension of the next tumultuous months.[3]

As summer progressed, rumors, intrigues, and personal rivalries began to surface, causing friction and mistrust between the Indians and the authorities. There was conflict too between Crazy Horse and the reservation Indians, who felt, with some justification, they had remained loyal to the government and had not gone to war in 1876, whereas Crazy Horse, who had fought the whites for years, was now receiving special treatment from the army and the OIA.[4]

The distrust and resentment of Crazy Horse was exacerbated by poor translation at a meeting at which Crazy Horse was present. Some at the meeting claimed Crazy Horse had said he planned to go to war against the whites.[5] Frank Grouard, who had interpreted that day, was accused by some of deliberately betraying Crazy Horse by misinterpreting what he said. Attitudes hardened and conspiracy theories flourished: Red Cloud and his fellow reservation Indians were accused of planning to murder Crazy Horse, Crazy Horse was accused of planning to assassinate General Crook at their next meeting, and Crook himself was accused of conspiring with the Indians to have Crazy Horse murdered.[6] By mid-August, Crazy Horse had become increasingly suspicious of the intentions of both the authorities and his fellow Indians. With all the tension, speculation, and uncertainty surrounding Crazy Horse, General Crook decided he should be moved away from the northern plains to Florida and ordered Colonel Bradley to put him under house arrest.

On September 4, when he learned a group of soldiers and reservation Indians were about to arrest him, Crazy Horse fled to Spotted Tail's agency. Spotted Tail told him he did not want any trouble, and together with the Indian agent and the Camp Sheridan post commander, he urged Crazy Horse to return to Camp Robinson. Crazy Horse was eventually persuaded and left the next day with an army escort, arriving at the Camp Robinson quadrangle in the early evening.[7]

In anticipation of Crazy Horse's arrival, hundreds of soldiers and Indians had gathered on the camp parade ground, swarming around the adjutant's office and the guardhouse. At around 10 p.m. Crazy Horse left the adjutant's office and walked toward the guardhouse, escorted by Captain Kennington and Little Big Man. As they approached, Crazy Horse suddenly realized he was going to be confined and began to struggle, pulling a knife on Little Big Man, who was holding him. What happened next is unclear. The consensus is that in the melee that followed, Crazy

Horse was stabbed by a soldier's bayonet. Whether he was deliberately killed or it was a tragic accident is still debated.[8] Whatever the truth, there is no doubt many Indians and whites were relieved to see the end of this influential, exceptional, but difficult Indian.

At sunrise the next day an army ambulance bearing Crazy Horse's body left the quadrangle at Camp Robinson. An Indian lament rent the air as the sad procession, led by Crazy Horse's parents and watched by soldiers, wives of the officers, a few journalists, and JW and his brothers, threaded its way slowly down the trail to Crazy Horse's village and the tepee of his parents. There his body was prepared for burial, dressed in new buckskin, securely rolled in a buffalo robe, and then transported by travois to Spotted Tail Agency, where, in the manner of their tribe, his family built a scaffold on which they placed his body.[9] A month later when the Brulé were forced to move to the Missouri, Crazy Horse's parents took their son's body to its final resting place—a place known only to his immediate family, but thought to be in Pine Ridge overlooking Wounded Knee Creek.

When Red Cloud signed the Manypenny Agreement he knew the Oglala would have to move, but it was not until August 15 that Congress confirmed they would move to the Missouri.[10] When they heard the news, Red Cloud and Spotted Tail immediately protested, and a meeting with President Hayes, who had taken office in March, and his newly appointed Commissioner of Indian Affairs, Ezra Hayt, was hastily arranged.

Hayes, a Republican like his predecessor, had made changes to his administration. On September 17, his new Secretary of the Interior, Carl Schurz, chose Ezra Hayt as his Commissioner of Indian Affairs.[11] Three years before, Hayt, a wealthy New York wholesaler with ties to the Reformed Church, had been appointed an unpaid member of the Board of Indian Commissioners and chairman of its Purchasing Committee.

Hayt, a small and officious man, was not a popular official. The general criticism of him was that he spent too much time managing his own personal affairs, he was an impractical theorist of questionable honesty and had little or no understanding of the Indians and no appetite to listen to advice. During his first year in office, he controversially replaced thirty-five of the seventy Indian agents working for the service.[12]

The Oglala and Brulé delegation, led by Red Cloud and Spotted Tail, traveled to Washington, DC, and assembled on September 27 in the East Room of the White House, where they met Commissioner Hayt for the first time. Over the course of the next few days, it was made clear to them that they had no alternative but to go to the Missouri, as their winter rations were already there and it was not possible at this late stage to make alternative arrangements. President Hayes did, however, promise that in the spring the Oglala could, if they wished, select a location on the Great Sioux Reservation away from the Missouri. It was a compromise the Indians reluctantly accepted.[13]

News of this decision reached Colonel Bradley at Camp Robinson on October 8. He was a practical and sensitive man who understood the plight of the Indians and their dislike of the Missouri and commented that yet again they were being treated badly. He wrote that evening to his wife: "The poor fellows love the White River as much as they hate the Missouri, and they hate to leave it. I wish some man of brains, with just a little sensibility, could be in charge of the Indians for a year or two, with power to use the money appropriated by Congress for the best good of the Government and the Indians. Such a man might save thousands of lives, and millions of money in preventing the outbreaks that occur almost every year."[14]

Indian Agent James Irwin's son had been killed by the Sioux, and he had no great love for them. But he also believed the Oglala were being unfairly and inhumanely treated.[15] Shortly after his arrival at Red Cloud Agency he wrote to his superiors suggesting an alternative location for the agency on the White Earth River, seventy miles short of the Missouri, but well clear of both the Black Hills and Nebraska.[16] His proposal was ignored, and Red Cloud and his demoralized and broken people were forced against their will to move to the Missouri.

JW's life and career were inextricably linked to the Oglala, so a new start for them on the Missouri was also an uncertain interruption for his business. By the time of the move, JW had forged a strong working relationship with Red Cloud and the Oglala, and like Colonel Bradley and James Irwin, he was not comfortable with the way they were being treated by the authorities. It worried him and increasingly influenced his decisions.

Over the four years since becoming an Indian trader, JW had seen a dramatic rise in his fortune. From a modest start in October 1873, he had built a thriving and profitable business employing more than seventy people, including his brothers, Richard and Luther. His main business was the trading store at Red Cloud Agency, which sat astride the major stagecoach and freighting route to the Black Hills and which had grown to include a hotel, restaurant, bar, and billiard room. In March his trading license had been renewed for a further twelve months, and in August the OIA confirmed that he could continue to trade with the Oglala when they moved to the Missouri, providing he built a new trading store and moved his stock there at his expense.[17]

His outgoings over the previous eighteen months had been substantial: he had lost money on his stage station investments, had sold his stage line and equipment at a loss to Stevenson & Marsh, and in July had paid off the final installment on Royal Oaks. Although money was tight, he was confident that his business at the new site would be successful. He was also comforted by the fact that his business on the old agency site, now referred to as "Old Red Cloud," was going from strength to strength.

The site had become the main overnight stop for the Sidney to Deadwood stage, which from February 1877 operated a daily service to the Hills bringing up to twenty passengers a day, all in need of food, drink, and often accommodation. In addition, since the opening of the Black Hills, up to a hundred ox wagons a day, carrying as much as five hundred tons of supplies from the railhead in Sidney to Deadwood, passed JW's trading store on their twelve-day journey to the Hills. This generated yet more business, as teamsters and bullwhackers also needed supplies, food, drink, entertainment, and sometimes a bed.[18]

All this activity made JW's complex the busiest transport and commercial hub for one hundred miles. In 1877, the Sidney to Black Hills trade totaled four million pounds of supplies. A year later this figure had risen to twenty-five million pounds, half of the total Black Hills imports for the year. JW's business benefited accordingly, and to help handle this growing volume he purchased Frank Yates's old trading store for $600 and "erected a large commodious barn and stable at an expense of hundreds of dollars."[19]

JW was confident that he was financially secure and his parents and younger siblings had been well provided for. He was still ambitious, but he was thirty-two years old and had been separated from his loved ones in Virginia for nine years. He longed for their company and to share his life with the person he loved. He was now ready for the next phase of his life.

His romance with Mary Ann had blossomed. Over years of correspondence and snatched moments together during infrequent visits back home, they had developed a closeness and an understanding. They both knew that when the time was right and JW was confident his future was secure, they would marry. Mary Ann understood that this would mean leaving Virginia, but it was a sacrifice she was happy to make. She wanted to be with the man she loved. The couple set the date for March 1878, which gave Mary Ann five months to plan for their wedding in Virginia and for JW to move with the Oglala to the Missouri and establish his new business there.

Agency staff, the army, and the Indians began to prepare for the move in early October. JW had the daunting task of restructuring his existing business at the old agency site, transporting much of his stock and equipment to the Missouri, and building a new trading store and accommodation there.

Although the OIA had built a new agency at Medicine Creek it had made no practical plans to move six thousand five hundred poorly clad Indians, which included the old and infirm, the young and vulnerable, all their worldly goods, and five weeks of rations, to the site. The move involved a three-hundred-mile trek across uncharted territory with ox wagons crossing and recrossing rivers and creeks with the dangers of quicksand and the ever-present threat of Indian hostilities. All these challenges had to be overcome at the start of a Dakota winter where high winds, rain, hail, snow, and freezing temperatures were the norm.

By October 11, the army recognized the attempt by the OIA to cobble together the transport necessary for the move was woefully inadequate, and General Crook ordered his staff to provide what support it could "by scraping together all the available Army transportation within reach, improvising many teams of broken down cavalry horses."[20]

Despite this, Agent Irwin still considered the arrangements inadequate and obtained agreement for JW to move 42,861 pounds of Indian rations three hundred miles at a cost of $1/100 pounds/100 miles.[21] This required a train of ten ox wagons each drawn by six oxen. In addition, JW needed a further six wagons to transport the stock and equipment required for his new trading store.

Indians started the process of packing up their villages: ponies were saddled, tepee poles balanced on each side, and packs loaded by women. Occasionally, a brave could be seen holding a restive pony until the poles were securely fastened. Their bundles were compactly stacked in skins and a framework erected over the poles, where a papoose could be carried. Rations were issued for ten days. Whatever could not be carried by pony was loaded onto ox wagons and carefully marked with the name of the chief of each band.[22]

On October 25, seventeen days after learning of the OIA's decision, Red Cloud and the Oglala left Red Cloud Agency for the last time. They were accompanied by Agent Irwin, contract surgeon Dr. McGillycuddy, two companies of the 3rd Cavalry, two thousand head of cattle, and one hundred twenty ox wagons and bullwhackers. The column was led by the army, next came the chiefs, followed by Indians with their ponies

JW's ox-wagon train leaving Red Cloud Agency for Medicine Creek, October 1877.
Dear Family Collection

and travois, then the ox wagons laden with equipment and supplies. The cattle and the second cavalry company brought up the rear. A team of twenty-five scouts, working in relays, went ahead of the column to map the safest and shortest route across the rivers and creeks that crisscrossed the inhospitable and uncharted terrain. During their journey they crossed the White River on at least ten separate occasions. On the march the total column was eight miles long, and when the Indians set camp at night their tepees were scattered for more than three miles along the trail.

JW and Richard both started with the Indians, but Richard soon left the column to ride ahead to Medicine Creek to oversee the building of JW's new trading store. Their younger brother, Luther, remained at Old Red Cloud to help run JW's stage station and trading post, while Clay, as post trader to the army, went with Spotted Tail and seven thousand Brulé Indians to the old Ponca Agency on the Missouri. The army officer in charge of moving the Brulé was Major William J. Pollock, with whom Clay struck up an enduring friendship.[23]

The Oglala journey to the Missouri was a nightmare. It took almost five weeks for them to reach the point where they finally pitched camp. Many unshod Indian ponies were simply not up to the task and died along the trail. Hundreds of Indians, including women and children, were forced to make the journey on foot.[24] On November 11, James Irwin wrote to Commissioner Hayt: "Bad winds and storms, want of sufficient transport, we are progressing very slowly."[25]

After weeks of great hardship and suffering during the coldest November on record and with their rations running low, the column reached the right fork of the White Earth River, seventy miles short of their intended destination at Medicine Creek. This was the site James Irwin had earlier proposed to the OIA for the permanent home of the Oglalas. It was here that Red Cloud pitched camp and, to avoid further suffering, made it his winter quarters.[26] JW with his ox wagons still laden with Indian rations, remained with Red Cloud, but Irwin continued to Medicine Creek where he arrived on November 25.

At the time of the move both Commissioner Hayt and General Crook recognized the inhumane consequences of moving so many inadequately clad and equipped Indians so late in the season. In his first annual report Commissioner Hayt wrote on November 11, 1877:

> The removal of fourteen thousand Sioux Indians at this season of the year, a distance of three hundred miles from their old agencies in Nebraska to their new quarters near the Missouri River, is not a pleasant matter to contemplate. Neither the present Secretary of the Interior [Schurz], nor the present Commissioner of Indian Affairs [Hayt] is responsible for the movement, but they have carried out the law faithfully, though reluctantly. The removal is being made in accordance with the act. . . . it is proper to say here, that I cannot but look on the necessity thus imposed by law on the executive branch of the government as an unfortunate one, and the consequences ought to be remedied as speedily as possible.[27]

When the exhausted and starving Indians pitched camp, they requested that food and supplies be brought to them from the agency at Medicine Creek. However, despite Irwin's strong argument for this to be done, the Commander of the Army, General Sherman, angered by what he saw as Red Cloud's act of defiance by not completing the journey, instructed General Sheridan on December 1 that no rations should be issued to the Indians unless they came to the agency to collect them.[28]

Exhaustion, appalling weather, and the state of the Indian ponies made it an almost impossible task to travel a further seventy miles. On December 15, Irwin again protested, arguing Sherman's decision was a direct violation of the president's promise, and asked to be relieved of his duties if the decision was not rescinded. Eventually, Sherman was overridden by the politicians, but not before further unnecessary suffering had been inflicted on the Indians.[29]

During December and a bitterly cold January, many Indians succumbed to the harsh conditions and lack of food, and an unknown number starved and froze to death. As a result, hundreds of Indian tree graves lined the White Earth River.[30] JW provided food and clothing for the Indians from his own stock and helped them obtain their annuities from the agency seventy miles away at Medicine Creek. This humanitarian act contributed to the growing bond between Red Cloud and JW.

CHAPTER 26

Mary Ann and the Third Red Cloud Agency: 1878

WHEN RED CLOUD AND MORE THAN SIX THOUSAND FIVE HUNDRED Indians pitched camp on the White Earth River in late November 1877, the post trader at Camp Robinson, Major Paddock, used his excellent political connections in Omaha to have himself also appointed Indian trader to the Oglala.[1] He had no intention of running the trading post himself and immediately recruited thirty-seven-year-old George Blanchard, a fellow member of the Douglas County Legislature, to man-age the store on his behalf.[2] This meant there were now three licensed Indian traders: JW, Frank Yates, and Major Paddock.

The strain of trading during the Great Sioux War, the constant fear of an Indian attack, the death of his brother at the Battle of Little Bighorn, and the complete redevelopment of his business required by the move to Medicine Creek had taken its toll on JW's old friend, Frank Yates.[3] He began to drink heavily and hired a partner to assist him with the move.[4] However, he still couldn't cope, and on January 25, 1878, he resigned and recommended that Thomas Cowgill, who was working for him as a clerk, replace him as trader. On March 14 Cowgill replaced Yates to become one of the three traders at the new agency.[5]

JW spent only a limited amount of time at Medicine Creek during the first quarter of the year. He was preoccupied with overseeing his other business interests and preparing for his wedding to Mary Ann in Virginia. For much of the time Richard was left in charge of the trading

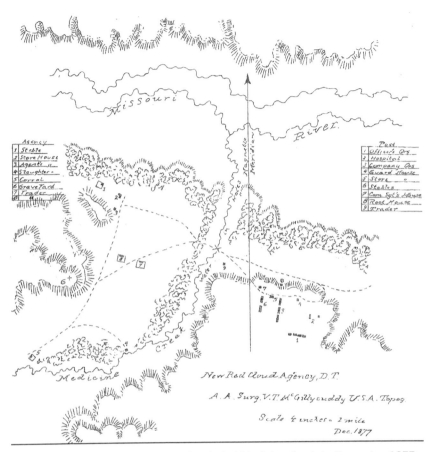

Agency	
1	Stable
2	Store House
3	Agente "
4	Slaughter -
5	Corral
6	Graveyard
7	Trader
8	

Post	
1	Officer's Qrs
2	Hospital
3	Company Qrs
4	Guard House
5	Store "
6	Stables
7	Com. Sgt's House
8	Root House
9	Trader

New Red Cloud Agency, D.T.

A. A. Surg. V. T. McGillycuddy U.S.A. Topog

Scale 4 inches = 1 mile

Dec. 1877

Plan of the third Red Cloud Agency located at Medicine Creek in December 1877. The agency closed in December 1878 after Red Cloud and the Oglala moved one hundred seventy miles southwest to Pine Ridge. M234, Roll 723, Letters Received by the Office of Indian Affairs 1824–1880, National Archives Building, Washington, DC

stores. On January 26, JW left the agency by steamship for Yankton, where he met Clay. A few days later the brothers traveled together by train to Omaha en route to the Rogerses' family home, Willow Cottage in Loudoun County, for JW's marriage to Mary Ann.[6]

The Rogers family had owned the house since the 1780s. Over the years it had been modified, extended, and then rebuilt, and by the time of their marriage it was no longer a cottage but a substantial family home.

Nevertheless, the name Willow Cottage was retained. The fine stone house stood proudly forty yards back from the road running south from Hamilton, and a large wooden barn was located fifty yards beyond it, the sturdy posts carved with generations of family names. The Rogerses farmed one hundred fifty acres of land, most of it arable, but some was set aside for a stud farm, which was a passion of the family then, and remains so to this day. Mary Ann's brother Sam managed the farm for their widowed mother. Sam's wife, Lizzie, and Mary Ann had become inseparable, and a bond was established between the two young women that lasted for the rest of their lives.

Mary Ann was a remarkable woman. Poised and self-confident, she was resigned to living at home, waiting to marry the man she loved. She was a schoolteacher, very sociable with a wide circle of friends, and extremely devout—she often attended religious gatherings during the week and thought nothing of attending two or three sermons at different churches on Sundays. Like all the Rogerses, she loved horses and was an accomplished rider. She enjoyed dinner parties and good conversation and had a passion for fashionable clothes. She spent months before her wedding planning the great day, and local dressmakers were engaged making fine dresses for the wedding, together with more practical clothes for Mary Ann to wear out West.

On Thursday, March 14, 1878, almost ten years to the day after JW had gone West, her wait ended, and Mary Ann and JW were married.[7] The ceremony was held in the parlor in Willow Cottage. If the wedding had been later in the year when the weather was warmer, it would have been held in the great barn, which over the years had played host to many summer parties and Fourth of July celebrations. But the weather on their wedding day was dull and gloomy with the temperature barely rising above fifty degrees Fahrenheit.

A small group of family and friends gathered in front of a table set at one end of the parlor, where Mary Ann's cousin, the Reverend Alfred Rogers, conducted the ceremony.

Mary Ann, now married at the age of thirty-five, would have to adjust to a new life out West to live among the Indians and rough frontiersmen on the dry and barren plains of Dakota Territory. Their plan was simple. At the time of their marriage JW's businesses were successful, and another few years out West would ensure his fortune. The couple then planned to buy a country estate in Loudoun County where they could farm and raise a family. They had no plans to live in Royal Oaks—JW had bought that for his family. They had their eyes set on a large country estate closer to Mary Ann's family home. It was a dream they shared, and a dream that, as it turned out, helped them get through many dark days in the West.[8]

Two days after the wedding JW learned the OIA had renewed his trading license for another year.[9] This was expected but still a relief, as it meant he and Mary Ann could plan their future together with confidence. On April 13, while the couple were in Omaha en route to the agency, JW met his backers, Stephens & Wilcox, and negotiated a short-term loan of $6,000.[10] It provided the cash he needed to maintain his expensive ox-wagon train, which was lying idle, and to prepare for the Oglala's anticipated move from Medicine Creek in a few months. It was a large and potentially lucrative contract both he and Stephens & Wilcox were confident of winning.

JW and Mary Ann arrived at Medicine Creek on April 20, happy to be together at last and excited by what the future might hold.[11] However, during JW's absence matters had not gone smoothly for either Red Cloud or Agent Irwin. At the meeting with the president the previous September, it had been agreed that provided the Oglala and Brulé moved to the Missouri they would be allowed to choose a new and permanent site for their agencies in the spring, "located in a country where they may eventually become self-supporting and acquire the arts of civilized life."[12]

After two very stressful months, the Oglala held councils at which they selected Big White Clay Creek, 170 miles west of Medicine Creek near the Nebraska border, as the site of their permanent home.[13] It was land they knew, and it had the advantage of having plenty of timber and good water. On March 14, Red Cloud sent a letter to the president confirming their decision and pleading with him to support their choice. "We have done what you asked us to do when we were in Washington . . . and ask you Great Father, today as friends to try and let us have this place for our agency."[14]

There was no response. Five weeks later a frustrated Red Cloud warned the commander at Camp Robinson that the president "told me come and get [our rations] this winter and in the spring go and look for a good place . . . I set a stake at White Clay, and that is the place I ask for. . . . We have sent our decision four times. . . . We have a new moon soon. When we get our next beef we will all go for rations and then move."[15] However, by this time attitudes were hardening within both the army and the OIA. General Sherman and Commissioner Hayt now regarded Red Cloud as difficult and hard to manage.

Hayt very rapidly came around to the army's view that the Indians should stay on the Missouri and not be allowed to relocate to the interior, where transport costs were higher and control of the Indians more difficult. Hayt, supported by Congress and the army, obtained President Hayes's agreement to have one final attempt to persuade Red Cloud to remain on the Missouri. As a result, the Oglala were not allowed to move in the spring. Red Cloud lost face with many of his people and found it increasingly difficult to prevent his young braves from traveling north to join Sitting Bull.

Irwin was shocked by what he considered to be inhumane treatment of the Oglala, and by yet another broken promise, this time by the president himself. On February 20 and then again on April 27, he tendered his resignation, but on both occasions, it was rejected by Hayt.[16] However, this put Irwin on a collision course with the commissioner, who saw Irwin as someone whose sympathies lay with Red Cloud and the Oglala rather than with the commissioner and the OIA. The future of both Red Cloud's and Spotted Tail's tribes remained unclear for the next few months.

Despite the tension and uncertainty that surrounded the agency, Mary Ann immediately threw herself into her new life. She was soon on good terms with James Irwin and Dr. McGillycuddy and their wives, and the three couples regularly spent time together.[17] Her brother-in-law, Richard, was based at the agency, so when JW was traveling on business, she could turn to him for company and advice.

Soon after her arrival Clay arranged for a small group, which included Mary Ann and Judge Peter Shannon's wife and daughter, to visit

Spotted Tail's agency, where Clay was the acting post trader. Judge Shannon was a good friend of Clay's and on several occasions went out of his way to help his career. He was an interesting character. Abraham Lincoln described him as a "patriot without ambition for personal aggrandizement," a rare trait in those who served in the Wild West of the 1870s and 1880s. In 1873, President Grant had appointed him Chief Justice of the Dakota Territory Supreme Court, and his nine-year tenure was marked by the social and judicial stability he brought to his lawless territory. His "forceful administration of justice" cleared out the rough elements in his territory but stirred some opposition among the lawyers who represented those elements of Dakotaian society.

Among the many colorful cases over which Judge Shannon presided, perhaps the most famous was the trial of Jack McCall in December 1876 for the killing of Wild Bill Hickok during a poker game in Deadwood. McCall's conviction resulted in the first legal hanging in Dakota Territory.[18] Shannon was also the judge at the April 1879 federal grand jury of three Indian agents charged with corruption.[19]

Shannon's status required a grand residence, and he rented one of the grandest in Yankton. It was an ornate, three-story Italianate mansion on Magazine Hill, surrounded on all four sides by a wide pillared veranda, and surmounted by a square cupola with a balustraded viewing platform with views for miles in every direction.[20] The judge, his wife, and their large family, including several eligible daughters, used this grand residence to host many balls, parties, and soirees at which Clay was a regular fixture on the guest list.

The small party bound for Spotted Tail's agency and led by Clay left Yankton on the steamer *Far West* on May 9. When they disembarked, they were met by a guard of honor provided by both the army and the Indians. They visited the Indian village and were introduced to Spotted Tail and his fellow chiefs. They were then shown around the agency, and after a few hours, carriages were organized to take them back to the jetty, where they reboarded the *Far West* for their return to Yankton.[21] Two months before, the farthest Mary Ann had ventured was to Washington, DC. Now, she was the guest of a famous Indian chief in his lodge on the

Great Sioux Reservation. The contrast between this and her privileged and cultured former life in Virginia could not have been greater.

In July, after several frustrating months of inactivity and indecision, the three-man Stanley Commission, with Hayt's son controversially acting as secretary and "disbursement officer," traveled to the Missouri to meet the Oglala and Brulé to settle the vexed question of the permanent location of their agencies.[22] JW, confident that the Oglala would be allowed to move to Big White Clay Creek, had left with Mary Ann a few days before the commissioners arrived to meet Stephens & Wilcox in Omaha, to discuss how they should handle the anticipated tender to move the Indians.

The commission first visited Spotted Tail's Indians arriving at their temporary agency on July 5. The meeting went badly. Spotted Tail was "arrogant and dictatorial," called Hayt a "bald-headed liar," and declared that he would leave for the place he had selected on the Rosebud River near the south fork of the White River in ten days and burn all the agency buildings.[23] He didn't burn the buildings, but the Brulé did move to the site of their choice, which became known as the Rosebud Agency.

After the disappointing meeting with Spotted Tail the commission moved upriver where it met Red Cloud a week later. Although not as aggressive as Spotted Tail, Red Cloud made it clear he would not stay on the Missouri and, taking "from his wallet a pamphlet containing the account of proceedings of the delegation in Washington the previous fall," insisted the president honor his promise to allow him to move to the site of his choice at Big White Clay Creek.[24]

Hayt tried to persuade Red Cloud to reconsider his decision and offered money and supplies if he stayed on the Missouri, but to no avail. Hayt was annoyed by Red Cloud's defiant stance and the support he received from James Irwin, which put further strain on the relationship between the two men. Nevertheless, Hayt reluctantly agreed the commission should survey Big White Clay Creek.

When JW arrived back at the agency from Omaha on the steamer *Durfee* on July 23 he learned from Irwin that although the final decision on the site had yet to be confirmed, Irwin considered it likely the Oglala would move to Big White Clay Creek within weeks. While in Omaha

JW had secured Stephens & Wilcox's agreement to back his tender, so before receiving formal confirmation of the move, but with Irwin's tacit approval, he put in place his plans to move two million pounds of supplies and equipment to the Oglala's new agency.

In August he took the steamship *Far West* to Fort Pierre to recruit a gang of ox-wagon teamsters.[25] He also began planning to move his trading store from Medicine Creek and to build a trading complex at the new agency site. But, as always, the wheels of the Washington bureaucracy turned slowly. Winter was fast approaching, and the OIA, which had expected the Oglala would be persuaded to stay on the Missouri and had made no plans to move them, was forced to wait until the proposed site had been inspected and approved by Congress.

The OIA's lack of foresight and general incompetence drew criticism from all quarters. The Oglala were angry; they felt promises made were being broken and that once again they were being cheated by the authorities. Irwin and his staff, JW, and the other traders all complained bitterly, as they feared the prospect of another forced march through the depths of winter accompanied by untold suffering and many deaths.

The press and the army, never slow to criticize the OIA, joined the fray, and the governor of Dakota Territory sent a telegram to President Hayes on August 14 expressing his concern:

> The Red Cloud Indians claim they had your promise to move them to agency last spring. They think the Indian Bureau means to cheat them. The new commission has selected the new location. The Spotted Tail Indians have gone. They are restless. I think prompt removal or a strong military force are necessary to prevent violence—prompt removal will enable them to make preparations for winter with the aid of Agent and assistants. Delay will bring cold weather, suffering and death. The Agency has no farms. Before they cut hay, wood etc, they had better go where the hay and wood are. One hundred and seventy miles will require too long a scythe for a common Indian. All suspicion of bad faith should be removed.[26]

Commissioner Hayt believed James Irwin was behind the governor's intervention, and in a telegram to Secretary of the Interior Carl Schurz he declared, "There is more trouble with the agent [Irwin] than with the Indians."[27]

During this period JW employed Billy Garnett to help him and Richard at his trading store.[28] He knew he could trust and rely on him. JW had known Billy since he first met him at the Sod Agency in Wyoming. Since then, Billy had worked for the OIA and the army as an interpreter and was highly regarded by both whites and Indians.

Congress finally approved Big White Clay Creek as the Oglala's new permanent home on August 28—five months after President Hayes had promised the Indians they could move in the spring.[29] But even then, to the growing frustration of both Irwin and Red Cloud, the OIA prevaricated and still did not allow the Indians to move. Special Agent Colonel O'Bierne, a hard man of limited experience, was drafted in to supervise the building and equipping of the new agency and to oversee the move. Within days of his arrival, he had clashed with both Irwin and Red Cloud.

The OIA was in chaos. With mounting criticism from all quarters, a siege mentality prevailed. As winter approached, JW, Irwin, and Red Cloud all feared the tragic lessons of the previous winter's move to Medicine Creek when many Oglala had died had not been learned, and that history would repeat itself. On September 4 James Irwin submitted his annual report and was extremely critical of the delay in moving the Indians:

> I am less fortunate in explaining the present delay to their satisfaction, as they know that the board of commissioners approved their selection of land for their new agency and have so reported. It is not easy to convince them of the necessity for longer delay. It is a fact known to every intelligent man who has been with Indians on the frontier, that the most damaging effects have heretofore resulted from broken promises made by the government and its officials, causing the greater part of the troubles with the Sioux since the treaty of 1868.[30]

The next day he wrote directly to Secretary of the Interior Carl Schurz, criticizing Commissioner Hayt for his insensitivity and indecisiveness, warning him that Hayt appeared to have learned nothing from

Billy Garnett, the interpreter and mixed-race son of General Garnett, who worked for JW during the summer of 1878. National Anthropological Archives, Smithsonian Institution, BAE GN 03698A

the disastrous move of the Oglala to Medicine Creek the previous winter, and that he was running the risk of repeating the experience and subjecting the Indians to yet more inhumane treatment and suffering during the coming winter.[31] The letter had no effect except to seal Irwin's fate.

Having called for quotes to move the Oglala to their new home, the OIA rejected all the tenders they received, including JW's, which had been underwritten by Stephens & Wilcox for $47,600. This was a shock—JW had expected to win the tender. He was the best organized of all the contractors with his team of drivers and wagons ready to move and his quote reasonable and competitive. At considerable expense, and with Irwin's support, he had kept his ox-wagon team waiting in anticipation of the move for over nine months. This change of policy cost him dearly and put a strain on his relationship with Stephens & Wilcox.

Trust between James Irwin and Commissioner Hayt had by now broken down, and Hayt and O'Bierne both believed Irwin had in some way conspired with JW and other freighters to tender artificially high prices. Against all advice Hayt and O'Bierne decided the Oglala should do the freighting themselves, for what they estimated to be a quarter of the cost, an estimate that proved to be wildly inaccurate.[32]

Red Cloud and the Oglala, impatient with the interminable delays, defied the authorities and without an army escort or taking their winter rations with them, left camp on the White Earth River on September 25 to travel southwest to the new agency site at Big White Clay Creek.[33] Red Cloud's unilateral decision to move infuriated Hayt, but there was nothing he could do to prevent it.

A large body of Indians on the move always alarmed settlers, and newspapers were happy to stoke the flames. The *Daily Press and Dakotaian* sensed trouble and speculated that Dull Knife and the Northern Cheyenne, who on September 9 had broken out from Indian Territory and were causing mayhem as they fled north, would join the Oglala "and stir up their bad blood . . . and cut loose for a season of plundering and murdering."[34] But Red Cloud had no appetite for making war and arrived with the main body of Indians at Big White Clay Creek on Monday, November 11.

The OIA decided to name the new agency Pine Ridge, a slight against Red Cloud, and the first time that an agency had not been named after him. JW and Mary Ann, James Irwin and his wife, and the rest of the agency staff arrived a week after the Oglala, where they found a barren and desolate building site with only one completed dwelling, which was occupied by Agent O'Bierne. Everyone else was forced to live under canvas for several very cold and miserable weeks.

CHAPTER 27

Pine Ridge, the Fourth Red Cloud Agency

TEN YEARS AFTER RED CLOUD SIGNED THE FORT LARAMIE TREATY, when he committed his people to reservation life, the Oglala finally put down roots in the location of their choice at Pine Ridge.

It had been a difficult and harrowing decade for the Oglala, marred by violence, broken promises, the loss of their ancestral lands, the erosion of their traditional way of life, and now, their total dependence on government annuities. They had been forced to move to three different locations and had lived at three different agencies. And every time they moved, JW moved with them.

An article that appeared in the national press graphically captured a sense of their plight and how their way of life had changed since JW had moved West:

> [In 1868] the Indians owned and occupied nearly all the country west of the Missouri river, from British Columbia to the Gulf of Mexico. . . . The almost unlimited extent of the country was occupied by two vast herds of buffalo, one grazing in the north, the other in the south, and each herd numbered from 2,000,000 to 3,000,000 of animals, and in the same region were herds of elk, antelope, deer and other large game of almost every variety, and in numbers innumerable, while in the valleys were to be found wild roots, vegetables, berries, and fruit in abundance. Nature had produced everything necessary for the subsistence of the Indians. . . . This . . . was their condition in this vast extent of the country about ten years ago, and this was good enough for and satisfied the wants of the savage, while constant feuds among

themselves gave them active occupation, as war was their only profession, and they disdained work. . . . Along came the nineteenth century progress . . . to disturb their happy condition. The white men crowded on to the grounds of the Indians and made encroachments on their rights which no government could stop. . . . The Government made treaties, gave presents, made promises, none of which were honestly fulfilled, and like all original treaties with the Indians in this country, they were the first steps in the process of developing hostilities. The Indian became jealous; he made in his simplicity blind bargains; he began to see his lands wrested from his possession, his herds of buffalo, which he believed the Great Spirit had given him, rapidly diminish, and the elk, deer, and antelope killed for the market and by the sportsman.

By 1878, all this land:

had passed into the hands of the whites, with the exception of the limited reservations assigned to the Indians, and with no compensation beyond the promise of religious instruction, schools, supplies of food and clothing, and an opportunity of learning the ways in which the white man cultivated the ground—most of which promises have never been fulfilled. In other words, we took their country, and their means of support, broke up their mode of living, their habits of life, and introduced disease and decay among them, and it was for this, and against this they made war. Could any one expect less? Then why wonder at Indian difficulties?

No quarter was given by the savages, and the officers and men had to enter on their duties with the most barbarous cruelties staring them in the face in case of defeat. Nor was this misfortune confined to the soldier; it extended to the settler, who was himself killed, or came home to see his wife and children murdered and his stock stolen. Such, in truth, has been the contest on our Western frontier during the past ten years.[1]

Forcing the Lakota onto reservations was probably inevitable, but the coming of the railroads and the discovery of gold in the Black Hills contributed to it happening so quickly and decisively. Gold brought tens of thousands of whites flooding into the area that the government was unable or unwilling to control, and the railroad made the slaughter of millions of buffalo possible, which opened the plains to settlers and open-range cattle ranching. By 1889, it was estimated there were less than six hundred buffalo left in America.[2]

When Red Cloud and JW arrived at Pine Ridge, they believed that the uncertainty and hardship they had suffered over the previous eighteen months was behind them. Red Cloud had resisted pressure from the OIA and avoided staying on the Missouri; he had secured Pine Ridge as the permanent home for his people and could now look forward to a more stable and less traumatic future. JW was confident that the revenue from his businesses at Pine Ridge and Old Red Cloud would enable him to clear debts accumulated from the latest round of forced moves.

A few days after the Oglala arrived at Pine Ridge, Agent O'Bierne arranged for teams of Indians, under the guidance of white teamsters, to return to Medicine Creek and collect their winter rations and ferry them back across one hundred seventy miles of inhospitable terrain to their new agency. The Oglala had virtually no experience of using wheeled wagons, and their unshod ponies struggled to do such demanding work during the depth of a Dakota winter. They managed to complete one trip using ninety-seven wagons to move one hundred thousand pounds of supplies, a fraction of the two million pounds that had to be moved. As a result, late in the season, freighters had to be hired at great cost to transport supplies from both the Missouri and Sidney to Pine Ridge.[3] The total cost of the exercise far exceeded JW's original tender and caused yet more unnecessary hardship and suffering.

JW was involved in the move and helped the Oglala settle into their new home, but his precise role is unclear. Mary Ann's diary records that he spent $18,000 of his own money transporting and feeding the Indians that winter.

In his annual report of 1878, Hayt attempted to gloss over the disaster he had presided over, writing: "In all the large Indian removals heretofore undertaken the government has had to pay enormously by reason of the misrepresentations put afloat by parties interested in getting profitable transportation contracts. . . . Fortunately the department was too well advised of the real situation of affairs to yield to panic, and the removal has been made peacefully and at a comparatively small outlay. As a result, there is sufficient money in hand to feed these Indians."[4]

This was refuted by Agent Irwin's letter of January 4, 1879, to Secretary Schurz describing the same incident:

> The Indians have returned from the Missouri River with ponies worn out, Indians frost bitten and discouraged. We now have an enormous Indian train of one hundred and fifty wagons and six hundred ponies that must eat corn or starve. Freight by this train costs the Government four cents per pound and will exceed that if the severe weather continues. I have just one month's provisions on hand. Annuities all at the river—Indians destitute of clothing, tepees torn and open. Thermometer running from ten to thirty degrees below zero. Half breeds and full bloods with their own wagons and American horses have had to be commissioned at two and half cents per pound [to move supplies from the Missouri and Sidney].[5]

In a report nine months later, and still in denial, Hayt painted an even more glowing picture of the same infamous incident when he wrote:

> After advertizing twice successively for bids for transportation without obtaining reasonable proposals, [in September 1878] it was determined to . . . hire the Indians with their four-pony teams to remove nearly 4,000,000 pounds of freight an average distance of nearly 150 miles . . . the task of teaching wild Indians to haul supplies with their unbroken ponies began October 11, 1878, and before January 1, 1879, their ability to perform the work had been successfully demonstrated, and 13,000 Indians were comfortably fed and clothed on supplies and annuity goods hauled by themselves without loss or waste.[6]

On October 25, 1878, General Sheridan's annual report to the War Department, in which he was highly critical of the OIA, was leaked to the press, and the "Transfer Issue" once again became a key topic, which was debated at the highest levels of government. He was frustrated and irritated by what he considered to be the OIA's mismanagement, initially with the lack of planning in the disastrous move to the Missouri, then the Oglala's unauthorized move from the Missouri to Pine Ridge. Sheridan wrote that "wretched mismanagement [by the OIA] has given . . . constant anxiety during the last year . . . loss of life and loss of property, attended with dreadful crimes and cruelties. There has been an insufficiency of food at the agencies, and, as the game is gone, hunger has made the Indians in some cases desperate, and almost any race of men will fight rather than starve."[7]

The gloves were off and, on December 2, a Congressional committee met to consider the arguments for and against transferring responsibility for the Indians back to the War Department. Carl Schurz and Ezra Hayt represented the Department of the Interior, and Generals Sherman, Sheridan, Terry, and Crook represented the War Department.[8] In the end the committee was persuaded by Schurz's arguments and responsibility for the OIA stayed with the Secretary of the Interior.

As the arguments raged between the army and the politicians in Washington, JW, Clay, and Richard were busy establishing a new business. In late November JW had been appointed the postmaster at Pine Ridge by the US Post Office. A few weeks later the brothers secured a mail delivery contract to provide a three-day-a-week service from Camp Robinson to Rosebud Landing and the Bijou Hills on the east bank of the Missouri, via the Pine Ridge and Rosebud agencies, a round trip of five hundred eighty miles.

To meet the exacting schedule demanded by the Post Office, they required six stagecoaches, a stable of over thirty horses, stage stations strategically placed along the two-hundred-mile route, and a team of twelve drivers. Establishing and managing this was a complex and demanding exercise that required an investment of many thousands of dollars. Although the brothers were equal partners, the new business was registered in Clay's and Richard's names, as JW had outstanding debts and was anxious to protect his assets against possible future claims.

All four brothers were to be involved in the new business. The plan was for JW and Mary Ann to be based at Pine Ridge alongside Red Cloud, where JW was both postmaster and Indian trader and expected to quickly build a thriving business. Luther would live with them and manage the stage station. Richard would be based at Old Red Cloud to manage JW's trading and stagecoach complex on the Sidney to Deadwood trail, and Clay would be stationed at Spotted Tail's Rosebud Agency, to run the stage operation and oversee the business interests of the brothers at Rosebud Landing. The mail service made its inaugural journey in early December.[9]

By mid-December, construction of JW's trading store and accommodation at Pine Ridge was progressing well. On December 22, JW, Mary Ann, and Clay abandoned their rough and freezing temporary tented accommodation to travel two hundred fifty miles by stagecoach, braving the snow and mud, to spend Christmas and the New Year together in the relative comfort of Cheyenne, which until recently had been "inhabited by rowdies and desperadoes, the scum of advancing civilization . . . and where murders, stabbings, shooting, and pistol affrays were at times events of almost hourly occurrence." By 1878, however, it had become the biggest and most prosperous town in Wyoming Territory.[10]

While JW and Mary Ann were still in Cheyenne, the War Department announced on December 30 that, with immediate effect, the temporary army cantonment at Camp Robinson would become a permanent

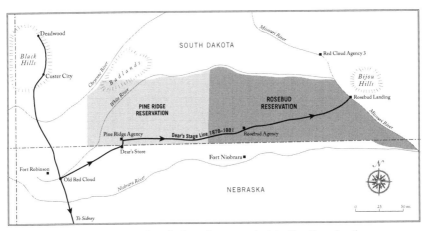

Map 5.   The passenger and mail stage line operated by the Dear brothers between Old Red Cloud, Rosebud Landing, and the Bijou Hills, from December 1878 to February 1881.

base and its name changed from Camp to Fort Robinson. It would be several months before JW fully appreciated the implications of the change.

Their seasonal break over, the three parted company early in the new year. Mary Ann remained in Cheyenne, and Clay traveled back to Rosebud Agency, while JW visited his brother Richard at Old Red Cloud to check on his business and to see his friends.

CHAPTER 28

Fort Robinson and the Cheyenne Outbreak: January 1879

ON THE BITTERLY COLD NIGHT OF JANUARY 9, 1879, A FEW DAYS AFTER he arrived at Old Red Cloud, JW dined with officers at the recently renamed Fort Robinson. A mile and a half away Richard was playing billiards in JW's bar at Old Red Cloud, when an incident occurred that resulted in the deaths of sixty-four Indians and eleven soldiers. The US Supreme Court called the shocking story "one of the most melancholy of Indian tragedies."[1]

The seeds were sown in March 1876 at the start of the Great Sioux War, when Colonel Reynolds had attacked and destroyed a peaceful Northern Cheyenne village on the Powder River. Eight months later, as part of General Crook's Winter Campaign, troops under Colonel Mackenzie once again ransacked their village. The survivors were forced to seek refuge in Crazy Horse's camp, and on April 21, 1877, nearly a thousand Northern Cheyenne, proud, starving, and in rags, surrendered to Crook at the Red Cloud Agency.[2]

The Fort Laramie Treaty dictated they must join their cousins, the Southern Cheyenne, in Indian Territory seven hundred fifty miles away. At the end of May they left the Red Cloud Agency on foot under military escort and arrived at their new home seventy days later.[3] The heat and humidity were unbearable. They found that mosquitoes, ticks, and horseflies were a constant plague; malaria was endemic; and there was little game in the area. A year later they were in a pitiful condition, suffering from starvation due to inadequate rations and unable to hunt to augment their meager allocation.[4] They were ravaged by disease, with little or no medical care to prevent fifty of their children from dying, and were at odds with their southern cousins.[5]

A report reached the OIA that "the Northern Cheyenne are very turbulent. If not fed, they might fight."[6] The report was right. In desperation and filled with superstition that they would all die if they remained in that unfamiliar territory, many resolved to flee the thousand miles back to their homeland—the Powder River Country of Wyoming and Montana.

On the night of September 9, 1878, a group of Cheyenne led by Dull Knife and Little Wolf, with ninety-two young braves and old men, one hundred twenty women, sixty-nine boys, and seventy-two girls, slipped away and headed north.[7] As soon as their escape was discovered they were pursued by cavalry companies from nearby Fort Reno, and the entire Military Division of the Missouri was placed on high alert. Settlers panicked, as the Cheyenne were regarded as desperate and dangerous and would have to "live off the land," in other words, from cowmen and white settlers, as they traveled north. The authorities were also concerned the Cheyenne might unsettle the Oglala and encourage them to leave their reservation to join Sitting Bull and the northern Indians on the Canadian border.

Traveling lightly and skillfully avoiding pursuing troops, the Cheyenne fled north through Kansas and Nebraska. They stole horses, mules, clothing, and food and killed and committed atrocities on white settlers and ransacked their homes. More than forty white citizens were killed and panic spread, embellished by newspaper reports of the activities of "the red devils." Shortly after they reached the Niobrara River, they split into two groups. Dull Knife's group of one hundred fifty Indians headed for Old Red Cloud on the White River, where they hoped to be reunited with their Oglala cousins, not realizing they had already moved to Pine Ridge. As the Indians moved toward their destination, a small group broke away from the main band and, on the night of October 13, stole nine horses from JW's Snake River Ranch stage station.[8]

The second group, led by Little Wolf, moved to the Sandhills of northern Nebraska, where they planned to lie low before heading north in the spring to join Sitting Bull on the Canadian border.[9]

A week later, in a blinding snowstorm, Dull Knife's group unexpectedly met two companies of the 3rd Cavalry and were escorted by them to Chadron Creek, twenty miles east of Camp Robinson, where they camped overnight.[10] Tense discussions resumed the next day. Faced with a superior force and the prospect of being fed, the Cheyenne were persuaded to disarm and dismount and move to Camp Robinson. Their surrender, however, was accompanied by one cogent, passionate plea, not to be returned to Indian Territory.

Although disarmed by their captors, the Cheyenne managed to secrete five rifles, and a further eleven other guns were broken apart and their parts distributed among the women and children.[11] The Indians were housed in a disused cavalry barracks at Fort Robinson, where they waited patiently for the OIA to decide their fate.[12] During this period the atmosphere was relaxed. The Indians were fed well, they mixed freely with the soldiers, and Dull Knife and his daughters even dined with officers at the fort. Red Cloud and other Oglala chiefs visited the Cheyenne on November 8, to impress upon them the helplessness of their position and the futility of resisting the authorities. But their arguments fell on deaf ears.[13]

After weeks of indecision the OIA finally decided that the Cheyenne must return to Indian Territory and the perpetrators of the atrocities committed on their journey north sent to Fort Leavenworth for trial, where, if found guilty, they would be hanged.

On January 3, the commanding officer at Fort Robinson, Captain Henry Wessells, told five Cheyenne leaders that the Great Father had decided they must return south at once. Dull Knife was intransigent. To attempt to march to Indian Territory in such weather inevitably meant that many would perish on the way. He told Wessells that if the Great Father wished them to die, they would die right there where they were—if necessary, by their own hands.[14] "I am here on my own ground. . . . You may kill me here, but you cannot make me go back."[15]

Little Wolf and Dull Knife, who led the Cheyenne flight from Indian Territory in September 1877. NAA Photo Lot 176, BAE GN 00270B, National Anthropological Archives, Smithsonian Institution

The standoff continued. The Cheyenne remained locked in their barracks, and after days of continued resistance, Wessells withdrew their food, fuel, and water. Lieutenant William Carter wrote in his book *Sketch of Fort Robinson*: "To add to the wretched plight . . . [they] were all but naked, for no clothing had been issued since their capture and they were clad only in tattered blankets and fragments of tent canvas . . . half-naked, without food or water these people starved and shivered for five days."[16]

To break the deadlock Wessells seized two Cheyenne leaders and put them in chains. This convinced the others they had to act, and on January 9 they ripped up the barracks floor where they had hidden their weapons. Doors and windows were barricaded, and rifle pits were dug in the earthen floor. "The barrack rang with the shrill, terrible death chant."[17]

Lieutenant Carter describes the events of that evening:

the barracks were soon darkened and the troops retired. The night was cold and the ground was covered with snow. At ten o'clock just as "all's well" was passing between the sentries, a buck fired through a window and killed a man on post . . . then two or three bucks ran out of the west door where they quickly shot down Corporal Pulver and Private Hals. . . . Their desperate captives, maddened by injustice and wild with hunger left the barracks through doors and windows. The bucks opened fire on the guardhouse . . . thus they held the garrison in check until the women and children, the old and the infirm were in full flight.[18]

When the firing began JW, who was a guest of the officers that evening, joined them when there was a call for reinforcements. Richard was in JW's trading post at Old Red Cloud playing billiards. He grabbed his gun, mounted his horse, and joined a group of civilians who galloped toward the fort.

The scene that confronted them when they arrived at the barracks was one of chaos and carnage. Over a dozen Indians and soldiers had lost their lives in the initial outbreak, and their bodies lay in the blood-stained snow around the barracks. Knowing they were going to die, five braves had turned to face the pursuing troops, jumping up and down screaming their war cries to attract attention and to allow time for the women and children to escape. The five managed to shoot about ten rounds each from their carbines before three were killed and two severely wounded.

The Indians were desperate, crazed with hunger, thirst, and hate, and had sworn to fight to the death. The Board of Inquiry later commented, "they literally went out to die."[19]

As the Cheyenne fled, Captain Wessells took command. Understanding the desperation of the moment as he raced across the parade ground from the officer quarters, he shouted, "Follow them up and kill them! Don't let them get away!"[20]

The soldiers, piling out of their barracks, some still in their underclothes, pursued the Indians to stop them before further lives were lost. At least twenty were killed before they reached Soldier Creek. Many were women and children, some shot as indistinguishable shapes in the darkness, others deliberately killed at point-blank range, perhaps from the madness and blood lust that overcomes those in terror for their lives or to defend themselves—"The soldiers had been merciless in their moonlight slaughter."[21]

A map drawn a month after the outbreak shows the trail of the retreating Cheyenne, running southeast to the frozen White River, where, crazed with thirst, some Cheyenne paused to break the ice to drink from the freezing water before heading westward. Once past the sawmill the Cheyenne continued parallel with the river before crossing it once more. They then headed across open ground for two miles to reach a hidden path up the sheer escarpment of the buttes.

The pursuit by the soldiers and civilians continued until they reached the buttes. At that point the extreme weather conditions, with the temperature thirty degrees below freezing and up to two feet of drifting snow, forced many to abandon the chase until sunrise, and JW and Richard returned to their beds at Old Red Cloud.

The journey taken by the Cheyenne that night and over the following days in the conditions that prevailed is extraordinary. Clad in rags, starved, and parched, they stumbled and ran through deep snow in temperatures far below zero, carrying babies and shepherding their women and older men, all the time holding off a determined and well-armed pursuit, largely on horseback. The exact choreography of that night will probably never be known. Soldiers found it difficult, if not impossible, to differentiate who was or was not a warrior. In the chaos of the moment, they took no chances and shot at whatever dark object presented itself.

Lieutenant Carter reflected: "Had the bucks gone alone they would probably have all escaped, but they resolved to die together and to protect the women and children to the last. All frontier history affords no record of a more heroic forlorn sacrifice than the Cheyenne sortie."[22] The Cheyenne body count filed the next day totaled eighteen men and twelve women and children killed. Thirty-five Indians had been recaptured, and eleven soldiers were dead.

Over the following days the army continued to hunt for the remaining Cheyenne. Richard resumed his duties at Old Red Cloud, and JW traveled back to his new trading complex at Pine Ridge. Once there he and Red Cloud discussed the events that had led to such a catastrophic loss of life.

Red Cloud called a council meeting three days after the outbreak to consider how the Oglala could help their Cheyenne cousins, and the following day JW left Pine Ridge to join Mary Ann in Cheyenne. The *Cheyenne Daily Sun* reported that "Red Cloud came to bid Mr Dear good-bye on his departure . . . [JW confirmed] the Sioux had held a council where it was resolved to apply to the government for the care and custody of the Cheyenne prisoners now confined at Fort Robinson."[23] Secretary of the Interior Schurz responded positively to Red Cloud's request and agreed that all the surviving women and children should be moved to Pine Ridge.

The army eventually tracked down the remaining Cheyenne on January 22, and after the final bloody battle—an act of suicidal resistance against a vastly superior force—all but a handful of Indians had been killed or arrested. One of the few Indians who escaped was Dull Knife, who eventually found sanctuary on the Pine Ridge Reservation. Seven warriors were sent to Fort Leavenworth for trial—all were eventually acquitted. "On January 31 thirty-three women and twenty-two children survivors . . . left Fort Robinson for Pine Ridge Agency" to be cared for by Red Cloud and their Oglala cousins.[24]

The whole sequence of events had been a disastrous catalog of inhumane ineptitude and mismanagement. General Sherman, Commanding General of the Army, when asked by a reporter about the Cheyenne Massacre was typically trenchant in his response: "Massacre! Massacre! Why do you call it a massacre? A number of insubordinate, cunning, treacherous Indians, who had no more regard for the lives of our officers and soldiers than if they had been dogs, attempted to escape from the custody of our troops, and used violence to carry out their rebellious act. They were treated just as they deserved, and it is folly to attempt to extenuate such a crime by soft-sounding words."[25] On January 15 the US Senate passed a resolution to investigate the circumstances behind the outbreak, and an internal army inquiry was quickly ordered by General Crook.[26]

Crook was suffering from malaria and unable to travel to Fort Robinson, but the three members of the board that met three weeks after the outbreak were all army officers, one a member of Crook's staff, judging their own. They convened on January 25 and heard evidence from forty eyewitnesses, including two civilians, nine Indians, and twenty-nine military personnel. JW, who was at Pine Ridge, and Richard, who was still at Old Red Cloud, were not called to give evidence.

During the testimonies it emerged that not only had many women and children been killed, but the day after the outbreak some bodies had been mutilated and at least one had been scalped. Civilians, probably bounty hunters, were seen in the vicinity that morning, but whether they or the soldiers were responsible was never established.

The inquiry's findings were inconclusive, and nobody was found accountable for the escape, deaths, or the atrocities committed. The board considered that Captain Wessells had acted appropriately and that "no one else, of equal experience or judgment, could have done any better." Nonetheless, the press was highly critical of the army, which was keen to downplay what became widely known as the Cheyenne Massacre.

On February 12, twenty days after the last Indian had been killed, General Crook signed the report adding, "I have nothing to add to the findings of the . . . Board which are very complete, and which are approved."[27] With that Crook expected the whole incident to be consigned to history.

But he was proved wrong, as the tide of public and press opinion turned against the "measures enforced." JW, Richard, and even Clay, although he was three hundred fifty miles away in Yankton, later found their presence in support of the army that night was held against them. And "one of the most melancholy of Indian tragedies" became one of the most infamous and talked about incidents of all the "Indian Troubles."[28]

PART IV

RED CLOUD AND JW FIGHT FOR SURVIVAL: 1879–1883

CHAPTER 29

Greed, Cronyism, and Corruption

RED CLOUD'S ACT OF DEFIANCE IN MOVING AWAY FROM THE MISSOURI without authorization had made Commissioner Hayt finally lose patience, and by early January 1879 he determined to isolate Red Cloud and introduce radical changes. The Lakota way of life, their tribal customs and beliefs, would be molded to fit the white man's way. Teaching them to farm their allotted acreage, educating their children, and encouraging the adoption of Christian values—the policy adopted by the OIA to assimilate Indian tribes—would now be enforced with renewed vigor. To Hayt, Agent Irwin was too sympathetic to Red Cloud and the Indian cause and would have to be replaced with a more forceful and determined man.

On January 1, Irwin played into his hands. Appalled by how the Oglala were being treated, Irwin wrote to Hayt resigning for the fourth time. "I am thoroughly discouraged with your management of the Indian service . . . the failure of your plans causing unnecessary expense to the Government . . . you having tied my hands . . . I can no longer serve the Department with justice to it or credit to myself, it becomes my duty to retire."[1]

Three days later he wrote an even more caustic and critical letter to Secretary Schurz detailing complaints about the shortcomings of both Hayt and O'Bierne:

Commissioner Hayt has met me at every point with an unjust and arbitrary exercise of his power. He delayed the authority to move the

261

Indians back from the Missouri River until they moved themselves. He refused to contract for transportation to new agency when the price was as low as ever offered by a responsible party [JW] in this country.

He kept a large ox train which was purchased for this Agency out of reach at heavy expense and doing nothing one whole year, which could and should have had transporting supplies all summer. . . . If he could not have organized this train before November, he should not have attempted it in the Winter. As it now is, they have made two trips to the Missouri River, have returned with ponies worn out, Indians frost bitten and discouraged, and which is calculated to drive many of them away from civilized pursuits.

He delayed the building of warehouse and other important buildings at the new agency until Fall and then sent a man [O'Bierne] to plan and supervise the work, whose total ignorance of the requirements of an Agency, and inexperience in the country . . . has not only been a loss to the Government of thousands of dollars, but has caused much suffering of employes living in tents . . . The fact is I have offended Commissioner Hayt by positively and determinedly obeying the behest of President Hayes and your honor . . . and am now ready to submit my record and retire from the service.[2]

Commissioner Hayt accepted his resignation with alacrity.[3] The more forceful and determined man that Hayt had his eye on as Irwin's replacement was the feisty agency physician, Dr. McGillycuddy. By December 1878, after spending a physically draining year with the Oglala, McGillycuddy had decided to leave the Indian Service and return to civilian life. However, in view of the extreme weather conditions, he was persuaded by the army to do one last job—to accompany the troops back to Fort Robinson.[4] They left Medicine Creek on December 9 and after a dangerous and harrowing journey arrived at the fort on January 3. Almost immediately McGillycuddy was summoned to a meeting with the OIA in Washington, where he was offered the job as the Pine Ridge Indian agent. He accepted, and his appointment was agreed by the Senate on January 29. For the next six weeks McGillycuddy and his wife, Fanny, busied themselves preparing for their new life together at Pine Ridge.[5]

In the period of calm before the arrival of the new agent at Pine Ridge, Clay and Luther enjoyed a relaxed social life. Clay spent some of his time in Yankton, boarding at the Merchant's Hotel and socializing with friends, including Judge Peter Shannon, his wife, and daughter Bessie. At the end of January Clay was a guest at a party at the Judge's palatial house, and the press reported that it "was one of the most elegant and pleasurable affairs ever given in Yankton. There was present in full force the elite of the city, beauty, fashion, and youth vying with each other for supremacy. H. C. Dear and Miss Bessie Shannon led in the dance."[6] Bessie was a bit of a paragon, very bright, well educated, and clearly the apple of her father's eye. Although Clay clearly loved a party, and despite Bessie's charms and probably those of many others, he never married.

Luther remained at Pine Ridge managing JW's businesses and, like any other red-blooded twenty-three-year-old, enjoyed an active social life. On January 19 a white employee at the agency and an Indian girl were married by Dr. Irwin. Luther was a guest at the reception and dance following the ceremony held in George Blanchard's warehouse. A colorful description of the event appeared in the local press:

> Not a white woman was present, the female dancers being entirely half or full-blooded Oglalas. Yet the pulsing rhythm of the music never met with better response from flying feet, and the daughters of the prairie endowed the poetry of motion with an accuracy and zest often foreign to it. As for the men, they were the men of the frontier, yet each was famous for some particular deed. There, for example, was William Irving, scapegrace son of a wealthy Philadelphia family, who, as Broncho Bill, is conceded all over the border, to have no equal as a rider, and who sits the wildest horse with an ease and assurance that is the continued envy of his fellows. There, too, was William Garnett, half savage and half aristocrat, the son of the rebel General Garnett by a squaw, next to Leon Palliday the best interpreter in the country; and Luther Dear . . . [younger brother] of JW Dear, once the most daring of Mosby's Men, and now the bravest freight and Indian supply contractor in the West.[7]

By mid-February, despite JW's mail and passenger stage generating more than $5,000 a month, cash flow problems surfaced, and he struggled to pay his creditors. The move of the Oglala to the Missouri in the fall of 1877 and their subsequent move to Pine Ridge a year later had been expensive, as had the investment in his new trading stores and stage line.[8] To help ease his short-term problems he sold his ox-wagon train for $4,000 and put Snake River Ranch on the market.[9]

There was more bad news a few days later. On February 28, JW learned that the US Post Office had unexpectedly terminated his position as postmaster and replaced him with trader Thomas Cowgill.[10] This was a blow, as he had been postmaster at three Red Cloud agencies since April 1873. Fortunately, the loss of his postmastership did not affect their mail delivery service, which continued to operate as normal.

Two weeks later he received further devastating news—his trading license would not be renewed.[11] The life of a licensed Indian trader was lucrative but precarious. The license was renewed, or not, annually, and the decision to renew was at the whim of the OIA. Many an Indian trader received his license by directly lobbying the administration, and the substantial sums earned by a trader did not go unnoticed by those with power and influence. By maneuvering their own appointee into the post and taking a percentage of the profits in return, they could add a comfortable annual sum to their own income.

Surprisingly, in the face of such potent threats to his position, JW had survived and prospered working alongside Red Cloud at four agencies, one of the longest serving of all Indian traders and a testament to his capability, personality, and sheer hard work. But in March 1879 his time had come, and he was unceremoniously removed from his post. As a Southern Democrat and an ex-Confederate guerrilla, he was vulnerable to political change, but it was greed and cronyism that led to his demise. Remarkably, the correspondence that lays bare the behind-the-scenes maneuvering to oust him is still on file in the National Archives in Washington, DC.

Over the previous eight years JW had built an extremely profitable and diversified business. Not only was he the licensed Indian trader to the Oglala, but he was also a restaurateur and hotelier of some distinction whose hospitality was renowned, he and his brothers ran passenger stage-coach and mail lines and the stage stations that supported them, and he had a large freighting business with its own ox-wagon train. His success, however, was coveted by others, principal of whom was the post trader at Camp Robinson, Major Joseph Williamson Paddock.

Paddock, a New Yorker, had moved to Omaha in 1855, where he had become a member of the Omaha Old Settlers, a club of early set-tlers and merchants who shared the plum appointments in the civic and state legislature between them. Before long Joseph's younger cousin, Algernon Sidney Paddock, a New York–trained lawyer, joined him, and in 1865 Algernon was elected the US Senator for Nebraska. The cousins were clearly well connected in the political and commercial worlds of Omaha.[12]

The position of post trader at any army base was profitable and highly sought after, and often influential backers were needed to secure such a lucrative appointment. In January 1877, at the age of fifty-two, Major Paddock left Omaha and moved five hundred miles west to become post trader at Camp Robinson, a job he held until the War Department abol-ished the position in the early 1890s.

Paddock arrived at the camp as the Great Sioux War was drawing to a close, but fifteen hundred troops were still billeted in the area. Paddock and his post store serviced the Camp Robinson troops, while Clay Dear's and Richard Dear's temporary post stores at Camps Canby and Custer serviced the other troops that had been drafted into the area. Paddock saw the booming business the Dear brothers were doing and took note of JW's extensive activities as Indian trader.

When the Oglala moved to Medicine Creek in October 1877, Paddock had been post trader at Camp Robinson for nine months. On November 23 with the support of his Omaha friends, Paddock, in addi-tion to his role as post trader, was appointed the third Indian trader to the Oglala. He then employed George Blanchard to manage the busi-ness on his behalf. Within months of his appointment Paddock began lobbying behind the scenes to have the number of traders reduced from three to two.

Senator Algernon Paddock. Brady-Handy Photograph Collection, Library of Congress, Prints and Photographs Division, LC-DIG-cwpbh-03804

By March 1878, the three Indian traders—Paddock and his manager, Blanchard; Thomas Cowgill; and JW—were all established at Medicine Creek. From the time Blanchard became manager of Paddock's store, he and Paddock had an understanding that Blanchard would eventually take over as the licensed trader, on condition that he paid Paddock and his Omaha backers a percentage of his profits.

Cronyism and the "old boy network" of family and Masonic lodges were a way of life in America's institutions and the burgeoning Western frontier towns and cities. In many ways, they helped facilitate the smooth and rapid development of both political and commercial interests. In Omaha the men of vision who founded the city in the mid-1850s very quickly introduced a legislative framework that helped them protect and control the commercial interests of the city. Thus, the founding fathers ensured they and their friends and families were the major beneficiaries from the financial rewards associated with living in one of the fastest growing cities in America. Outsiders, like JW, were tolerated and even admired, but preference would always be given to Omaha's early settlers with Republican and Union loyalties, and to their families and friends.

Alvin Saunders, a shamelessly corrupt Republican politician, was a friend of Joseph and Algernon Paddock.[13] In 1861, Abraham Lincoln had made Saunders governor of the Territory of Nebraska as a reward for his contribution to the Republican Party, a position he held until 1867. After this he continued to play an active part in both the public and commercial development of Omaha. During the 1870s he was a member of the first commission to look after Indian welfare, and it was then that he met Ezra Hayt, who later became Commissioner of Indian Affairs.

These were the actors in JW's downfall. At a private meeting in May 1878 between US Senator Algernon Paddock, Alvin Saunders, and Ezra Hayt, the Commissioner of Indian Affairs, the commissioner agreed that when the location of the fourth Red Cloud Agency was finalized, he would reduce the number of Indian traders from three to two and replace JW with their candidate George Blanchard.

Alvin Saunders, now president of the State Bank of Nebraska, supported by Senator Paddock, wrote to Commissioner Hayt on July 23, asking for confirmation that JW would be dismissed:

The Honorable Alvin Saunders, one of the principal architects of JW's downfall. Brady-Handy Photograph Collection, Library of Congress, Prints and Photographs Division, LC-DIG-cwpbh-03922

Mr Blanchard says if you continue the three traders at that agency, no money can be made. . . . I told Mr Blanchard that you had told us (that is Senator Paddock and myself) that you would dismiss one of the traders and thus leave but two—that Mr Dear being the last one appointed, his license would be revoked as soon as it was settled as to whither the Indians were to be removed.[14]

This was not true, as they knew, but they needed a pretext. JW was by far the longest-serving trader; the others had been in post for less than a year. Paddock had been granted his license in November 1877 and Cowgill in March 1878.[15] Realizing this was obviously a ploy, Hayt later changed his grounds for not renewing JW's license to his involvement in the Cheyenne outbreak.[16] The army's role that night was under intense press scrutiny, which provided a convenient smoke screen for Hayt's maneuver.

Hayt's decision to remove JW was kept from him for eight months, by which time JW had built a new trading store, office, and accommodation at Pine Ridge, which Hayt knew JW would never profit from.[17] On January 24, 1879, Hayt kept the promise he made to Senator Paddock and Saunders, and Blanchard replaced Paddock and received his trading license. Six weeks later JW was told his license had not been renewed and he was ordered to remove his assets and leave the reservation by May 3.[18] The highly profitable business in which he had invested and had grown over the previous eight years was summarily taken from him and given to a group of Omaha businessmen.

By this time, it was general knowledge that Saunders was corrupt, but little was done to stop him. In January the governor of Wyoming, John Wesley Hoyt, complained to Secretary of the Interior Schurz that a trading license "had been brought about by Senator Saunders . . . as a means of providing for one of his friends." He added that "the deal 'smited of the old hand in the till,' which for so long had disgraced the Indian Office."[19]

Against this background one can only speculate how many of the thirty-five Indian agents and many more Indian traders that Commissioner Hayt replaced during his short tenure were because of bribery. Hayt attracted many serious accusations of corruption. Whether motivated by corruption or not, the decision to remove JW from his post was at the behest of a notably and undeniably corrupt politician, and the reason given was manifestly false.[20]

Hayt's drive to replace JW stemmed from two considerations: he would gain financially, and it would remove a potential problem. He knew both JW and James Irwin were strong supporters of Red Cloud and that by removing them, he believed Red Cloud would be easier to manage.

JW was completely unaware of Commissioner Hayt's duplicity and that his fate had been decided in a secret meeting many months earlier, and he misguidedly believed that Thomas Cowgill had played a significant part in the loss of his license. Cowgill was no friend of JW. He was an ambitious and aggressive businessman who coveted JW's business and wanted to see him removed, and to this end he spread malicious rumors about JW's role in the Cheyenne outbreak.

Cowgill's rumormongering was successful, and Hayt, ever the opportunist, used his argument to persuade the US Post Office to cancel JW's position as postmaster. The loss of his trading license and role as postmaster, his two steady sources of income, could not have come at a worse time for JW, as he was already in debt to his backer, Stephens & Wilcox, for $6,000 and to the wholesaler Tootle & Livingston for $1,901.[21]

Additionally, JW had also been denied the lucrative contract to move the Indians from Medicine Creek to Pine Ridge, despite being the cheapest bidder and the agent's preferred contractor. Yet he was allowed to keep his ox-wagon train laying idle for almost a year on the understanding it would be used. The cost of the eventual move was substantially more than JW's bid. These decisions by a corrupt government official contributed to his losing at least $18,000.[22]

By the end of March both JW's and Red Cloud's optimistic hopes for the future were in ruins: JW was fighting for his financial life, and Red Cloud was locked in combat with the OIA to retain his position as head chief of the Oglala.

CHAPTER 30

Agent McGillycuddy Humiliates Red Cloud

AGENT MCGILLYCUDDY ARRIVED AT PINE RIDGE ON MARCH 10, 1879, to assume his new role as Indian agent. Commissioner Hayt had warned him to be wary of any whites who were close to Red Cloud. He advised him not to employ anyone who had been recruited by Agent Irwin, and, continuing his pretext for not renewing JW's license, he blackened his name by questioning his role in the Cheyenne outbreak, saying he was not fit to be in the Indian Service.[1]

When he arrived at Pine Ridge, McGillycuddy was thirty years old with no previous experience of running a large and complex organization, nor did he have firsthand experience of dealing with over six thousand five hundred Indians. He did, however, have boundless energy and an unshakable belief in his own ability and was a good administrator. He was also considered by many to have "a bitterly revengeful and unrelenting nature . . . and . . . was overbearing and tyrannous."[2]

In contrast, the man McGillycuddy would be dealing with, fifty-seven-year-old Red Cloud, had led his people successfully during Red Cloud's War of 1866–1868 and then made the brave decision to lead them onto reservation life. He had worked closely with the authorities at the first three Red Cloud agencies. He had negotiated on behalf of his people with senior government officials in Washington, DC, and had met Presidents Grant and Hayes in the White House on four separate occasions.

Dr. Valentine McGillycuddy, the controversial Pine Ridge Indian agent, 1879–1886. Photographed in 1880. Minnilusa Historical Association

After ten years of struggle, he had finally secured the permanent home of their choice at Pine Ridge for his people. Despite having been deposed by General Crook two years earlier, he was still recognized as the head chief of the Oglala by the subchiefs, and he was determined to remain so. He accepted that their way of life would have to change. Their children would go to school, war paint and beads would be replaced by Western clothes, and farming would play an increasingly important part in their lives. Red Cloud was not totally opposed to these changes, but he wanted them made in a steady and measured way.

But McGillycuddy was in a hurry. His brief was to advance Indian assimilation into mainstream American life to make them self-sufficient as quickly as possible, to adopt American values and become civilized, to establish an Indian police force under the control of the agent and not the tribal chiefs, to teach the Indians to farm and do their own freighting, and to establish the Episcopal Church on the reservation. It is not surprising, therefore, that these two very different but strong characters clashed and that within weeks of their first meeting, their positions rapidly hardened and each set out to destroy the other.

For his ambitious program to succeed, Hayt believed the power of the traditional chiefs, like Red Cloud and Spotted Tail, had to be broken. One of the first symbolic steps he took was to name the new agency Pine Ridge and not Red Cloud. It took time, however, for the name to become accepted, and for at least a year it was still regularly referred to as the new Red Cloud Agency.

McGillycuddy was aware he had a formidable task ahead of him. He was someone who liked to be in control, so he gathered a team of people he knew and could trust around him.[3] He wanted to employ his elder brother, Francis Stewart McGillycuddy, but employing relatives contravened OIA rules, and it was vetoed by Hayt.[4] Undeterred, he employed him anyway, overcoming the problem by registering him as Frank Stewart on the agency payroll.[5]

McGillycuddy's first few weeks were chaotic. When Red Cloud and his fellow chiefs learned JW's license had not been renewed, their immediate reaction was one of outrage. Between 1871 and 1879, Red Cloud and JW had lived alongside each other at four different agencies. They had witnessed the high and low points in each other's lives, their successes and failures. This had brought the two men together and established an understanding and trust between them. Now, at the whim of the commissioner, and without consultation, JW was to be replaced.

Red Cloud immediately called a council meeting, at which forty senior chiefs, including Red Dog; American Horse; Blue Horse; George Sword; Young Man Afraid of His Horses; and the Oglala shaman, Afraid of Bear, all signed a petition to the Great White Father asking for JW's license to be renewed.[6] They marched to the council room, where they demanded their new agent pass their request to the OIA and the president. There is no record in the National Archives that the petition was received by the OIA, and it is quite probable that like other controversial and embarrassing correspondence, it was conveniently lost or destroyed.

Undeterred by the unrest caused by JW's dismissal, McGillycuddy's first formal meetings with Red Cloud and his fellow chiefs were held on March 24 and 26, when he outlined his plans for the Oglala. He pinned a map of the reservation on his office wall and explained how he wanted the Indians to move away from the agency complex and disperse over the reservation to establish small communities where they could farm the fertile valleys that crisscrossed their land. McGillycuddy saw this as a way of reducing Indian dependence on government handouts, breaking up the old tribal system, and reducing the power of the traditional chiefs. At the same time, he outlined plans to introduce a much-expanded Indian police force, which reported to him and not to tribal chiefs.

McGillycuddy's plans were not well received. At a meeting on April 22, the Indians expressed their opposition to his proposal to move their lodges away from the agency and argued against the establishment of an Indian police force that reported to the agent.[7] McGillycuddy listened to their concerns but made no comment and left for Rosebud Landing.

In the days following McGillycuddy's departure, JW and Mary Ann prepared to leave Pine Ridge. Dear family legend recounts that before they left, Red Cloud honored JW at a special Lakota *Hunka* ceremony in which two people committed to a relationship that bound them together "by ties of fidelity stronger than friendship, brotherhood or family."

Respect between JW and Red Cloud had grown over the years, but it was JW's actions ensuring Red Cloud's people received food and supplies in the depth of winter on their march to the Missouri River that cemented their relationship. A year later, JW again helped Red Cloud move at considerable cost, this time to Pine Ridge. These acts prompted Red Cloud to honor JW and demand his reinstatement as their Indian trader.

The *Hunka* ceremony was always conducted by a shaman or medicine man to ensure the rites were performed correctly. It was unusual for a white man to be honored in this way and to become a *Hunkayapi*, but it was not unknown—the Oglala shaman Afraid of Bear, who had signed the petition calling for JW's reinstatement as their trader, said "I can perform the ceremony for anyone who is chosen in the right way. I can do it for a white man."[8]

Magnificent gifts were presented to JW: an eagle feather headdress, a tomahawk, a red stone clay pipe made from sacred pipestone from quarries in Minnesota, council moccasins, a tobacco pouch, neckpiece, and a buffalo-hide saddle blanket.[9]

On Saturday, May 2, 1879, after eight years as the Indian trader to the Oglala, JW, Mary Ann, Luther, and three ox wagons loaded with the residual stock from his store, left Pine Ridge Agency, and headed southwest to his premises at Old Red Cloud, a seventy-mile journey that took two days to complete.

JW's mind must have been in turmoil. He was angry with his fellow trader, Thomas Cowgill, whom he mistakenly believed had orchestrated his removal; concerned about the growing tension between Red Cloud and McGillycuddy and the way the old chief was being treated; and unsure about what to do to fix his short-term financial problems. He was struggling to pay his creditors but was still confident he would receive payment from the OIA for the costs he had incurred in the fall of 1878, which would more than cover his debts.

Although the future was uncertain, JW was comforted by the fact that his hotel, restaurant, bar, and trading store at Old Red Cloud were all doing well, and the stage service to Rosebud Landing and the Bijou Hills was growing steadily. The plan was for JW to run the businesses at Old Red Cloud and for Clay, Richard, and Luther to concentrate on the stage business.

Before long the animosity between McGillycuddy and Red Cloud came to a head. During the agent's absence on a visit to Rosebud Landing, Red Cloud and three fellow chiefs wrote to President Hayes urging him to replace McGillycuddy with his predecessor, Dr. James Irwin.[10] A similar letter was sent to the president by twenty-two subchiefs.

When he returned to the agency on May 15 and learned about the letters, McGillycuddy was furious. He knew JW was close to both Red Cloud and Irwin and suspected that JW, Irwin, or both had initiated the letters.[11] A few weeks later he took his revenge. On June 4 the OIA authorized the expenditure of $2,500 for the construction of a house for Red Cloud in his capacity as head chief of the Oglala Sioux.[12] In a deliberate attempt to humiliate Red Cloud, McGillycuddy arranged to have this reduced to $500 and the balance spent on other agency buildings.[13] By contrast, a large house costing the allocated $2,500 was built for Spotted Tail at Rosebud Agency.[14]

For thirteen years, since the start of Red Cloud's War, whites and Indians alike had recognized Red Cloud as head chief. Yet within three months of his arrival, the young agent had challenged Red Cloud's standing with the Oglala and publicly dishonored and insulted him. The act of a vindictive and petty man, this established a pattern of behavior that continued throughout McGillycuddy's years at the agency. One either agreed with him and was his friend or disagreed and became his enemy. For McGillycuddy there was no middle ground.

His ability to upset people and make enemies was not confined to the Indians. By mid-April he had quarreled with his opposite number at Rosebud Agency, Special Agent Bullis, over the allocation of rations to their respective agencies.[15] The dispute dragged on for weeks before a grudging compromise was reached, but from then on McGillycuddy was at odds with all subsequent Rosebud agents.

Pursuing his policy to isolate and break Red Cloud, McGillycuddy sought the support of the younger chiefs. The two he targeted were forty-three-year-old Young Man Afraid of His Horses, the son of the hereditary Oglala chief Old Man Afraid of His Horses, and George Sword (Man Who Carried the Sword), who, at Young Man's suggestion, was appointed captain of the Indian police.

Both men represented the next generation. They were intelligent, ambitious, and relatively open to new ways of doing things, and both had their supporters within the tribe. McGillycuddy gave them responsibility and encouraged their support by giving them preferential treatment. He allowed them to leave the reservation to hunt and devised various schemes to put extra money in his policemen's pockets.[16] Between 1879 and 1881 the agent listed many of his force as both policemen and freighters or laborers—a clear violation of OIA rules against dual employment.[17]

Although JW was banned from the Pine Ridge Reservation, his brothers continued to have access, as they, much to McGillycuddy's annoyance, were employed by the postal service to deliver mail to Pine Ridge, Rosebud, and Rosebud Landing on their stage line from Fort Robinson. This enabled them to have regular contact with Red Cloud and to counsel him in his fight with McGillycuddy. JW continued to support and advise Red Cloud, but it was Clay, and to a lesser extent Richard, who saw Red Cloud and Spotted Tail on a regular basis and bore the brunt of McGillycuddy's ire.

Both JW and Clay were close to the Lakota, but they were very different characters. JW was calm and measured, a calculated risk-taker and a hard worker; he was a man who got things done by pulling strings in the background; he was very sociable and was equally at ease with senior army officers, local businessmen, academics like Professor Marsh, and scouts and interpreters like Frank Grouard and Big Bat Pourier. Clay was more volatile and impulsive, but was well respected by Spotted Tail, and was an established member of the Omaha and Yankton business communities. He also had particularly good ties with several powerful Yankton politicians.

It was inevitable that the continued support for Red Cloud would put the brothers on a collision course with McGillycuddy, who saw them as working to undermine his authority as Indian agent. At Medicine Creek, according to Fanny McGillycuddy's diary, she and Mary Ann had been friends and visited each other frequently.[18] But the previous cordial relationship between the Dears and McGillycuddys had broken down, which had a major impact on all their lives.

Over the coming months the tension between the Red Cloud/Dear and McGillycuddy camps heightened, and attitudes hardened. When Secretary of the Interior Carl Schurz visited Pine Ridge in early September, McGillycuddy took him on two separate occasions to Young Man Afraid of His Horses's lodge but not to Red Cloud's.[19] He considered Red Cloud to be "an old man in his dotage, childish and not responsible for what he does," so he was relegated to meeting Schurz at a gathering attended by thirty subchiefs—a very deliberate public humiliation for the old chief.

A few weeks later, on the evening of September 28, McGillycuddy's recently formed Indian police force stopped the Dears' stagecoach when it arrived at Pine Ridge and insisted on searching it. Clay reacted aggressively and was reported by McGillycuddy to have threatened his staff with a gun. Soon after this incident McGillycuddy accused Richard of beating a man in Blanchard's trading store, and then a few weeks later, of writing to him threatening physical violence if his harassment of the Dear businesses by his Indian police did not stop.[20] The behavior of both sides became increasingly vicious and vindictive.

As tensions rose at Pine Ridge, JW and Mary Ann settled into their new life at Old Red Cloud. They set up home in a spacious log "cottage" in sight of the buttes, half a mile from JW's old office and trading station. JW concentrated on managing his businesses—his trading store, hotel, restaurant, and stage station. Luther joined Richard, who was already living at Old Red Cloud, to manage the mail and passenger service between Fort Robinson and Rosebud Landing. This meant they spent only one or two nights a week at Old Red Cloud. Clay continued to manage the Dears' stage station at Rosebud Agency and supervised their business interests at Rosebud Landing.

Mary Ann kept a diary in which she recorded in detail the minutiae of daily life—the weather, letters from home, who they met, how they felt, and what they did. She did her best to turn their simple cottage into a home. She enjoyed the finer things in life like fresh flowers, good furniture, and carpets on the floor. Her diary describes how JW's prized bureau and favorite paintings were carefully placed in their living room, and that the fine tableware JW had bought in Omaha was used for dining. They were forced to live frugally but were determined not to let standards slip.

They both took pride in their appearances. Mary Ann commented in her diary, "I completed my ironing today & my clothes look beautiful. It is such a relief to feel that our clothes are all clean and in order. I counted over Mr. Dear's collars tonight & found he has 10 collars, all done up beautifully enough it seems to last a life time. But when he is from home is always sure to buy more. My husband will always have nice looking linens which I love to see on a gentleman."[21]

During the short spring and summer months of 1879 Mary Ann watched the barren prairie around the old agency turn green and the land become carpeted with spring flowers, which she picked to bring color and fragrance to their home. By contrast in the fall and winter that followed, severe winds made the house rock and blew sand through the walls, covering everything in a film of dust, and snow piled in deep drifts when the temperature plummeted.

When he was not traveling, Richard boarded with them. Mary Ann made it clear in her diary that of all JW's brothers, Richard was her favorite. Occasionally, when there were too many overnight stage passengers for the accommodation at the trading post, she let them stay in her spare bedroom. Finding decent, honest, and upright staff to work in the kitchen and serve in the restaurant was a problem. Mary Ann, despite the gentility of her upbringing, rolled up her sleeves to help her husband and cooked, baked, cleaned, washed, and ironed as staff came and went.

Typical entries describe her predicament: "Will [JW] closely confined to the office, as Ratcliff and Thomas are not to be trusted, both half intoxicated all the time. Again I am chief cook. Herman has been so very disagreeable the last few days, cursing & abusive when I was in hearing. Mr Dear determined to correct him which made him still more angry. He picked up his coat & gun, & away he went out of the kitchen."

Two months after they arrived at Old Red Cloud, JW received further devastating news. The army decided that with effect from June 28, 1879, the exclusion zone surrounding Fort Robinson would be extended to cover an area of twenty square miles.[22] That meant JW's trading post and stage station, which he had built with the full approval of the authorities in 1873, and enlarged in the following years, was now on military land.

Extending exclusion zones around army installations was standard practice to secure control of good grazing land and the nearby timber reserve for fuel and building materials. It also wanted to shield military personnel from the temptations offered by unscrupulous traders—gambling, prostitution, and alcohol—and to protect the business of officially appointed army post traders, in this case, Major Paddock.[23] As a result, JW was ordered to close his store and vacate his premises by the end of the year.

He appealed and eventually, on December 10, was told he could sell his residual stock, but when that was cleared his store had to close.[24]

More bad news surfaced a few weeks later. As a result of a series of ill-judged investments, Stephens & Wilcox, JW's sponsor and major backer over the past six years, was struggling financially. The company was so desperately short of cash it pushed all its creditors, including JW, for settlement, but to no avail, and on June 15, 1879, the First National Bank of Omaha took over the management of its debt.[25] Immediately, the bank began identifying assets it could seize to offset creditors' liabilities. JW was now dealing with bank officials who were ruthless and, as it soon transpired, unscrupulous.

He was now in a precarious position. He had been forced to move his trading store at great expense three times in the previous eighteen months, he had spent his own money to help move and feed the Indians, and his misplaced confidence that he would secure the contract to move the Indians to Pine Ridge had been an expensive mistake that helped put him into debt. But the income he quite reasonably expected to generate from his ongoing businesses—his trading store and postmastership at Pine Ridge, his thriving business at Old Red Cloud, and his passenger and mail service would have been more than enough to cover any shortfall. However, with the loss of his Pine Ridge and now his Fort Robinson businesses, JW's only remaining assets were the stage line and the restaurant and accommodation that served it. As this was now the main source of income for the brothers, selling his stage line to pay his creditors was not an option. His plan was to buy time; push the OIA to settle his claim, which he was confident they would do; and use that money to pay his creditors.

Sensing trouble now that the bank had taken over Stephens & Wilcox's affairs, JW returned to Virginia in July to meet his attorney in his office in the Fairfax County Court House. They discussed his options and agreed the best way to protect JW's main asset would be to transfer Royal Oaks into Mary Ann's name.[26] Once this was done JW returned to Old Red Cloud, breaking his journey in Washington, where he stayed two nights at the Willard, at that time regarded by many as the city's premier hotel.[27]

When he arrived back at Old Red Cloud on September 23, he heard the news he had been dreading but half expecting: the bank had sought permission from the Fairfax County Court to force JW to sell Royal Oaks, which he had mortgaged to Stephens & Wilcox in December 1878 as security on his $6,000 loan.[28] JW and his attorney fought tooth and nail to prevent this. They challenged the accuracy of the bank's figures and argued that the court could not enforce the sale of a Virginian's primary residence. The bank countered that JW had never lived in Royal Oaks and that for the past eleven years Wyoming, Nebraska, and Dakota had been his places of residence. He had only transferred Royal Oaks into Mary Ann's name two months earlier to protect his assets. The legal argument dragged on for almost three years, and the uncertainty caused JW a great deal of stress.

The tense relationship between the McGillycuddy and Red Cloud factions continued into the early weeks of 1880, when there was an unexpected development. For some months there had been rumors in the press about Commissioner Hayt's honesty and adverse comments about his department's mismanagement of the Indians. Eventually, Secretary of the Interior Carl Schurz was forced to act, and in January he fired Hayt for his involvement to acquire a valuable coal mining area from the Apache White Mountain Reservation. The fraud was spearheaded by Edward Knapp, who was discovered to be Edward Knapp Hayt, the commissioner's son. Hayt, according to Colonel Hammond who had been sent to investigate, had knowingly approved of his son's illegal activity. Schurz was so incensed by what the head of the Board of Indian Commissioners branded "the stench in the nostrils of honest men" that he ordered Hayt to clear his desk and leave within the hour.[29]

Hayt's twenty-eight-month tenure as the most senior official in the Indian Service was over. The man who bore a grudge against both Red Cloud and JW was replaced by Acting Commissioner Edgar M. Marble, who held the reigns for the next six tumultuous months.

CHAPTER 31

Red Cloud and the Dears Clash with McGillycuddy: 1880

HAYT'S DISMISSAL GAVE JW AND RED CLOUD HOPE THAT THEIR CIR-cumstances might take a turn for the better. Banned from Pine Ridge, JW was removed from the brunt of the continuing clashes between his brothers and McGillycuddy. His focus since he had returned to Old Red Cloud was to keep his creditors at bay, press the OIA for payment of the money due him, and be reinstated as the Indian trader at Pine Ridge. With Hayt gone, JW considered this was now a possibility.[1]

In January 1880, to strengthen their stage and mail operation, JW agreed to terms to buy a business at Rosebud Landing. O. M. Carter was the owner of the trading post where the brothers leased office, storage, and stabling space for their stage line. As it was on the Rosebud Reservation it came under the jurisdiction of the OIA, and the transfer of ownership from Carter to JW required its permission. However, Hayt's replacement, Acting Commissioner Marble, refused to sanction the transaction but gave no reason for his decision—clearly the Dear brothers were still on an OIA blacklist.[2]

Red Cloud was also more optimistic about the future, as McGillycuddy now appeared vulnerable. Hayt, the man who had appointed and supported him over the previous confrontational nine months, was no longer there to protect him. Most of the Indians in his charge wanted McGillycuddy removed. Government employees at Rosebud and Rosebud Landing found him difficult to work with and would be happy to see him replaced, and Indian unrest in the OIA's largest and most high-profile agency was receiving widespread and often damaging press coverage. Hayt had plucked McGillycuddy from relative obscurity to transform the Oglala from uncivilized nomads to Christian farmers because of his uncompromising toughness and his devotion to duty. Those qualities would soon be tested.

With the trading store at Old Red Cloud about to close, the brothers built a new stage station and trading post near Pine Ridge. It was one hundred fifty yards south of the Dakota border in Nebraska and one and a half miles from the agency and, therefore, outside the jurisdiction of the OIA and the Pine Ridge Indian agent. The store was opened to compete with the two licensed agency traders, George Blanchard and Thomas Cowgill, and to enable JW to resume trading with the Oglala, with whom he had built a long-standing relationship, and to act as a post office and staging post on the Bijou Hills stage line.

Clay supervised the construction of the new store, which opened for business on April 8. McGillycuddy immediately regarded this as a provocative act and although it was not in his jurisdiction, a direct attack on his authority. He set out to obstruct their business and, if possible, to find a way to close it down.

His campaign started within a few days of the store opening. Three of Clay's wagons, carrying $2,000 worth of goods from Rosebud Landing to the new store, were seized by McGillycuddy's Indian police on the grounds that Clay was trespassing on the Pine Ridge Reservation.[3] McGillycuddy also convinced the OIA that Clay's stock at Rosebud Landing should be frozen until it had been properly inspected. This caused Major Upham, the commander at Fort Niobrara, considerable irritation, as the goods were destined for his recently opened fort.

Fort Niobrara had been commissioned by the army as a replacement for Camp Sheridan and was located on the Niobrara River in Nebraska, forty miles south of Rosebud Agency and one hundred twenty miles east of Pine Ridge. Its role was to police Indians on the Rosebud Reservation; to prevent horse thieves stealing Indian ponies; and to stop cowboys from grazing their steers on Indian land, a source of continuing aggravation to the Brulé.

Clay was on good terms with Major Upham, and, for a few months after the fort opened, he fulfilled the role of temporary post trader at the fort. And it was the consignment of goods that Clay had purchased for the fort that McGillycuddy had impounded. Upham demanded their immediate release. However, his demands went unheeded, and the OIA refused to release the consignment.[4]

Shortly after their new trading store opened JW saw an opportunity to unseat Thomas Cowgill and have McGillycuddy replaced. A warehouseman, John Heister, who had worked for Cowgill at Pine Ridge, left his job and moved to Old Red Cloud, where he boarded with JW and Mary Ann.[5] Heister and JW discussed developments at Pine Ridge; the relationship between Red Cloud and McGillycuddy; and how the two traders, Cowgill and Blanchard, were faring. It was during one of those sessions that JW learned Heister had seen Cowgill stealing government property. This gave JW the opportunity he needed.

With Heister's full support, JW with Red Cloud and Clay with Spotted Tail devised a plan to have Cowgill dismissed with a view to having JW reinstated as the trader at Pine Ridge and McGillycuddy replaced as agent. The fact that Spotted Tail agreed to give his support to the plan and to work so closely with Red Cloud was remarkable.

For years the two chiefs, while working together to confront white encroachment on their lands, had had an uneasy and fractious relationship. In 1869 Spotted Tail had killed Red Cloud's great friend and cousin Big Mouth in a leadership dispute. In October 1876 General Crook had publicly humiliated Red Cloud by deposing him in favor of Spotted Tail as leader of the two Sioux reservations. These events were never going to make them intimate friends, but here they were working together to get JW reinstated as Indian trader to the Oglala and have the Pine Ridge agent removed. Neither of these two objectives had anything to do with affairs at Spotted Tail's Rosebud Reservation and can only be a testament to his friendship with Clay and Red Cloud's support for JW.

JW accompanied John Heister to Fort Robinson on May 6, where Heister swore on oath that when he was working for Cowgill the previous November, he witnessed him stealing bags of government corn and transferring the contents into non-government sacks for resale. He also claimed Cowgill regularly brought alcohol onto the reservation to sell at gambling sessions held in his store.[6] If this could be proved, Cowgill would be fired and the way opened for JW's reinstatement as Indian trader. The incident would also reflect badly on McGillycuddy—was he aware, and maybe complicit, in what was going on?

As JW was hatching his plot to have Cowgill and McGillycuddy removed, he started to transfer his residual stock from his store at Old Red Cloud to their new store at White Clay. By mid-May this was completed, and, as the army had insisted, he closed his old store. A few weeks later the owners of the Sidney to Deadwood stage line also moved their stage station away from Old Red Cloud to avoid the army's new exclusion zone. That meant passengers no longer needed overnight accommodation or to be fed, so JW lost yet another source of income.

Once JW, Clay, Red Cloud, and Spotted Tail had presented Heister's sworn deposition to the OIA, JW and Mary Ann left for Virginia.[7] JW was keen to press his claim with the OIA in person and to work with his attorney to retain ownership of Royal Oaks.

The OIA reacted swiftly to the evidence presented to them, and the two chiefs were summoned to Washington, DC. Red Cloud traveled on the Dears' stagecoach from Pine Ridge to Rosebud, where he was joined by Spotted Tail. They then traveled together to Rosebud Landing, where they met Richard and discussed tactics for the forthcoming meeting in Washington. The next morning Red Cloud and Spotted Tail left by steamer for Yankton, where they stayed at the Merchant's Hotel and met Clay, who also counseled them on the issues they should raise with the OIA. From Yankton the two chiefs continued by train to Washington, where they met JW on June 15.[8]

Well briefed by all three brothers, Red Cloud and Spotted Tail met the OIA commissioners on June 19. They were questioned about Heister's affidavit and their knowledge of Cowgill's larceny.[9] Both confirmed they believed the charges to be true and used the opportunity to complain about McGillycuddy, accusing him of corruption and mismanagement, and called for his dismissal. As a result, Special Inspector McNeil was instructed to conduct an official inquiry into the charges against Cowgill and affairs at the agency, and to establish why Clay's goods, destined for Fort Niobrara, were still impounded at Rosebud Landing. Having delivered their accusations in person, Red Cloud and Spotted Tail then returned to their reservations.

Special Inspector McNeil spent most of July in Pine Ridge. He concluded the goods impounded at Rosebud Landing should be released, and Clay was informed on August 15.[10] Resolving the larceny charge against Cowgill was more problematic. When McNeil arrived in Pine Ridge, Heister was in the hospital in Fort Robinson, and when McNeil interviewed him, Heister withdrew all charges against Cowgill and claimed he had been pressured into making them by JW. Heister's contradiction of his initial deposition concluded in technical, legal, language, clearly dictated: "I, John Heister, do deny seriatim the allegations therein contained."[11]

Mary Ann's diary, however, records that, far from threatening Heister that he would be "kicked out on the prairie in a helpless condition," as he claimed when refuting his allegation, JW and Mary Ann were very concerned about his health and had taken him to Fort Robinson to seek medical help. On May 28, three weeks after Heister had signed his deposition, Mary Ann wrote, "Mr Dear drove up to the Post this afternoon with poor John [Heister]. He disliked to be moved on this day, but the day was calm & beautiful, & Buck board being in could not well wait. Poor fellow, I doubt very much if he ever gets about again. He has been growing worse all the time. I feel quite relieved to have him where he can receive medical attention." After JW and Mary Ann left Old Red Cloud for Washington, DC, in early June, someone, probably Cowgill, visited Heister while he was in the hospital and bribed him not to testify.

JW and Clay had feared that something like this might happen, and as a backup the brothers had used Clay's legal contacts in Yankton, probably Judge Peter Shannon, the Chief Justice of the Dakota Territory Supreme Court, to have a civil case against Cowgill heard by a Dakota court. The larceny charge against Cowgill was brought jointly by JW, Red Cloud, Spotted Tail, Clay, and warehouseman George Barnard and was scheduled to be heard by the grand jury in Deadwood in August.

McGillycuddy was apprehensive about the outcome, as he knew one of the main objectives of the plaintiffs was to have him removed.

On July 27, five days before he left for Deadwood, he wrote to the OIA saying, "Although the charges in the affidavit presented to the Dept & the Grand Jury are not made directly against me, there is no doubt that the same was intended to reflect on myself as agent . . . and that this movement had the openly expressed sympathy of the Govt employes and others at the Rosebud agency and Landing in the expectation that I would be dismissed as agent."[12]

Clay, McGillycuddy, Cowgill, and John Heister, together with fifteen whites and a party of Indians, were called as witnesses. JW was not among them. He had remained in Virginia, where discussions with his attorney and the OIA were entering a critical phase and he left the direction of their case in Deadwood to Clay.

The stars of the show in Deadwood were Red Cloud and Spotted Tail. Both must have had mixed feelings about their visit. This was the first time they had returned since they had signed the Manypenny Agreement under duress four years earlier relinquishing their right to the Black Hills. When they were last there, the Hills belonged to the Indians and were sparsely populated and undeveloped, a paradise of wooded hills threaded with clear streams and teeming with game of all kinds.

In a few short years Deadwood had become the rawest of frontier towns, pulsating with energy and home to an eclectic mix of miners, thieves, prostitutes, pimps, Chinese opium merchants, preachers, and saloonkeepers. The thousands who lived and worked there sought pleasure in drugs, drinking, gambling, and whoring, often fighting twenty-four hours a day. Deadwood's most popular entertainment center was Al Swearingen's notorious Gem Variety Theater on Main Street.

The Indians established their encampment at the Mammoth corral on the outskirts of town. And just as Red Cloud and Spotted Tail were interested in seeing Deadwood, so Deadwood was interested in seeing them.[13] Curious citizens, anxious to meet the legendary chiefs, visited their encampment, where the press reported they were courteously greeted by Red Cloud and Spotted Tail. Clay, together with almost everybody else involved in the trial, including the McGillycuddys and twelve members of the jury, boarded at Wentworth House Hotel at the north end of Main Street, one hundred yards from the courthouse.[14]

On the Thursday, Friday, and Saturday preceding the trial Al Swearingen exploited the excitement created by the Indians by persuading them to provide three nights of entertainment at his dance hall. The great and the good of Deadwood scrambled for tickets to watch "one of the most remarkable entertainments that was ever given in this, or any other city . . . the performance will commence at 8 o'clock sharp, and will consist of war and scalp dances, with other performances that are peculiar to the noble red man, to say nothing of the choral singing that will be howled by the entire troop."[15]

To promote the show Al Swearingen's band led the Indians from their camp along Main Street to the Gem Theater. The young daughter of a federal judge observed: "Along came the noisy band and behind it an array of war-bonneted Indians on horseback the like of which was of novel splendor even to us little Westerners. Their brilliant eagle feathers dipped and swayed as they rode. They were armed with bows and arrows and they let out blood-curdling whoops."[16] Hundreds of spectators jammed the narrow streets to catch a glimpse of this extraordinary spectacle.

The Indians dismounted outside the Gem, and Red Cloud and Spotted Tail led their entourage into the theater. Red Cloud opened the proceedings with a short speech: "It was I who sold you these Black Hills. I want peace with the white man in all circumstances."[17] Over the next few hours the Indians performed the Scalp and Omaha dances together with other traditional songs and dances.

The people of Deadwood had never witnessed anything like it—and they loved it.

During those crazy days in Deadwood, Clay stayed close to Red Cloud and Spotted Tail. However, the hearing before the grand jury on Monday, August 9 was an anticlimax, as John Heister, the chief prosecution witness, failed to appear. Eyewitnesses claimed he had been bribed and had fled the territory. His cross-examination challenging just why he had changed the testimony he had made under oath would certainly have been an embarrassment for several parties. The jury had no option but to declare the case yet again "not proven." Months of careful planning had come to nothing, and the prospect of JW returning to Pine Ridge as the Indian trader was now more remote than ever.

A subdued Red Cloud and his entourage traveled via Old Red Cloud back to Pine Ridge on Wednesday, August 11, and an equally despondent Clay and Spotted Tail returned to Rosebud.[18]

McGillycuddy's retribution was swift. On September 1, he banned Clay from the reservation and accused JW of perjury for encouraging Red Cloud and Spotted Tail to complain about him when he was in Washington. He then convened a council of chiefs and subchiefs at which he demanded they elect one head chief. He clearly believed his lobbying and grooming of Young Man Afraid of His Horses and George Sword over the previous months would bear fruit and Red Cloud would be deposed. However, he badly miscalculated the mood of his charges, and the council voted ninety-five to five in favor of retaining Red Cloud as their head chief.

McGillycuddy's response was to ignore the result, to carry on as if nothing had happened. He continued to treat Young Man Afraid of His Horses as head chief, bypassing Red Cloud and addressing him disparagingly as "ex-chief Red Cloud." Red Cloud and his fellow chiefs were determined not to let McGillycuddy's actions go unchallenged. Red Cloud and American Horse both wrote to President Hayes on September 4, probably with Clay's help and support, giving details of the vote and their agent's willful behavior in the face of so overwhelming a demonstration of their wishes.

American Horse's letter, signed by twenty-two subchiefs, was particularly powerful.

A council was called to determine who should be the head chief of the nation. Ninety-five votes were cast for Red Cloud and only five votes were cast against him. Our agent is trying through some of our young men and a few of his police to throw Red Cloud away.... This the nation does not want, and it is only bringing great trouble and bad feeling among our people. He has been our Head Chief, he is now and always will be, because the Nation love, respect and believe in him. We ask and beg of you to take our present Agent from us.[19]

Red Cloud's letter to the Great Father complained of Agent McGillycuddy's corruption and contemptuous treatment of him:

> The Agent Dr. McGillycuddy tells me you have ordered him to throw me away, and tells my people you do not want me to be the head chief any longer. . . .
>
> In a great Council of my people yesterday of over a hundred chiefs and head men, only five small chiefs out of them all voted against me. The agent has taken my horses and buggy and all my furniture which you gave me, away from me and he is now taking the cattle you sent my people away from many of them, because they want me as their head chief. . . .
>
> He tries to trample me in the dirt and make a dog of me and says I and my people have *no right* when we differ from *his opinion*. . . . All this is done because I told you of his stealing our goods when I was in Washington . . . things are very serious here . . . I write to beg you to take away our Agent who is bad and a thief, and give us a good man.[20]

Responsible for all affairs on a reservation, the agent had duties and powers that were virtually without limit. McGillycuddy's widow wrote in her biography of her husband that "at this time there was probably no more autocratic position under the United States government than that of an Indian agent at a remote agency."[21] A complaint about conditions or treatment could only be made either to the agent, who in many cases would have been the cause of the grievance, or by written protest or visits to Washington. Writing petitions, for most Indians, required finding someone who was sympathetic to their case and competent to express their problems in written English.[22] During this period JW and, after his return to Virginia, Clay, were acting for Red Cloud and the Pine Ridge Indians as their petitioners, as McGillycuddy well knew and attempted to expose in his many letters to the OIA.

Red Cloud and many of the older Indians were viewed by McGillycuddy with contempt. On the day that Red Cloud and American Horse wrote to the president, McGillycuddy wrote his annual report on the affairs at the agency for the commissioner:

I have necessarily met much opposition, notably from Red Cloud, who, with the neighboring chief Spotted Tail, form about as egregious a pair of old frauds in the way of aids to their people in civilization as it has ever been my fortune or misfortune to encounter. When these two old men shall have been finally gathered to their fathers, we can truly speak of them as good Indians, and only regret that Providence, in its inscrutable way, had so long delayed their departure.[23]

To ensure their voices were heard, Clay arranged for the contents of both Red Cloud and American Horse's letters to appear in the *Press and Daily Dakotaian.* The newspaper forced the OIA to respond, and on September 16 Acting Commissioner Marble demanded an explanation from McGillycuddy.[24] Two days later, in total denial of the seriousness of the situation, he replied, refusing to admit there was a problem. He claimed Red Cloud was isolated, that most of the chiefs supported him, and that Clay Dear was responsible for the letters to the president and for spreading malicious gossip. His superiors must have begun to have serious doubts about their agent's judgment.[25]

With this degree of turmoil at their largest agency the OIA ordered another investigation, and at the end of September Special Inspector Robert Gardner arrived at Pine Ridge. He immediately ordered McGillycuddy to write to Clay withdrawing the ban on visiting the reservation.[26] He inspected the Dear trading post and then examined the evidence of McGillycuddy's corruption.

On October 15, he reported that he had found no evidence of corruption by Agent McGillycuddy and nothing to indicate impropriety by the Dears or that they had been selling alcohol to Indians as McGillycuddy had claimed:

a Trading Post has been established by Messrs. Dear, the same is under the immediate control and supervision of Mr HC Dear . . . This Ranch is also used by the Messrs. Dears who are sub-mail contractors on the route from Fort Robinson, Neb to Bijoux Hills, Dak as a place where they change horses that are used in transporting the mail . . . In looking over his stock I failed to observe any article of contraband character, and saw no Indians lounging or trading around this place of business, as is the custom at Licensed Traders Stores.[27]

Rowland Trowbridge, a friend of President Hayes, replaced Marble as the commissioner of Indian Affairs on November 1. McGillycuddy, emboldened by the fact that the McNeil and Gardner enquiries and the Deadwood grand jury had found all charges against him not proven, decided to test the mettle of the new commissioner.

Five days later, he again banned Clay, Richard, and Luther from the reservation and a week later ordered the chief of Indian police to arrest any of the four Dear brothers "should they at any time be found on this reservation and not on a vehicle or horse used in carrying the US Mails."[28]

Having done what he could within his powers to banish the Dears, McGillycuddy wrote a fourteen-page letter to Commissioner Trowbridge on November 15 informing him what he had done, detailing his case against each of the brothers. He accused Clay of writing letters to the president on behalf of Red Cloud, "former chief of the Oglalas and an old man in his dotage," and American Horse, "a petty chief," and claimed he had the "deliberate and malicious intention of disturbing the peace and tranquility of affairs at this Agency and thereby forcing your Dept to ultimately dismiss me as an official of the Indian service."

He charged that the Dears were constantly tampering with the Indians and cited as an example: "On the visit of the Chiefs to Washington last spring, RB Dear counselled with them at Rosebud Landing, regarding my removal, Mr HC Dear at Yankton and still another brother, Mr JW Dear . . . in Washington." He stated what was at stake in the fight between the Dears and the agent was to "either control the management of affairs at this Agency as in former times, or cause the dismissal of myself."

He reminded Commissioner Trowbridge that "Myself and employes have now undergone, for the benefit and satisfaction of this Dear family, two investigations by Inspectors of your Department and one examination before the Grand Jury at Deadwood." He finished with a plea: "I am powerless on the reservation of which I am in charge." He asked for Trowbridge's backing for the Dear mail contract to be canceled.[29]

It was a bold move and a high-risk strategy. McGillycuddy effectively challenged the new commissioner to back him or fire him. Trowbridge backed him and in December asked the Postmaster General to cancel the Dear mail contract and find a replacement carrier.[30] Their immunity would then be revoked, and as ordinary citizens they would not be allowed on the reservation.

CHAPTER 32

Mary Ann, Old Red Cloud, and Virginia

As the battle between the Dear brothers, Red Cloud, and McGillycuddy raged that year, Mary Ann dutifully recorded events in her diary. By January 1880 she had been living at Old Red Cloud for more than six months and had established a regular routine. The old agency complex consisted of a community of around sixty people: stage drivers; catering staff; civilians working for the army; and the staff at Sal Morton's bar and brothel, which employed six working girls, a musician, and a barman.

Although her diary barely touches on the momentous events swirling around her and JW, it does give a glimpse of their lives together in a harsh and unforgiving environment and the love they had for each other.

JW's day was spent supervising the daily arrival and departure of the Black Hills stage and their three-days-a-week mail service to Rosebud Landing and the Bijou Hills. What time remained was spent managing his finances and planning to regain his tradership at Pine Ridge. Mary Ann was his greatest asset. She cooked, cleaned, and managed the staff employed in their restaurant and hotel. It was hard work, but they were still confident their difficulties would soon be behind them.

When their future had seemed assured in 1879, JW purchased Greenway Manor, an impressive nineteenth-century country estate a few miles from Mary Ann's family home in Virginia.[1] It was a large house, complete with maid's quarters, fruit cellar, smokehouse, carriage house, barn, and a substantial formal flower garden. This was the home JW had promised Mary Ann—the home where they would raise a family when they returned from the West.

Mary Ann had a love-hate relationship with her life out West. She saw the stark beauty and serenity of her surroundings, but also the harshness and isolation. She loved being by JW's side and sharing his life, but desperately missed her family and friends in Virginia.

By January 1880 she was looking forward to returning home. Extracts from her diary give a sense of her feelings:

> We are here at Old Red Cloud only temporarily for Mr Dear is heartily sick of this life, & is determined to make a change when the spring [of 1880] opens. This is truly a wearing weary life, & so far beneath his ideas & aspirations. God only knows what is in store for us, but we will trust Him & try & be cheerful & hopeful. These are truly dark days for us. I cannot but compare the present with my husband's days of prosperity. Dear Boy, how sensibly he feels it. How difficult to decide what is best to go at next, in order to recuperate lost money.

JW's growing preoccupation with his financial problems was a constant worry. He spent many hours in his office juggling his creditors and working out how to recoup his losses. Arrival times of the stages were unpredictable, which meant JW was often away from Mary Ann until late at night. As a result, she spent many days and nights alone in their cottage: "but my life just now is so monotonous I don't take the same pleasure in writing, day after day passes very much the same. The evening shades gather and find me sitting here alone in our cottage. I have had the blues all day. Sitting here I think so much."[2]

Mary Ann's isolation was partly relieved when the telegraph operator installed a telephone line between JW's office and their cottage, so at least they could talk to each other. The monotony of the winter months was made up for by the longed-for arrival of spring. Mary Ann was entranced by the sheer scale of the beauty that surrounded her:

> Slight snow this morning, & the surrounding bluffs obscured by heavy clouds, which is really beautiful at times. I love to watch the approaching storms as they gather around & surround these wonderful

looking bluffs. How different the scenery from anything we see East. I remember so well how peculiar these gigantic formations appeared to me when I first came west leaving Omaha . . . winter extends far into spring months in this climate. Not before May will we see the springing grass & the prairie dotted over with lovely flowers. how I love flowers & long to live where I can lavish my time upon them.

When the weather was fine and no passengers were expected on the stagecoach, Mary Ann walked alone to the bluffs behind their cottage. It was a round trip of two miles, and she loved the serenity and peace it brought. She walked across the flat, flower-covered prairie until she reached the foot of the bluffs, rising majestically above her. The cares and worries of the world lifted from her shoulders, she then retraced her steps to the cottage. On some days, she explored the surrounding countryside on horseback. She was an accomplished rider and loved the freedom of being alone on the open plains on her favorite horse. Residents at Red Cloud were both impressed and surprised by her horsemanship.

To this day, the sheer scale and natural beauty of the area is breath-taking; there is almost a spiritual quality about it—no wonder Mary Ann loved it so and the Oglala fought so hard to remain there.

Although life at the Old Red Cloud had its challenges, Mary Ann was more in love with JW than ever. On their wedding anniversary she wrote:

The buttes Mary Ann and JW saw every day, which formed the backdrop to their last days at Old Red Cloud. Dear Family Collection

This the 14 of March is the anniversary of our second year. We spent a pleasant morning together & now start out on our third year loving each other far more than when we did two years ago. May God help us each to live nearer to our Heavenly Father, & may another anniversary find us still happy & pleasantly situated. I have lived today amidst different scenes. Thoughts of home & loved ones are constantly before me.

Their social life was limited. Occasionally, they visited one of the few other married couples living in the area: Dr. Brewster, the surgeon at Fort Robinson, and his wife and Edgar Bronson and his family, who owned a large open range ranch five miles west of Old Red Cloud.[3] Some evenings they visited Sal Morton's bar, where they listened to music. "We had some real sweet music, as sweet an instrument as I ever heard, something entirely new to me, Zither. Such a rough common looking man to make such sweet music. I only wish I could perform as he does. Will is devoted to music. With the sweet sound of melody many cares are cast aside."

The harsh reality of living on the very edge of the frontier was brought home to Mary Ann when news of a devastating outbreak of diphtheria in Deadwood reached Old Red Cloud, spreading fear and apprehension along the Deadwood to Sidney trail. She wrote: "The Diphtheria rages in & around Deadwood at a fearful rate. Am told that 11 corpses are waiting to be transferred over this long stage route. O how sad I feel that we are not free from contagion at this point, meeting so constantly passengers who are making their escape. But I think this is a very healthy position. We surely have pure air in abundance & these high winds are sufficient to make it healthy."

Another entry soon followed: "Another dear little motherless babe on today's coach, the same sad story, the father in charge & the mother a corpse on top of the coach. It was crying pitifully when I went over, but I soon quieted it. I have been feeling real badly all day, death is sad at any time, but more so when loving hearts are separated far from other kindred."

But it was not just diphtheria victims who made up the colorful diaspora who passed through the old agency. Two girls arrived who

Mary Ann had hoped to employ as domestic servants, but she was soon disappointed:

> The two girls turned out to be fancy, for the "Hog Pen" as Will calls Sol Morton's. We talked over our trip to Va this morning. Willie says it will be to his advantage to go this spring. Can better attend to his claim in W [with the OIA in Washington] perssenally & I am so sick of this miserable country. I want some day to explore the Bad Lands & then I will be satisfied entirely never to return again. Would like to see Deadwood.

In early May the stage from Sidney arrived, and another colorful group of passengers disembarked for a meal:

> This has been an unusually busy day with me, late breakfast & coach from Sidney rather earlier than usual. There were six convicts in shackles, three chained together. It made me shudder the sound of their chains as they came in & out of the dining room, all of them young looking men doomed to imprisonment. But they were apparently indifferent. I could but think as I looked at them eating, was it highway robbery, murder, or what. This is a place to see all kinds of people.

A week later JW's store finally closed because of the expansion of the army exclusion zone around Fort Robinson; the Sidney to Black Hills stage now bypassed his restaurant and hotel. His financial affairs had reached a crisis point, and he was fighting for survival on several fronts. However, his persistent lobbying of the army had not been entirely in vain. On May 25, the army headquarters in Washington, DC, advised General Crook, "I have the honor to inform you that you are permitted to allow Mr Dear to remain on the military reservation of Fort Robinson with his buildings until further notice."[4]

Despite this welcome news, JW and Mary Ann returned to Virginia to deal with their two most pressing issues. The First National Bank of Omaha had obtained agreement from the court for the sale of Royal Oaks to proceed, which JW needed to discuss with his attorney in

Fairfax. He also wanted to visit the OIA in Washington to press his claim for the costs he incurred when he helped move the Oglala to Pine Ridge.[5]

The stress he was under was considerable, and the first signs of his failing health began to surface. Mary Ann wrote that "Will is feeling quite badly this morning. He complained yesterday of such a queer feeling about his heart, which I don't like to hear about. Has felt badly in that locality several times lately. When the heart is affected I always fear heart disease. But I think he is rather billious & will be all right again after taking some medacine."

A month later, "Will is feeling quite poorly today, billious attack I think. Will feel better I trust in a short while. Dear Boy, he has so much to worrie & try his patience, so many things bearing down on him at once. Truly misfortune never comes singly, but with his firm will, he will conquer. I will try to help him bear his crosses. I trust a way will be opened after while which will lead to more prosperous times for us."

On Wednesday, June 2, they spent their last night in the cottage that had been their prairie home for more than a year. Mary Ann had mixed feelings about leaving and was clearly apprehensive about what the future held:

> How pleasant after the day's work is over to return to our dear little home. After all, how painful the thought of breaking it up. I have had some precious hours within these old rooms. I stopped awhile & listened tonight to Dick and Willie singing, & as their clear voices rung out on the night air, "Am I a Soldier of the Cross," I could not keep back the tears. O that they both were Soldiers of the Cross, & I pray God that I may live to see them followers of the Lamb. I see many clouds above the brow of my dear husband and I feel tonight a presentment of trouble in the future. May God take care of us both & better prepare us to battle with the turmoils of life.

As dawn broke the next day a small group, including Richard and Luther, gathered by the stage station to see them safely on their journey. Mary Ann commented that "I could but feel sad at the thought of Luther's loneliness. I am leaving forever our Prairie Home, the scenes of many happy days."

Throughout her time at Old Red Cloud, Mary Ann had hoped to become pregnant, but as she left for Virginia, cryptic entries in her diary reveal that still hadn't happened.

The first leg of their journey to Sidney was a nightmare. It took twelve hours to travel the first thirty-four miles, and everyone was concerned they would miss their connecting train to Omaha. Mary Ann had cramps all day and only had coffee when they stopped for a break at JW's Snake River Ranch. There was little to alleviate the tedium and hardship of the journey. "Such a weary tiresome trip . . . this stageing is indeed dreadful to be cramped up night & day & jolted around against strangers, & it is so very cold at night here in June." They eventually reached their hotel in Sidney where an exhausted Mary Ann spent most of Saturday in bed.

At half past eight that evening they boarded the Union Pacific train bound for Omaha:

> We took dinner at Fremont, Nebraska, which was very nice indeed. Reached Council Bluffs early in the afternoon. Then three hours of waiting to make connections. We sit on the Platform of the rear Car & see all the Country. O how I enjoy this trip. We are now passing rapidly through Missouri & evry thing is so fresh & lovely. How delightful it looks when I compare our barren Country. We are flying homeward as fast as steam can take us.

Mary Ann was clearly elated at the prospect of returning home after more than two years of living on the Western frontier.

JW had expected to be in Virginia for only a month or two and had rented Greenway Manor, so he and Mary Ann planned to stay with their respective families.

On their arrival in Washington, the couple spent a few days in the city seeing friends. Mary Ann then left for Willow Cottage, but JW remained in Washington, where he met Red Cloud and Spotted Tail prior to their meeting with the OIA. He then left to meet his attorney in Fairfax to discuss the latest developments on Royal Oaks.

A week later JW organized a family reunion to introduce Mary Ann to the members of his family she hadn't yet met, and to show her Royal Oaks, which she had heard about but surprisingly had never seen. JW had described the house to Mary Ann, but nothing prepared her for what she saw. In her diary she recalls that first visit:

> This is really a lovely place [Royal Oaks]. Evry thing looks so thrifty [prosperous] & beautiful, & my heart is full of love & gratitude that I have such a good & noble husband. I see his tokens of tender love & care for his Parents, & the thought that we must toil on in the far away Western Country suffering privations, dear Boy. When I think of it my eyes are full of tears to think he has spent his best days on others & still must struggle on. But God will reward him, & I will help him all I can. But here they little know what their Boys are enduring in the West.

While they were staying at Royal Oaks, JW learned that Stephens & Wilcox had been declared bankrupt and had closed its doors forever.[6]

Over the next four months JW fought for his financial life. During weekdays he stayed with his parents, George and Sarah, at Royal Oaks, but most Fridays, however inclement the weather, he rode the thirty miles to spend the weekend with Mary Ann at Willow Cottage. She would wait anxiously for signs of his approach. "Just before I retired last night, I heard someone comeing up the Hill. As I hoped it to be my own dear Boy, I hastened to put on my clothes, & who but him, just as wet as could be & 11 O'clock & O so dark. I was so glad to see him, & yet uneasy about him taking cold. We had quite a time getting settled down for the night as the entire house is occupied."[7]

During their time together, they visited friends, went to church, or simply relaxed and enjoyed each other's company. Mary Ann had quickly slipped back into the routine of domestic family life. Her younger brother, Sam, and Lizzie ran the family estate. Lizzie was expecting her fourth child, so Mary Ann's time was spent supporting her sister-in-law cooking and sewing, leading an active social life visiting family and friends, and attending religious gatherings where she was an enthusiastic supporter.

Mary Ann's family home, Willow Cottage, where she lived throughout the second half of 1880 before returning West to join JW at Old Red Cloud. Dear Family Collection

In early August while Clay, Red Cloud, and Spotted Tail were in Deadwood giving evidence before the grand jury in support of the larceny charges they had brought against trader Cowgill, the fate of Royal Oaks hung in the balance. JW did not make the long journey west to Deadwood but remained in Virginia to argue in court for the sale to be postponed.[8] A few days later his decision to remain in Virginia was vindicated, as he obtained the delay he sought.

In the months that followed, JW divided his time between helping his aging parents at Royal Oaks and pursuing his claim against the OIA. On November 4 he had an important meeting, which he considered had gone well, and sent a note to Mary Ann saying he was hopeful he would be paid in full. However, despite further visits to Washington the issue remained unresolved.

Buying Greenway Manor, in the light of his growing financial distress, had proved to be a bad decision. In November, much to their relief, they sold the estate to Mary Ann's cousin and her husband, an attorney, and an old Mosby Ranger contemporary of JW. Although they had owned Greenway Manor for almost two years, Mary Ann had spent only a few nights in her dream home.

Realizing there was little to be gained by staying in Virginia, JW left Mary Ann at Willow Cottage in early December and returned to Old Red Cloud and his brothers. He planned for Mary Ann to join him in the new year.

Entries in Mary Ann's diary, written in the weeks before JW departed, give a sense of the deep love and affection the two had for each other:

> I had scarcely written the last few words last night when a low knock was heard at the door. I knew in a moment it was my own loved husband. How rejoiced I was to see him. We sat & talked quite a while, & when he went to look after his horse I sat him a nice lunch which he enjoyed after his long drive from Centerville. All had retired but myself. He is nearly always after night getting here. But darling husband, I am always rejoiced to see him. They all laugh because I am so devoted to him, & show him so much attention . . . Again I am left lonely. O how I miss him & wish that we could be settled somewhere together where we could enjoy home life. I think of my far away Prairie home with many pleasant recollections. With all its isolations we had a beautiful & happy home.

And on another occasion as she left JW after a visit to Royal Oaks she wrote, "Willie, my ever-attentive husband, was on hand to see me on the train. So we parted again, he to go his lonely midnight route whilst I returned to Old Willow Cottage. These partings are so painful. We had such a sweet little communion. I love to know that I am so beloved."

CHAPTER 33

The Feud Escalates and the President Acts: 1881

WHEN JW ARRIVED BACK AT OLD RED CLOUD IN MID-DECEMBER 1880, he learned from his brothers that the OIA had backed McGilly-cuddy and had instructed the Postmaster General to cancel their mail delivery contract. This meant they had to close their stage and mail service and that their sole source of income would now be their trading store near the Dakota–Nebraska border.[1]

A few fraught weeks later, JW was called back to Virginia for urgent discussions with his attorney. While in Washington, DC, he slipped on the ice, broke his leg, and was forced to convalescence in Virginia for the next three months.[2]

Despite JW's presence in Virginia the sale of Royal Oaks became bogged down with legal arguments. On April 11 he made a sworn statement to the Fairfax County Court in which he argued strongly for his right to retain Royal Oaks, but to no avail—the court granted permission for the sale to proceed.[3] Demoralized but now fully mobile, JW returned to Old Red Cloud, but this time Mary Ann accompanied him.

On a bitterly cold day in February the Dear stage made its last two-hundred-ninety-mile run to Rosebud Landing.[4] The winter of 1880–1881 was one of the most severe that century, and the driver and his passengers had to battle deep snow, temperatures thirty degrees below freezing, and gale force winds. Snow blindness was an ever-present threat.[5]

On completion of the run the brothers closed their facilities at the Pine Ridge and Rosebud agencies and at Rosebud Landing. Three stagecoaches and more than thirty horses were brought to Old Red Cloud. At this point Luther, who had worked for JW for five years, left to seek his future elsewhere.[6] He moved three hundred fifty miles northwest to Miles City, one of Montana's early gold rush towns, where he was employed as a clerk by a local wholesaler.[7]

Having succeeded in closing JW's stage and mail delivery service, McGillycuddy now turned his attention to their Nebraska trading store, where he believed Red Cloud and his supporters met to plot against him. His plan was to have the Dakota–Nebraska border moved so that the Dear store, and the mixed-race men living in the area just south of the border, would be incorporated into the Oglala Reservation in Dakota Territory and, therefore, come under his jurisdiction.[8]

James Garfield was sworn in as the twentieth President of the United States on March 4, 1881. The usual churn in government officials took place, and Secretary of the Interior Schurz and Commissioner Trowbridge were replaced by Secretary Samuel Kirkwood and Commissioner Hiram Price.

With the new administration in place Red Cloud tried to assert his authority by stopping the annual census. The Oglala had always been reluctant to be counted, fearing that it would in some way result in their annuities being reduced, but, on this occasion, he misread the situation: his fellow chiefs were reluctant to get involved, and when McGillycuddy cut off rations to Red Cloud's band, he was forced to back down and allow the count to proceed.[9]

Undeterred, Red Cloud continued to seek ways of having the agent replaced. On April 28, while McGillycuddy was in Washington hoping to get a sympathetic hearing from the new administration, Red Cloud wrote to the president complaining about McGillycuddy, pleading for him to be replaced because he was making the agency "more like a military post than an agency to civilize my people." He hoped the president would keep him in Washington and not let him return.[10]

It is likely the Dears were behind the letter—McGillycuddy was in no doubt about their involvement. Two weeks later Red Cloud redoubled his attack on the beleaguered agent. He sent a petition to the new president signed by ninety-six of his fellow chiefs demanding McGillycuddy's removal. "We as a people have lost all faith in him from his unjust treatment of us in many cases. He says we have no rights on our reservation when we differ from his opinion. He has tried to depose our head chief Red Cloud which the nation does not want and . . . he lies to us."[11]

McGillycuddy was apoplectic, and when he returned from Washington, he immediately accused the Dears of being behind the petition and forging names to swell the number of signatories. He also rounded on his OIA colleagues at Rosebud, whom he believed tacitly supported Red Cloud and the Dears and also wanted to see him replaced: "this movement [against me] had the openly expressed sympathy of the Govt employees and others at the Rosebud Agency and Landing in the expectation that I would be dismissed as agent."[12]

McGillycuddy struck back. He wrote to the commissioner on May 30, accusing the Dear brothers of bringing alcohol onto the reservation and requesting that the agent and superintendent at Rosebud and Rosebud Landing be instructed to ban the Dear brothers from their reservation.[13] Commissioner Price ignored him.

The following month at the annual Sun Dance, McGillycuddy's simmering anger boiled over, and he confronted Red Cloud, accusing him of colluding with the Dears against him. He made his accusations in front of Lieutenant John Bourke, who recorded their exchanges verbatim in his diary:

> Dr. McGillycuddy: This comes down to a question as to who has told a lie—you Red Cloud or Mr Dear? I blame you, Red Cloud, for this thing and so does the Great Father for counselling with Mr Dear or having anything to do with him. At the council we had last fall you promised the inspector and me you would have nothing to do with Mr Dear. As long as you or your people go to Mr Dear or have anything to do with him there will be trouble.
>
> Red Cloud: There is another thing I want to say about the letter which was written last and which Mr Dear knows nothing about.

Dr. McGillycuddy: I'll have nothing to do with you, Red Cloud, until you tell me who has been writing these letters.[14]

By now the distrust and dislike between Red Cloud, the Dears, and the agent had widened to a chasm. Although the feud between Red Cloud and McGillycuddy remained a major problem for the OIA, elsewhere their management and control of the Indians was gradually strengthening, and on July 19, this was given a further boost when Sitting Bull and his band, who had fled to Canada in 1877, surrendered at Fort Buford.

In August Commissioner Price invited a delegation of chiefs to Washington. Both Red Cloud and Spotted Tail were invited, but McGillycuddy's request to attend was refused. A few days before the meeting took place, Spotted Tail was shot in the chest and killed by Crow Dog at the Rosebud Agency, the tragic culmination of a long and bitter feud between the two men. Crow Dog was immediately arrested and sent for trial.

With Spotted Tail's death Red Cloud had lost a valuable and much respected ally. Although the two chiefs had had their differences, over the last three years they had put aside their petty jealousies and been united in their opposition to many of the OIA's initiatives and, as a consequence, had become much closer.

The meeting in Washington took place. The Oglala delegation led by Red Cloud included Young Man Afraid of His Horses and George Sword. Red Cloud dominated the discussions. Much to his satisfaction and McGillycuddy's subsequent annoyance, Red Cloud also secured permission from Secretary Kirkwood for white men ("squaw-humpers" as McGillycuddy called them) who had married Oglalas to remain on the reservation, subject to their good behavior.[15]

McGillycuddy saw nothing but trouble coming from this, and on September 1 he expressed his annoyance in his annual report to the Commissioner of Indian Affairs. In the same report he commented on the murder of Spotted Tail: "The old chiefs [Red Cloud and Spotted Tail], relics of a system that has ceased to be necessary in our dealings with the Oglalas, are as antagonistic as ever to all innovations and improvement. . . . But, with the death of the neighboring chief Spotted Tail, and the deposing of Red Cloud at this agency, their influence for good or evil is rapidly dying out."[16]

The contrast between McGillycuddy's comments and those of the Rosebud Agent, John Cook, could not have been greater. Agent Cook, who was no admirer of McGillycuddy, wrote in his annual report of September 1: "The loss of this chief [Spotted Tail] is irreparable. There is not one on the reservation who can fill his place. The value of his services to the government in the past cannot be too highly estimated, and he was regarded by all as a true friend to the whites. His influence was ever on the side of law and order . . . he never opposed innovations when he saw they were for the good of the people, whose interest he had at heart, and for whom he labored so long and so well."[17]

While Clay and Richard were battling with McGillycuddy, JW and Mary Ann had returned to Old Red Cloud in late April. The once bustling, crowded, noisy entrepôt was now eerily quiet, and only a handful of hardy old-timers remained. While Mary Ann busied herself making their old cottage comfortable, JW focused on his claim against the army.[18]

He was now desperately short of money, and on June 8 he again wrote to the War Department asking to be allowed to resume trading until the matter was settled:

> I respectfully ask if there are any prospects of being allowed by the government any compensation for my buildings near Fort Robinson. If the government cannot allow for the use of which I have been deprived of since the extension of the reservation at great loss to me as they cost me near $4000, will you not grant me permission to continue my trade there . . . until there can be something definite decided?[19]

His request went up the chain of command to Secretary of War George Ruggles, who instructed General Sheridan to resolve the issue. He in turn asked General Crook and the commanding officer at Fort Robinson, Major Sumner, for their recommendations on how to proceed. Eighteen days later Sumner wrote to General Crook stating he was opposed to JW resuming trading but proposed a board of officers should be appointed to recommend the financial settlement due to him.[20]

Sumner's proposal was accepted, and on August 5 JW's premises were inspected and all relevant documents reviewed by a board of officers, who unanimously recommended he should be awarded $3,000. Five weeks later this was endorsed by General Sheridan.[21] JW was satisfied and relieved by their decision. It was now clear that JW's store at Old Red Cloud would never reopen, so Richard accepted a job as bookkeeper with Thomas Kurtz, a Wyoming railroad contractor with the Union Pacific Railroad Company.[22]

September 19, 1881, was the day JW hoped would never come. He had still not received payment from the OIA or the army and was therefore unable to settle his debts. As a result, Royal Oaks was sold at auction by the Fairfax Court commissioners to the president of the First National Bank of Omaha, Herman Kountze. He reneged on the deal, and at a second auction one month later under controversial circumstances, a proxy for the bank acquired Royal Oaks for a substantially lower price. JW and his attorney challenged the integrity of the sale and accused the bank of fraudulent behavior.[23] For the next eighteen months this was the subject of heated debate between the opposing attorneys and the authorities.[24]

After Richard's departure, McGillycuddy directed the full force of his ire on the two remaining Dear brothers, JW and Clay. He once again lobbied for the Dakota border to be moved so he could close the Dear Nebraska store and rid himself of the main focus of support for Red Cloud. "Half-castes and squaw men," as McGillycuddy referred to them, were anathema to him and a constant target of abusive threats, and in November he banned Louis Shangrau from the reservation for what he claimed was disorderly conduct.[25] It was more likely to have been part of McGillycuddy's systematic campaign to rid the reservation of anyone who opposed him.

The dispute between the Dears and McGillycuddy reached the White House on January 22, 1882. President Chester Arthur, who had succeeded the assassinated President James Garfield the previous September, issued an executive order increasing the Pine Ridge Reservation by fifty square miles. This meant a rectangle of five by ten miles, known as the White Clay Extension—encompassing JW and Clay's store and not much else—now extended south of the previously dead-straight border. The store was no longer in Nebraska, but on the Oglala Reservation in Dakota Territory, and under McGillycuddy's direct control.

JW had been warned this was likely to happen, and in early January the brothers sold their store. To avoid arrest by McGillycuddy's Indian police Clay moved away from the area, and for the next few months alternated between living with JW and Mary Ann at Old Red Cloud and staying with friends in Yankton.

McGillycuddy had succeeded in closing the last of the Dear businesses, but he wasn't finished yet: he wanted Clay arrested and sent for trial for allegedly selling alcohol to Indians. In early January, the Nebraska district attorney issued a warrant for Clay's arrest, but the US

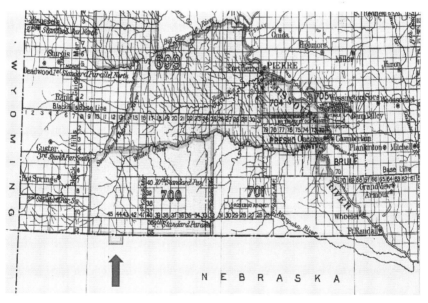

President Arthur's executive order of January 22, 1882, adjusted the Dakota–Nebraska border extending the Great Sioux Reservation, which resulted in the Dears' store being forced to close. Library of Congress, Image no. 13023487, Royce, Charles C, and Cyrus Thomas, Indian Land Cessions in the United States, 1899

marshal was slow to act. Clay had left the reservation and traveled via Fort Niobrara to Yankton, where he arrived on February 20. A week later McGillycuddy fired off yet another letter to Commissioner Price criticizing the Nebraska authorities for their slow response and demanding they take steps to arrest Clay. In the same letter he expressed his concern that Clay's powerful friends would bring pressure to bear in Washington to have him dismissed. "As this man Dear was strongly vouched for by the Ex-Chief Justice of Dakota [Peter Shannon] . . . and others, in his attack on the management of this agency in 1880, it is probable that he will sooner or later turn up in Washington, lobbying for the removal of the present Pine Ridge Agent."[26] McGillycuddy's efforts to have Clay arrested and brought to trial were in vain; Clay kept well clear of the reservation.

McGillycuddy must have believed that with the Dears gone his troubles were behind him and that he would have little difficulty in handling Red Cloud. He was wrong.

CHAPTER 34

Red Cloud Fights Back: 1882–1883

By the spring of 1882, McGillycuddy had been the Pine Ridge agent for three years. Having successfully forced the closure of the last of the Dear businesses so they were no longer able to support Red Cloud as they had in the past, McGillycuddy now channeled all his energy into curbing Red Cloud's power and influence. But Red Cloud was determined not to give up without a fight. He was committed to remaining the head chief of the Oglala and having McGillycuddy removed.

The first victim in McGillycuddy's renewed campaign was Cloud Shield, a lieutenant in the Indian police. He was a strong supporter of Red Cloud and was dismissed for purportedly aiding Red Cloud in causing dissention and desertion from the police force.[1] Red Cloud immediately called for McGillycuddy's removal, claiming he favored the Indian police when distributing annuities and that he diverted goods for personal gain. On April 5 McGillycuddy responded, warning Commissioner Price that "Ex-chief Red Cloud is holding his usual Spring councils with the intention of securing if possible the removal of the present agent."[2]

As the weather became warmer and summer approached, the animosity between the two factions grew. Most of the Oglala supported Red Cloud and even those who did not objected to the humiliating way in which he was treated by McGillycuddy. They resented his being patronizingly referred to as their ex-chief.

Just as the Indians were divided, so were the whites. McGillycuddy's main supporters were his brother Frank Stewart; his wife's relative, the engineer R. O. Hoyt; interpreter Frank White; trader George Blanchard; George Sword; and many Indian police. He also had the backing of the OIA, which considered he had done a good job establishing an Indian police force, encouraging the Oglala to send their children to school, and promoting self-sufficiency through farming and freighting.[3]

The anti-McGillycuddy faction consisted of JW and Clay; JW's old nemesis Thomas Cowgill, who McGillycuddy now accused of "irregular and unjustifiable acts" and wanted removed from the agency along with his clerk; the agency physician; the chief of police; most of the older subchiefs; and the mixed-race interpreters and freighters working at the agency.[4] It also had the support of most government employees at Rosebud Agency and Rosebud Landing who had experienced McGillycuddy's abrasive personality.

Matters came to a head on August 13. After weeks of planning, Red Cloud and fifty-two subchiefs illegally left the reservation, without a pass, to gather at the ranch of Red Cloud's friend and JW's former clerk and interpreter, Louis Shangrau, who was now living in northwest Nebraska. There, at a secret meeting, they met fellow conspirators to discuss an extraordinarily audacious plan designed to force McGillycuddy's removal. Clay was one of the chief plotters. Also present was William J. Godfrey, a shadowy figure from Colorado who McGillycuddy later claimed was a friend of Secretary of the Interior Henry M. Teller.[5]

The conspirators plotted carefully, as the OIA had ignored previous Indian petitions to have McGillycuddy removed. If their demands were not met, they planned to forcibly eject the agent from the Pine Ridge Reservation. Godfrey came armed with a letter addressed to Secretary of the Interior Teller for the Indians to sign warning that "if the incumbent as U.S. Agent is not removed from this Agency within sixty days, or a proper person sent out in the mean time to fully investigate his gross misconduct here, we will upon the expiration of the above stated time take upon ourselves the responsibility of politely escorting him out of our country, and let the consequences be what they may."[6]

This was an unprecedented move with potentially serious consequences, but Red Cloud and his supporters were confident they had sufficient backing to execute the threat. To demonstrate the seriousness of their intention and that their action did not constitute a wider rebellion against the authorities, the conspirators advised both Secretary Teller and Major Sumner, the commander at Fort Robinson, of their plan.[7]

The OIA ignored the niceties, regarded the petition as a threat to the established order and tantamount to insurrection, and immediately gave McGillycuddy their unqualified support. They ordered him to arrest Red Cloud and to use the threat of bringing in troops if the unrest continued. The prospect of armed troops entering the reservation was something the Indians had not anticipated, and they backed down.[8]

With the pressure off, and much to the annoyance of Commissioner Price, McGillycuddy left the agency on August 20 to attend to other business in Yankton and Omaha. In his absence both camps for and against McGillycuddy furiously lobbied Washington, and on August 26, Commissioner Price, now becoming concerned by the opposition to McGillycuddy and the strength and sophistication of the Indian challenge, sent special investigator Major William J. Pollock to Pine Ridge to investigate.[9]

Major Pollock was no friend of McGillycuddy. He had been the officer in charge of the troops that accompanied Spotted Tail and the Brulé on their long trek to the Missouri in the fall of 1877, which was when he first met Clay. Later, they cemented their friendship when Pollock became the acting agent at Rosebud Agency and he worked alongside Clay when he was the post trader.

Pollock arrived at Pine Ridge on September 1 and filed his first report to Secretary Teller and Commissioner Price on September 15. In it he attributed most of the blame for the troubles to McGillycuddy, vindicating Red Cloud's refusal to work with the agent.[10]

> It could hardly be expected the old chief would work in harmony with a man who lost no opportunity to humiliate and to heap indignity upon him, who called him liar, fool, squaw, refused to shake hands with, deposed him, ordered the Agency employees not to entertain him in their houses, and no doubt sought to enforce a condition of affairs on August 19th that would result in his death.[11]

Pollock suspended McGillycuddy on October 4 for "established malfeasance in office," but he was immediately overruled by Commissioner Price.[12] Ten days later, Pollock filed his second report, in which he itemized the irregularities he had found citing "the agent was living high at the expense of the Indians; he had taken credit on vouchers that were not paid; he had unlawfully deprived Red Cloud of rations while giving the Indian police and other favorites more than they could use; he had permitted agency employees to convert government supplies for their own use."[13]

McGillycuddy spat back in one of his characteristically caustic letters, describing Pollock as "a disappointed office-seeker and was associated with the 'Indian Ring,'" and accused him of "carrying on his investigation with a high hand" and eagerly accepting "the testimony of every squaw man and half-breed."[14]

To validate Pollock's assessment, Commissioner Price sent a second agent to Pine Ridge, Special Agent E. B. Townsend. He endorsed Pollock's findings and added that "not only was McGillycuddy fraudulent in the management of the agency, but the fraud was being perpetrated willfully and as the result of collusion which dated back to 1879, when the agent had assumed his post."[15] At this point McGillycuddy tendered his resignation.

Worried by McGillycuddy's threat to resign and not content with the findings of two inspectors, Commissioner Price asked yet another inspector for his views. On November 15 Inspector S. S. Benedict's report "completely exonerated McGillycuddy of any but 'technical irregularities'" and claimed he "was one of the best agents in the service."[16] Perhaps not surprisingly Commissioner Price, having received the answer he wanted, accepted Benedict's version of events.

A few days later, emboldened by Commissioner Price's support, McGillycuddy took his revenge on Thomas Cowgill and banned him from the reservation. Price wrote to McGillycuddy, "information having been received at this office of certain irregular and unjustifiable acts on the part of Thomas G. Cowgill, a licensed trader at your agency, his licence is hereby revoked, to take effect not later than January 1 [1883]."[17] Alas, it was too late to help JW.

Shortly after defeating Red Cloud's challenge, McGillycuddy suffered a severe setback, the seeds of which were sown in late October 1882 when the Edmunds Land Commission arrived at Pine Ridge Agency. The three-man commission, headed by a former governor of Dakota Territory, was instructed to discover whether the Lakota would sell "surplus land." Their proposal was that the Indians should "cede all of their land between the White and the Cheyenne Rivers, thus opening a wide corridor from the Missouri to the Black Hills"—an area of approximately eleven million acres, accounting for more than 40 percent of the Sioux Reservation.[18] In return, the head of each family would be allowed to select three hundred twenty acres of land plus eighty acres for each minor child, and the government would provide twenty-five thousand head of stock cattle and one thousand bulls to be divided among the reservation Indians accepting the offer.[19]

The commission convened meetings at which they presented the various Lakota tribes with a glowing account of how it would be better if they agreed to their proposals.[20] The Oglala elected Red Cloud to speak for them and then went into council for several days. When Red Cloud delivered the council's response it was an uncompromising message to the commission. "We will not sell our land. Why ask us why? I will tell you. . . . We signed away the Black Hills; they were full of gold. Have we ever received an equivalent for them? Look at my people. We have no money; our pockets are empty, and we are poor. This is our land by mutual consent of the Indians and of the whites. We shall never willingly yield it to the whites."[21] In spite of this unequivocal response, the commissioners, with McGillycuddy's support, continued to push hard to have their proposals accepted.

They obtained what they claimed was the support of a representative number of chiefs and headmen. But the numbers fell well short of the 75 percent of adult males required under the terms of the Fort Laramie Treaty.[22] When this was discovered by liberal politicians and Washington activists, they worked tirelessly to prevent the agreement from being passed by the Republican-controlled Congress.

Secretary Teller and Commissioner Price reflected on the recent dramatic events at Pine Ridge and invited Red Cloud to Washington to hear his side of the story.[23] He arrived with his interpreter on December 21, and over the next two months he had a number of inconclusive meetings with the authorities. Red Cloud complained yet again about McGillycuddy's corruption. He restated his opposition to the land agreement and again pressed for recompense for the 722 ponies taken from his and Red Leaf's bands by General Crook more than six years before.[24] But progress was slow, and the discussions dragged on into late February.

Red Cloud was kept fully occupied during his visit. He was fêted by East Coast liberals and political activists and enjoyed an active social life. He was invited by his old friend Professor Marsh to stay with him at his New Haven, Connecticut, home. The *Sunday Globe* reported that "Red Cloud, the Indian chief, arrived to-day on a friendly visit to Prof. Marsh, of Yale College. He was accompanied by an interpreter. The day was spent visiting the Peabody Museum, examining among other curiosities the fossils procured by Prof. Marsh in the Indian country in 1874."[25] At the end of January he attended a reception at the White House, where he was introduced to President Chester Arthur by Secretary Teller.[26]

The Indian activists Cora Bland and her husband, Dr. Thomas Bland, editor of the Indian reformer's magazine *Council Fire*, were strong supporters of Red Cloud and his opposition to the land agreement. They and Professor Marsh organized a series of soirées and meetings at which Red Cloud outlined the injustices done to his people.[27]

Red Cloud was a charismatic and persuasive orator. His opposition to the land agreement gained support, and before it could be implemented, Indian reformers challenged its legality. On March 2 the Senate passed a resolution creating a commission, with Senator Henry Dawes of Massachusetts as its chairman, to investigate the "feasibility and propriety of the proposed reduction of the Sioux Reservation." Red Cloud returned to the agency having set in motion considerable senatorial opposition to the Edmunds Commission's proposals.

In late June, ignoring strong opposition from McGillycuddy and the OIA, Red Cloud presided over the last Sun Dance to be held before

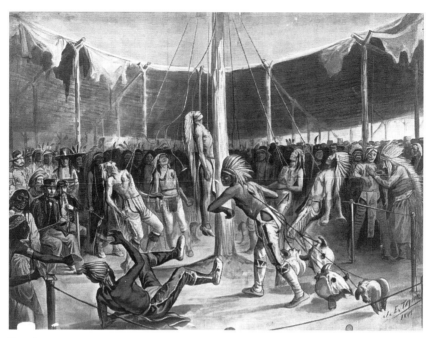

The Sun Dance, considered by the government to be a barbaric practice, was banned in 1883. Painting by James Earl Taylor in 1881. MS 4605, James E. Taylor Scrapbook of the American West, National Anthropological Archives, Smithsonian Institution

it was banned by the authorities.[28] Thousands of Indians from the surrounding area attended the ritual reaffirmation of the Oglala's cultural and spiritual identity.

Although the Sun Dance marked the end of an era, it also heralded a resurgence in Red Cloud's fortunes. After gathering evidence over the summer months, the Dawes Commission met in September 1883 at Pine Ridge, where it concluded that Edmunds and the commissioners had lied to the Indians. They found the Indians were almost unanimous in their opposition to the land agreement. As a result, it was declared null and void.[29] McGillycuddy and the commissioners came out of this exercise badly. But Red Cloud gained stature, and many of the younger Indians, who had previously supported McGillycuddy, now transferred their allegiance to the old chief.

This proved to be the turning point in the battle between the two adversaries. From that moment Red Cloud's star gradually rose while McGillycuddy's faded.

CHAPTER 35

The Final Days

WHILE RED CLOUD WAS GAINING THE UPPER HAND AT PINE RIDGE, JW spent most of 1882 in his cottage at Old Red Cloud with his beloved Mary Ann by his side. It was a sad and melancholic experience for them both. When JW had left the agency in the fall of 1877 to move with Red Cloud and the Oglala to the Missouri River, he was thirty-two, unmarried, wealthy, and a successful and respected businessman, comfortable in the knowledge that he had achieved nearly everything he had set out to do.

The agency had been the vibrant hub for six thousand five hundred Indians; his bar and restaurant were full every night with colorful characters wining, dining, gambling, and playing billiards; and his trading store did a thriving business with travelers and bullwhackers toiling up and down the Sidney to Deadwood trail. The whole area had been alive with people coming and going—miners, frontiersmen, freighters, Indians, and military men. He could look forward to his marriage to Mary Ann, confident they would raise a family and have a long and full life together.

But now, just five years later, the site was silent, inhabited only by the spirits of the past: the Indians had gone; the agency had been dismantled and the timber used to build Pine Ridge; the buildings surrounding JW's trading post now stood empty, abandoned, and suffering from neglect; and the Sidney to Deadwood trail, once the agency's lifeline, bypassed the military reservation.

The worries of the world were on his shoulders. His every waking hour was spent challenging the integrity and validity of the forced sale of Royal Oaks to the First National Bank of Omaha and pursuing his claims against the army and the OIA.[1]

But officialdom and bureaucracy moved slowly. At the end of 1882 his attorney had made little progress on resolving the Royal Oaks dispute, and although JW's claims were under review, they had not been settled. The uncertainty took its toll. He feared that if he lost Royal Oaks he would be declared bankrupt and his aging parents would be homeless. He couldn't sleep, and his physical and mental health suffered.

Throughout the year Clay had kept on the move to avoid McGillycuddy's vengeful pursuit. Maintaining his active and vociferous support for Red Cloud, he saw friends at Rosebud Agency, Fort Niobrara, Yankton, and Omaha and regularly visited JW and Mary Ann at Old Red Cloud. However, because of the change in their circumstances, he decided to radically reshape his life. At the end of the year, after twelve years as an Indian goods wholesaler, post trader to the army, and stagecoach proprietor and having had a career that had brought him into contact with many diverse and colorful characters, his peripatetic lifestyle came to an end.

Clay, then thirty-six years old, settled down and became one of the first pioneers to move to Valentine, Nebraska, a fledgling frontier community five miles west of Fort Niobrara. He was elected to various public offices, continued to support Red Cloud, and helped JW pursue his claim against the OIA. In April 1883, he obtained permission to visit "that portion of the Pine Ridge Reservation in Dakota recently added by Executive Order from the state of Nebraska . . . for the purpose of obtaining the affidavits of certain parties residing there."[2] He continued to do everything in his power to ensure JW's claims were successful.

As winter set in and 1882 drew to a close, Mary Ann was becoming increasingly concerned by their precarious financial position and the effect it was having on JW's health. In December her brother Sam threw them a lifeline. He suggested they should return to Virginia and that he and JW should go into business together. It was the break they desperately needed, and early in the new year JW and Mary Ann left Old Red Cloud for the last time. After stopping in Omaha, where they said an emotional and tearful farewell to Clay and Richard, they boarded the train for Virginia.

Soon after they arrived home at Willow Cottage it became clear that the business venture that Sam had proposed to JW wasn't going to work—JW's health was deteriorating; he was unable to focus and had difficulty sleeping. In mid-March he suffered a complete mental and physical breakdown, and Sam arranged to have him admitted to a specialist and reputable sanitorium in Baltimore sixty miles away. When he returned home two months later, he could remember nothing of his time in Baltimore: it was as if he had been in "a dreamless sleep." However, they were both optimistic he would make a full recovery, and their spirits were lifted by the news that Mary Ann was pregnant, something they had longed for.[3]

They marked the occasion by having their photograph taken. It shows a devoted Mary Ann standing protectively beside a vacant and expressionless JW. Clearly, he had not yet fully recovered. On the photograph he wrote enigmatically: "Wide awake & fast asleep."[4]

A few weeks later, he wrote a poignant but rambling letter to his brother Richard:

> My Dear Precious Bro, . . . Thank God I am here but still very weak. Cannot walk but short distance without tiring out . . . The storm was there brewing in the distance, the weary tired brain required rest. In March the storm came. I was in a life unknown to me, floating almost in space. . . . The last thing I remember at home was my Mamie, my darling noble wife, crying in the bed, crying. . . . Thank God dear Bro, I soon shall be myself again with a comparative new brain.

It was not to be. JW's health did not improve, and their troubles were not over. In early July they learned that their hard-fought efforts to retain Royal Oaks had failed and the property had been granted to the First National Bank of Omaha.[5] JW's parents, George and Sarah, would have to leave the home that he had worked so hard to provide for them.

Then, a few harrowing days later, on July 14 and just eight days after his thirty-eighth birthday, JW died. Given his severely weakened

A protective Mary Ann, four months pregnant, and a pensive JW posed for the photographer. JW died two weeks later. Dear Family Collection

condition it was probably a heart attack or a stroke. Mary Ann was inconsolable, for she had devoted all her adult life and love to him and now he was gone. She was pregnant and alone, with only her memories to console her. It was her unborn child, her deep faith, and her family that gave her the strength and a reason to continue.

JW was buried in the Union Cemetery in Leesburg, where a large gathering of family and friends came to pay their respects and say farewell. Sam Rogers, his closest friend, brother-in-law, and future guardian of his unborn son, delivered a moving eulogy, which was later printed in the *Loudoun Mirror*:

> To the great world, the above simply records the closing of another human life. But to many dear friends who he gathered to him and "bound with bonds of steel" the announcement of Will Dear's death will come as sad news indeed. He was born and raised in Loudoun County. When but a youth he was called to do a man's service for his country; and right manfully he did it. He served in Company D of Mosby's Battalion from its organization until its disbanding in 1865. For several years after the war he was engaged in the publication of the *Sentinel* at Warrenton, Va. Then the tide of enterprise and fortune bore him to the Western wilds, and the more mature years of his life were spent among the vicissitudes and dangers of Dakota and the far frontiers. Wherever he went his clear judgment and wonderful energy and tact won him rank amongst the foremost in business; and his traits of character and disposition brought him warm and staunch friends. With the element of strength which commanded for him prominence among the iron men who inhabit our western boundaries, he combined a frankness and unselfish generosity which bound men to him, and those tender graces of heart and mind which made him almost an idol in the family circle. Amid all the cares and excitement of his busy life, substantial tokens testified that he ever had thought and love for the dear ones in their far-away home.
>
> In the spring of 1878, he returned to his native county and bore away with him one of our worthiest daughters to share and cheer his hardy western life. For years they bore its toils and endured its trials together. Separated as it were from the rest of their kind, they were truly all in all to one another, and their beings became perhaps more

closely and tenderly knit together than is common even unto husband and wife. But death is no respecter of the "ties that are so close." Disease lay its hand heavily upon him, and sadly he and his faithful companion turned their steps eastward for him to come home to die. In manhood's prime, and when all the things that make life lovely had taken hold about him, he was stricken down.

But thanks be to God who gave the victory through faith, the life which here seems as the column broken half way up, will be completed and rounded out in the great Hereafter—and may the rainbow of promise which arches over his early grave shed the light of the same hope into the hearts of those who mourn that Will Dear is dead.[6]

Throughout their short time together as man and wife, Mary Ann had been troubled by the time and energy JW had devoted to providing for others, something she frequently commented on in her diary. He had always put their needs before his own and had toiled tirelessly to provide a home and an income for his parents, employment for his siblings, and justice for Red Cloud. That is reflected in the epitaph Mary Ann chose for JW's grave:

BLESSED ARE THE DEAD WHO DIE IN THE LORD:
THEY REST FROM THEIR LABORS.

Five months later Mary Ann's despair at the loss of her beloved husband was eased by the arrival of their son, who brought joy and purpose back into her life. On December 7, forty-year-old Mary Ann gave birth to another remarkable Dear, William Richard Dear, who grew to have a life as filled with drama and incident as his father. But that is another story.

Grave of JW and Mary Ann in the Union Cemetery, Leesburg, Virginia. Dear Family
Collection

PART V

THE AFTERMATH

Chapter 36

Red Cloud

For three years following JW's death Red Cloud remained locked in battle with McGillycuddy. In March 1885 Grover Cleveland became the twenty-second President of the United States, and Red Cloud's East Coast liberal friends arranged for him to meet the new Democrat president.[1] Clay, together with other supporters, raised the money to finance Red Cloud's sixth visit to the White House, where once again he aired his grievances and asked the president for McGillycuddy's removal.[2] "I am head chief of my people, . . . My people have been treated very bad, . . . Now I tell you I want a new agent."[3]

By this time support for the troublesome and combative agent was on the wane, and the new Democrat administration decided to engineer his dismissal. McGillycuddy was ordered to replace a Republican employee. Predictably, he refused, and in May 1886 McGillycuddy was removed from office by the Secretary of the Interior with the full approval of the president.[4]

Red Cloud was then sixty-four years old. He had survived seven years of being bullied, belittled, and humiliated by McGillycuddy. He had weathered General Crook's ill-judged decision to try to replace him as head of the Oglala and Brulé in October 1876. He had emerged victorious and was still recognized by Indians and whites alike as the head chief of his people.

With McGillycuddy gone, Red Cloud and Young Man Afraid of His Horses reconciled their differences and, at a council meeting at Pine Ridge on July 26, 1887, joined forces in the fight to retain their tribal lands.[5] Although the Edmunds Land Agreement had been rejected in 1883, the question of the division of Sioux land had not gone away, and in 1887 Congress passed the Dawes Act.[6] This was an attack on the communal ownership of Indian land—a cornerstone of tribal existence whereby tribal lands could be divided and given to individual Indians in an attempt to turn them into homesteaders. The government made it clear that only those Indians who accepted their conditions would be recognized as US citizens.

The subsequent Sioux Act, passed by Congress in March 1889, partitioned the Great Sioux Reservation into five smaller reservations and opened nine million acres of former reservation land for settlement by whites.[7] In spite of Red Cloud, Sitting Bull, and Young Man Afraid of His Horses's vehement opposition, the authorities eventually obtained the required signatures from 75 percent of the Indian adult male population. Although stories of vote fixing and bribery abounded, the result of the two acts was that the Lakota lost a further 40 percent of their reservation and received very little in return.[8]

Red Cloud was scathing in his address to the commissioners in his campaign against the dismantling of the reservation: "the Great Father has not paid the things promised us, but wants us to give more land before we are paid for what is due. I looked around to see if you had any boxes full of money to pay us, but I see none. I presume you are to pay us in sugar talk, as you have done before."[9]

The loss of their land, the systematic extermination of the great buffalo herds, and the banning of Indian tribal practices all contributed to the Indians' growing sense of despair and disillusionment.[10] This prompted the rise of the Ghost Dance movement, which swept through the Sioux nation in the winter of 1890. This movement promised a return to a world that had vanished and a spiritual answer to their sense of alienation.[11] As long as they performed the required rituals they would once again see their ancestors, the buffalo would return, and the white man would be miraculously removed from their lives.[12]

The movement rapidly gained support, and the authorities, sensing the possibility of a general uprising, took an uncompromising stance by ordering that all dancing must stop. Many Indians refused. One of the

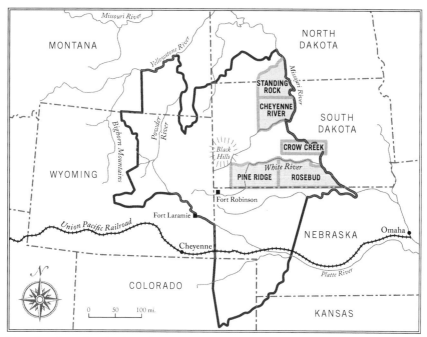

Map 6.   Sioux Lands: As defined by the Act of March 1889, which created five separate reservations and reduced Lakota Sioux land by a further 40 percent.

early casualties was Sitting Bull, wrongly suspected of being a driving force behind the movement, who was shot dead by Indian police while resisting arrest at his home at Standing Rock Agency on December 15.[13] It was a sad and tragic end for one of the most revered and influential of all Indian chiefs.

Troops were sent to Pine Ridge in anticipation of trouble. On December 29, a bitterly cold winter's day, they corralled a large group of dancers at an isolated location near Wounded Knee Creek, sixteen miles northeast of the agency, and called on them to surrender their weapons. The Indians refused to disarm, and in the ensuing clash more than two hundred Indians, including women and children and at least twenty-five soldiers, lost their lives.[14] It would come to be known as the Massacre at Wounded Knee.

One hundred years later Congress passed a resolution of "deep regret" for the massacre, and the site is now a National Monument. Red Cloud's role in the movement is unclear. He was probably supportive but was by now strongly opposed to the use of violence.[15] Having shown no firm leadership either for or against the Ghost Dance movement he effectively lost the confidence of both the whites and his own people. The tragic events of that day effectively marked the end of Red Cloud as a political force among the Oglala.[16]

Red Cloud and his wife, Pretty Owl, lived in the same simple two-story house on the Pine Ridge Reservation in South Dakota for the rest of their lives. They often dressed in Western clothes and increasingly adopted the outward appearance of the white man.

Red Cloud abdicated as head chief of the Oglala Lakota on July 4, 1903. His final speech to his people demonstrates his remarkable powers of oratory:

My sun is set. My day is done. Darkness is stealing over me. Before I lie down to rise no more, I will speak to my people.

The Great Spirit made us, the Indians, and gave us this land we live in. He gave us the buffalo, the antelope, and the deer for food and clothing. . . . We were free as the winds and like the eagle, heard no man's commands. . . . Where the tepee was, there we stayed and no house imprisoned us. No one said, "To this line is my land, to that is yours." In this way our fathers lived and were happy.

I was born a Lakota and I have lived a Lakota and I shall die a Lakota. Before the white man came to our country, the Lakotas were a free people. . . . The white man came and took our lands from us. They put [us] in bounds and made laws for us. We were not asked what laws would suit us. But the white men made the laws to suit themselves and they compel us to obey them. This is not good for an Indian . . . the white man has taken our territory and destroyed our game so we must eat the white man's food or die . . . where the Lakota could ride as he wished from the rising to the setting of the sun for days and days on his own lands, now he must go on roads made by the white man; and when he crosses the bounds the white man has set about us, the white man says to us Indians, "You must not be on lands that are not on the road."

The commissioners and the white people sent to us by the president tell us that the white people know what is best for us. How can this be? No white man was born an Indian, then how can he think as an Indian thinks?

As a child I was taught the Supernatural Powers were powerful and could do strange things; that I should placate them and win their favor; that they could help me or harm me; that they could be good friends or harmful enemies. . . . When the Lakotas believed these things they lived happy and they died satisfied. What more than this can . . . the white man . . . give?

Shadows are long and dark before me. I shall soon lie down to rise no more. While my spirit is with my body the smoke of my breath shall be towards the Sun for he knows all things and knows that I am still true to him.[17]

Two months later Red Cloud made his last appearance at a tribal council at which the discussion focused on obtaining compensation for the Black Hills, which, to this day, has not been resolved.[18]

Red Cloud in 1901, nearly blind, with his wife, Pretty Owl. Library of Congress Prints and Photographs Division, LC-USZ62-39083

In his later years Red Cloud's health gradually declined. He became nearly blind and increasingly frail and infirm. He died peacefully at his home on the Pine Ridge Reservation on December 10, 1909, in his eighty-seventh year. He and Pretty Owl had been married for fifty-nine years. They were both baptized as Catholics in 1884, and the day following his death, Red Cloud was buried with the full rites of the Catholic Church in a little cemetery that now bears his name. A simple cross marks his final resting place, which overlooks the Sacred Heart Church at Pine Ridge and the plains beyond.[19] Pretty Owl was laid to rest beside him when she died in 1940, aged one hundred five.

In death Red Cloud received many tributes. The *New York Times* described him as "the boldest and fiercest of the Sioux leaders and a diplomat of rare ability."[20] Unlike his contemporaries Spotted Tail, Dull Knife, Crazy Horse, and Sitting Bull, Red Cloud did not die young, nor surrender, nor flee his country in exile. In 1868 he took the brave decision to lead his people onto reservation life and fought unstintingly for their cause until his death forty-one years later.

Grave of Red Cloud and Pretty Owl at Red Cloud Cemetery, Pine Ridge. Dear Family Collection

CHAPTER 37

The Dear Family

FOUR WEEKS AFTER JW'S FUNERAL, HIS FATHER, GEORGE, DIED UNEX-
pectedly at the age of sixty-seven. At the same time, the family learned
JW had not left a will. The court valued his assets, mainly books and
furniture, at just $209.[1] After George's death, Sarah moved to the home
she owned in Aldie, where she was joined by Mary Ann, and for the next
five years, the two recently widowed women devoted themselves to giving
Mary Ann and JW's son, Willie, the best possible start in life.

During this time Mary Ann fought to recover the money owed to
her husband. JW's estate had two outstanding claims, both of which
would have, if successful, transformed Mary Ann's financial position. The
first was for $18,000 against the OIA for moving and feeding the Oglala
when they relocated to Pine Ridge.[2] This claim was complex and difficult
to unravel. Moving the Oglala to the Missouri in 1877 and to Pine Ridge
the next year had been chaotic and badly planned and had caused untold
suffering, something the authorities were keen to conceal. The OIA was
in a state of flux, and by the time JW had started pressing for payment,
the Commissioner of Indian Affairs had been bribed and already agreed
not to renew JW's trading license. It is unlikely, therefore, that his claim
received a sympathetic hearing. Mary Ann's diary and Dear family papers
refer to the case JW and Clay were preparing in early 1883 to submit to
Congress, but JW died before it was completed and there is no record
that it was ever presented.[3]

The estate's second claim was for $3,000, which had been agreed to
but never paid by the army, for the forced closure of his business on the

Fort Robinson Military Reservation. His executor, Sam Rogers, together with Richard's wife, Ridie, and Mary Ann, fought for eleven years for payment of the compensation. Their claim was considered by Congress on four separate occasions before finally being rejected on appeal in 1894.[4] The voluminous file in the National Archives in Washington, DC, documents the proceedings in depressing detail. A distraught Ridie reportedly burned all the papers associated with the claim so no other member of the family would have to suffer the distress the case had caused. Mary Ann was resigned to live the rest of her life in genteel penury, dependent on her family for her financial well-being.

Sarah Dear died in 1892, and a year later, when Willie was ten, Mary Ann moved to Washington, DC, where she ran a "boarding house for gentlefolk." The house was owned by the Rogers family, and both Willie's cousins, Sam and Joseph, boarded with their aunt for more than fifteen years.[5]

Of all the Dear brothers, Mary Ann had been closest to Richard.[6] After McGillycuddy had forced the closure of the Dear trading store, Richard moved to the railway town of Laramie, Wyoming. In early 1884, he joined Winston Brothers, a successful railroad and mining company based in Minnesota, and became the partner responsible for their mining division. Having tasted success, Richard returned to Virginia to marry Ridie Jamesson, thirteen years after her father, Malcolm, had issued the prospective groom his challenge, telling Richard to come back "when he had made something of himself."

By 1893, Richard was one of the richest men in northeast America. Years earlier he had been part of a consortium that had made a speculative investment in land in Utah. Large quantities of iron ore were discovered, and the land was sold in 1893, giving Richard a profit of $300,000.[7] That same year the Winston-Dear Company was formed, and Richard was appointed president. The largest iron ore deposits in America were discovered at Hibbing, Minnesota, and Richard's company won the contract to strip the mines.

The crowning glory of Richard's career came a few years later, when his company was awarded one of the biggest civil engineering contracts in America. The Winston-Dear Company built the 1.7-mile St. Paul Pass tunnel through the Bitterroot Mountains in Montana, completing the railroad from Chicago to Seattle.[8]

Shortly after the tunnel opened, Richard's health declined. On Sunday, December 12, 1909, two days after Red Cloud's death, he died at the age of fifty-nine surrounded by his family in his magnificent Wisconsin mansion overlooking Lake Superior. Richard was buried in Glenwood Cemetery, Washington, DC, and his substantial collection of ceremonial robes and Indian artifacts was given to a museum in Wisconsin.

The National Cyclopaedia of American Biography stated in 1920 that "Few men started with less and accomplished more than he, and his unusual career may be taken as strikingly emblematic of those laudable characteristics which reveal American manhood in its most virile and inspiring form."[9]

Like JW, Richard employed members of his family. Frank worked for him for over twenty-five years. Clay joined him in 1889, and when Richard bought Woodgrove Farm, a historic five-hundred-acre estate in Round Hill, Loudoun County, Virginia, in 1895, he appointed his brother-in-law Thomas Wynkoop, who was married to his sister Frances, as his estate manager. Although Richard and Ridie's main home was in Wisconsin, the couple spent a considerable amount of time at Woodgrove, which remained in the Dear family until 1944. Luther, who had been brought out West by JW, married, had two children, and continued to live in Montana until his death in 1929.

Clay lived in Valentine for six years. He became the postmaster, and the owner and editor of the local newspaper, *The Valentine Reporter*, and, as County Superintendent for Schools took a special interest in teacher training. Valentine was a colorful frontier town, and "a Democratic stronghold where anti-McGillycuddy sentiment ran high."[10]

Clay and Red Cloud met regularly, and when Red Cloud learned that Mary Ann was pregnant, he presented Clay with a pair of ceremonial moccasins for her unborn child. These tiny moccasins are now one of the author's most treasured possessions.

During the bitter winter of 1885–1886, Clay had an accident that changed his life. Hunting with a group of officers from Fort Niobrara, he

Tiny deer skin ceremonial moccasins given by Red Cloud to Mary Ann in 1883 for her unborn child. Exquisitely decorated with white, gold, yellow, red, green, blue, and black beads. Dear Family Collection

fell through the ice on a lake south of the fort and nearly froze to death. Although he survived, he never fully recovered. He walked with a limp and suffered from rheumatic fever for the rest of his life. In mid-1889, ill health forced him to leave Valentine and move to Wisconsin, where he lived with Richard and his family until his death on September 1, 1905—the day after his fifty-eighth birthday.

Clay never married, and forty years after the end of the Civil War he returned to where he was born and fought as a Mosby Ranger. He was laid to rest in a simple grave next to his parents in Middleburg, Virginia—the very heart of Mosby's Confederacy.

Mary Ann died of pneumonia in 1918, thirty-five years after JW's death. She never remarried and was buried alongside her beloved husband in the Union Cemetery in Leesburg. Their son, Lieutenant Colonel William Dear, led the small group of family and friends that gathered at her graveside to pay their last respects.

JW's son, William, who wore the moccasins Red Cloud gave to Mary Ann, was an outstanding student, an accomplished horseman, and a world-class sprinter, who in 1903 won the 60-yard dash at the American

The author's great-grandmother, Mary Ann Rogers Dear, about 1915. Eugenia Newberg

Championships.[11] Three years later, he graduated with a degree in medicine from the University of Pennsylvania; he joined the Medical Corps of the US Army and was an officer for thirty-eight years.

He served in two world wars and rose to the rank of general. His postings took him to China, the Philippines, Germany, and Russia. The stories he told of the extraordinary events he witnessed in those exotic, far-flung locations mesmerized his grandchildren: China, during the

343

JW's son, General William Dear, circa 1950. Dear Family Collection

period of unrest leading up to the Chinese Revolution of 1911; the Philippines from 1910 to 1916, where the author's father was born; the American Zone in Koblenz, Germany, at the end of the First World War; and Russia, where he was the medical director of the American Relief Association in the Tatar Autonomous Soviet Socialist Republic, then in the grip of a widespread typhus epidemic during the Great Famine of 1922.

William died on September 7, 1956, aged seventy-two. He served his country well and was buried with full military honors in Arlington National Cemetery. JW, the father he never knew, would have been proud of him.

Afterword

The quest to unravel the twists and turns of JW's extraordinary life led to fascinating and often remote places and introduced us to many knowledgeable and kind people who helped piece together my great-grandfather's story. Of all the many remarkable incidents that occurred during our research, one stands out.

On a hot and dusty June day in 2017 in Whiteclay, Nebraska, an isolated settlement one and a half miles from the site of the old Pine Ridge Agency, we stumbled across what we thought could possibly be JW's last trading post. It is now a much-altered wooden building called the Fireside Inn.

It was around midday and a few locals were having lunch. We asked the owner about the history of the diner. She and her elderly mother told us they thought it had been an old mail station because the previous owner had found a bundle of undelivered letters from the early 1880s behind paneling. Reality dawned. We were standing inside my great-grandfather's trading post, where he and Red Cloud used to meet one hundred forty years ago.

After a pause to take this in, we asked the owner where we could find Red Cloud's grave, which we knew was nearby. One of the diners, who had been watching us intently, came forward and kindly gave us directions. She then asked why we were interested in visiting his grave. I told her of my quest to learn more about my great-grandfather, who had been a friend of Chief Red Cloud. A look of surprise spread across her face, and she replied, "I am Red Cloud's great-great-great-great-granddaughter, Lymona Red Cloud Hawk," and gesturing to her companion, "this is my husband, Steve Hawk, who is a direct descendant of Sitting Bull."

Since that remarkable chance meeting we have remained in constant contact with Lymona and her family. It was a meeting that has enriched all our lives.

The author with Lymona Red Cloud Hawk in Pine Ridge, June 2017. Dear Family Collection

Acknowledgments

Absolutely fundamental to writing this book has been our friend Michael Dover, whose knowledge of the publishing industry and editorial skills have been invaluable. Our thanks also to his long-suffering wife, Ruth, who gave the project her unwavering support despite having to share her husband with us for many hundreds of hours.

The fact the book has seen the light of day is largely thanks to two people who helped kickstart the project. Sadly, neither are still with us. Marilyn's aunt, Francis Dewey, in whose New York attic we found the original drawing of JW's trading store at the Red Cloud Agency, and the late Tom Buecker, the curator at the Fort Robinson Museum, who took us under his wing, introduced us to JW's old haunts, and enthusiastically supported our tentative first steps into the world of research and writing.

We are deeply grateful to the many others who filled gaps in our knowledge, helped us track down leads, and offered advice that brought our story alive. The Rogers family still owns Willow Cottage, and Patty and Donna Rogers opened their homes to us and provided an invaluable insight into Mary Ann's life. Rogers Fred's observations on the Civil War were constructive and helpful, and Gene Dear and Eugenia Newberg were instrumental in helping to piece together the story of the early Dears. Eugenia also kindly made available images from Richard Dear's private collection, several of which appear in the book.

Marilyn's sister, Wendy, and her cousins Fred and John Dewey indefatigably searched attics, cellars, and storage units and unearthed reams of previously forgotten family history, much of which we have used in the book. Bill Ray's and Lewis Leigh's encyclopedic knowledge of Mount

Gilead and the Civil War helped trace JW's life growing up as a teenager in the hamlet during the war.

We are indebted to all those who believed in our project, have read our manuscript, and provided objective criticism. The book is better as a result. A particular mention to Sarah and Paul Nelson, whose editorial skills and clear uncluttered vision shamed their father, and additional thanks to Paul who worked wonders on the many old images included in the book.

We are thankful for the unbridled enthusiasm and support we have received from Neil Osborn and Holly Smith, who were, and still are, a font of innovative ideas; Pat Short for her creative observations about her native city, Omaha; and Wayne Taylor, who has dispensed wise advice and enthusiastically monitored the project from Sydney, Australia.

Others who have made a significant contribution are Lymona Red Cloud Hawk; Bry Dear; our friends, Mike and Les McCann, who introduced us to the Dovers; Ronnie and Susy Leon, who suggested the book's title; Michael and Tash Crawford; John and Judy Tole of the Little Washington Historical Society; Jane and Bunk Riley from the Manassas Museum; Eugene Scheel, who has unsurpassed knowledge of the history of Northern Virginia; Eric Buckland, with his knowledge of Mosby's Rangers; Fairfax County historian, Debbie Robison; Elaine McRey and Chris Barbuschak of Fairfax County Library's Virginia Room, where many of JW's letters and the Royal Oaks collection are held; the late Mary Fishback at the Thomas Balch Library, Leesburg, who was generous with her time at the outset of this project; Sandra Lowry at Fort Laramie; Rose Kor at the 1881 Courthouse Museum, Custer City; Paul Horsted, who contributed rare stereo cards from his impressive collection; and our friends Greg Carlow, Paul Gillingham, John Mottram, and John O'Reilly, who read the manuscript and made valuable observations.

Our thanks to the superb staff at the National Archives in Kansas City and Washington, DC; the Library of Congress; the National Anthropological Archives, Smithsonian Institution; and the many curators and volunteers in the libraries, historical societies, and archive centers listed below who have so generously given their time and advice.

From Virginia: Library of Virginia; Fauquier County Historical Society and Public Library; Prince William Library, Manassas; Confederate Museum, Front Royal; Rappahannock County Court House Archives; Loudoun County Court House Archives; the H. Furlong Baldwin Library.

From South Dakota: Red Cloud Heritage Center, Pine Ridge; Rosebud Sinte Gleska Heritage Center; Crazy Horse Monument Library; Deadwood City Hall and Library Archives; and the Adams Research Center, Deadwood.

From Nebraska: Nebraska State Historical Society, Lincoln; Douglas County Historical Society, Omaha; The Steamboat Bertrand Museum; Dawes County Historical Society Museum, Chadron; Museum of the Fur Trade, Chadron; Cherry County Historical Society, Valentine; Crawford Museum; Sidney Library; Cheyenne County Court House Archives, Sidney.

From Wyoming: Wyoming State Archives, Cheyenne; Pioneer Memorial Museum, Douglas; Casper Fort Museum; National Historic Trail Center, Casper; and Denver Public Library.

And finally, our thanks to Sarah Parke, the acquisitions editor at TwoDot, who believed in our book and whose calm and wise counsel has been instrumental in bringing our efforts to fruition.

Abbreviations

AG	Adjutant General
BIA	Bureau of Indian Affairs
BIC	Bureau of Indian Commissioners
CA	Chronicling America: Historic American Newspaper, Library of Congress
ColA	Commissioner of Indian Affairs
CWSS	Civil War Soldiers & Sailors System Records
DFC	Dear Family Collection
DPR	Department of the Platte, Records from the US Army Continental Commands
FCL	Fairfax County Library
FLNH	Fort Laramie National Historic Site
FRM	Nebraska State Historical Society Museum at Fort Robinson, NE
GPO	Government Printing or Publishing Office
LLPC	Lewis Leigh Private Collection
LS	Letters Sent
NAB	National Archives Building, Washington, DC
NACPR	National Archives, Central Plains Region
OIA	Office of Indian Affairs
PRA	Pine Ridge Agency
RG	Record Group
SDSH	South Dakota State Historical Society
SPL	Sidney Public Library
WHFC	Wrenn/Harrison/Fitzhugh/Cross Family Papers

Notes

Prologue

1. Richard Irving Dodge, *The Black Hills Journals of Colonel Richard Irving Dodge*, ed. Wayne R. Kime (Norman: University of Oklahoma Press, 1996), Diary entry, October 9, 1875.

Chapter 1

1. US Office of Indian Affairs (OIA), *Annual Report of the Commissioner of Indian Affairs* (CoIA) *for the Year 1845* (Washington: Government Printing Office [GPO], 1845), Statistical Appendix.

2. The seven Lakota Sioux tribes were the Oglala, Brulé, Hunkpapa, Miniconjou, Sans Arc, Blackfeet, and Two Kettle.

3. David C. Posthumus, "Transmitting Sacred Knowledge: Aspects of Historical and Contemporary Oglala Lakota Belief and Ritual" (PhD diss., Indiana University, 2015), 58, 71, 73.

4. Charles Wesley Allen, Red Cloud, and Sam Deon, *Autobiography of Red Cloud: War Leader of the Oglalas*, ed. Eli Paul (Montana Historical Society Press, 1997), 65.

5. Tom Drury and Tom Clancy, *The Heart of Everything That Is* (New York: Simon & Schuster Paperbacks, 2013), 109, 111; Allen and Deon, *The Autobiography of Red Cloud: War Leader of the Oglalas*, ed. R. Eli Paul (Helena: Montana Historical Society Press, 2020), 78–80.

6. Fort Kearny (1848), Fort Laramie (1849) along the Oregon Trail, and Fort Randall (1856) on the Missouri.

7. James C. Olson, *Red Cloud and the Sioux Problem* (Lincoln and London: University of Nebraska Press, 1965), 5.

8. The OIA, also known as the Bureau of Indian Affairs (BIA). Curtis Emanuel Jackson and Marcia J. Galli, *A History of the BIA and Its Activities Among the Indians* (San Francisco: R&E Research Associates, 1977), 43, 57.

9. Eric M. White, "Interior vs. War: The Development of the BIA and the Transfer Debates, 1849–1880" (Master's thesis, James Madison University, 2012), 1 et seq.

10. The 1851 Fort Laramie Treaty was also known as the 1851 Peace Treaty.

11. Olson, *Red Cloud*, 6–7.

CHAPTER 2

1. Dear Family Collection (DFC).

2. Ralph Beaver Strassburger, *Pennsylvania German Pioneers; A publication of the original list of arrivals in the Port of Philadelphia on 1727–1808*, I, ed. William John Hinke (Baltimore Genealogical Publishing Co., Inc., 1980), 339.

3. Farley Grubb, "Morbidity and Mortality on the North Atlantic Passage: Eighteenth Century German Immigration," *The Journal of Interdisciplinary History* (MIT Press) 17, no. 3 (Winter, 1987): 565–85.

4. Johannes Dear's will of 1881. "Germanna Colonies 1714–1717," RootsWeb, http://wc.rootsweb.ancestry.com/cgi-bin/igm.cgi?op=GET&db=germanna&id=160618.

5. In 1833 Little Washington became part of Rappahannock County.

6. DFC; 1840 Federal Census.

7. Now part of the Inn at Little Washington.

8. DFC; *Fauquier County, Virginia Marriage Bonds*, Book 5, 189.

9. DFC.

10. Fauquier County Records, 1848, Warrenton.

11. *Virginia Select Marriages 1785–1940, Fauquier County, Virginia Marriage Bonds*, Book 5, 189.

12. 1840, 1850, 1860 Federal Census; 1850 Fauquier Co. Slave Owners Census.

13. William C. Ray, *Mount Gilead, History & Heritage* (Grantville, PA: Wert Bookbinding, 2013), 69.

14. DFC.

15. *Alexandria Gazette*, August 29, 1862.

16. Ray, *Mount Gilead*, 34, 57.

17. Federal Census, 1830, 1840, 1850, and 1860.

18. Library of Virginia, Published Resources/Manuscript Collection: Secession, https://www.lva.virginia.gov/public/guides/civil-war/Secession.htm.

19. Ray, *Mount Gilead*, 69.

CHAPTER 3

1. Eppa Hunton, *Autobiography of Eppa Hunton* (Richmond, VA: The William Byrd Press Inc., 1933), 22–23.

2. John E. Divine, *8th Virginia Infantry* (Lynchburg, VA: H. E. Howard, Inc., 1983), 1.

3. Hunton, *Autobiography*, 32.

4. J. David Hacker, "A Census-Based Count of the Civil War Dead," *Civil War History* (Kent State University Press) 57, no. 4 (December 2011): 307.

5. Briscoe Goodhart, *History of the Independent Loudoun Rangers U.S. Vol. Cav. (Scouts), 1862–65* (Washington: McGill & Wallace, 1896), 23, 27.

6. Taylor M. Chamberlin and John M. Souders, *Between Reb and Yank, A Civil War History of Northern Loudoun County, Virginia* (Jefferson, NC and London: McFarland & Company, Inc., 2011), 117.

7. *Alexandria Gazette*, August 29, 1862.

8. Chamberlin and Souders, *Between Reb and Yank*, 164–65.

9. Hunton, *Autobiography*, 82–85.

Chapter 4

1. Hunton, *Autobiography*, 86; 1860 Federal Census.

2. J. Marshall Crawford, *Mosby and His Men: A Record of the Adventures of that Renowned Partisan Ranger, John S. Mosby* (New York: G. W. Carlton & Co., 1867), 96.

3. Order enclosed with letter to Captain John S. Mosby from W. H. Taylor, Assistant Adjutant General (AG), March 23, 1863.

4. *Hunton Autobiography*, 90–99. Permission to use text granted by William Byrd Press owned by Cadmus Communications since 1984.

5. James A. Ramage, *Gray Ghost: The Life and Times of Col. John Singleton Mosby* (Lexington: University Press of Kentucky, 2010), 96.

6. Company B was formed in October 1863; Company C, in December 1863; and Company D, in March 1864.

7. Hugh C. Keen and Horace Mewborn, *43rd Battalion Virginian Cavalry Mosby's Command* (Lynchburg, VA: H. E. Howard, Inc., 1993); Ramage, *Gray Ghost*, 96.

8. John S. Mosby, *The Memoirs of Colonel John S. Mosby*, ed. Charles Wells Russell (Boston: Little, Brown and Company, 1917), viii–ix.

9. Ramage, *Gray Ghost*, 98.

10. James J. Williamson, *Mosby's Rangers: A Record of the Operations of the Forty-third Battalion of Virginia Cavalry from its Organization to the Surrender* (New York: Ralph B. Kenyon, 1896), 368.

11. Crawford, *Mosby and His Men*, 192.

12. John W. Munson, *Reminiscences of a Mosby Guerilla* (New York: Moffat, Yard and Co., 1906), 31.

13. Ramage, *Gray Ghost*, 103; Munson, *Reminiscences*, 25.

14. John H. Alexander, *Mosby's Men* (New York: The Neale Publishing Company, 1907), 21.

15. Munson, *Reminiscences*, 23.

16. Crawford, *Mosby and His Men*, 144.

17. Ramage, *Gray Ghost*, 96.

18. Ramage, *Gray Ghost*, 248; Jeffrey D. Wert, *Mosby's Rangers* (New York: Simon & Schuster, 1990), 74.

19. *The Salina Journal*, January 23, 1879.

Chapter 5

1. Munson, *Reminiscences*, 102–09.

2. Williamson, *Mosby's Rangers*, 221.

3. Wert, *Mosby's Rangers*, 197.

4. Ramage, *Gray Ghost*, 193–94.

5. Mosby, *Memoirs*, 283–311.

6. *Richmond Times*, September 24, 1899.

7. Mosby, *Memoirs*, 312–26.

8. Mosby, *Memoirs*, 320.

9. *The War of the Rebellion: A Compilation of the Official Records of the Union and Confederate Armies*, 43, pt. 2, 910.

10. Mosby, *Memoirs*, 303; Munson, *Reminiscences*, 149–51.

11. Major Jordon D. Walzer, USMC, "Chasing the Gray Ghost: Blazer's Independent Union Scouts and the Shenandoah Valley Guerrilla War of 1864" (Master of Military Studies, United States Marine Corps Command and Staff College, 2008), 16.

12. Mark E. Neely Jr., *The Fate of Liberty: Abraham Lincoln and Civil Liberties* (New York: Oxford University Press, 1992), 133.

13. George Baylor, *Bull Run to Bull Run, or Four Years in the Army of Northern Virginia* (Richmond: B. F. Johnson Publishing Co., 1900), 294–95; Mosby, *Memoirs*, 333.

14. Eugene M. Scheel, *Loudon Discovered: Communities, Corners & Crossroads* (Leesburg, VA: The Friends of the Thomas Balch Library, 2002), 177.

15. Chamberlin and Souders, *Between Reb and Yank*, 301. Public Domain, Papers of the Janney and Related Gilmour and Pollock Families, Accession #8409-a,-b,-c, Special Collections Dept., University of Virginia Library, Charlottesville, VA.

16. *The Years of Anguish: Fauquier County, Virginia 1861–1865*, compilers Emily G. Ramey and John K. Gott (Westminster, MD: Heritage Books, 2008), 129.

Chapter 6

1. Baylor, *Bull Run to Bull Run*, 320.

2. Munson, *Reminiscences*, 27.

3. Williamson, *Mosby's Rangers*, 84, 369–70.

4. Baylor, *Bull Run to Bull Run*, 303.

5. Tom King gave the name of his previous regiment, the 7th Virginia Cavalry, when captured to avoid being identified as a Mosby Ranger.

6. Don Hakenson, *Reminiscences of Frank H. Rahm of Mosby's Command* (Alexandria, VA: Donald C. Hakenson, 2008); Mosby, *Memoirs*, 318–19.

7. *Charleston Mercury*, March 2, 1864; Baylor, *Bull Run to Bull Run*, 92; *The Daily Dispatch*, Richmond, September 29, 1864.

8. *The Wheeling Daily Register*, April 22, 1865.

9. Baylor, *Bull Run to Bull Run*, 315.

10. Williamson, *Mosby's Rangers*, 369–70.

11. John Stewart Bryan, *Joseph Bryan: His Times, His Family, His Friends* (Richmond: privately printed by Whittet and Shepperson, 1935), 148.

12. Salem, today known as Marshall, is in Fauquier County.

13. Wert, *Mosby's Rangers*, 284.

14. "Mosby to His Troops, Fauquier, April 21, 1865," J. S. Mosby, Colonel Commanding Battalion, *The New York Times*, May 5, 1865, 1.

15. Keen and Mewborn, *43rd Battalion Virginia Cavalry*, 274–75.

16. Robert E. Denney, "Deaths in Northern Prisons," *Civil War Prisons and Escapes: A Day by Day Chronicle* (New York: Sterling Publishing Co.: 1993), 381.

17. Civil War Soldiers & Sailors System Records (CWSS), National Archives, Washington, D.C. (NAB).

18. JW's signed parole. CWSS, NAB.

CHAPTER 7

1. Thomas L. Livermore, *Number & Losses in the Civil War in America: 1861–65* (Boston and New York: Houghton, Mifflin & Co., 1901).

2. Hunton, *Autobiography*, 144.

3. Ramage, *Gray Ghost*, 106–07.

4. *The Daily Dispatch* (Alexandria), May 31, 1861.

5. Kathi Ann Brown, Walter Nicklin, and John T. Toler, *250 Years in Fauquier County: A Virginia Story* (Fairfax: George Mason University Press, 2008).

6. *Alexandria Gazette*, October 21, 1865.

7. The *Virginia Sentinel* masthead stated: "Published by CANNON & DEAR. OFFICE—One door from Warren Green Hotel."

8. Ramage, *Gray Ghost*, 276; and Hunton, *Autobiography*, 144.

9. "Soil Survey: Fauquier County Virginia," United States Department of Agriculture, Series 1944, no. 7 (August 1956): 14.

10. Clay Dear obituary. *Washington Post*, September 3, 1905; JW was in contact with Mosby until he became US consul to Hong Kong in 1878. Mosby to Stephens & Wilcox, July 29, 1878; Red Cloud Agency (RCA), 1871–1883; (M234, roll 7231); NAB.

11. John T. Toler, Cheryl H. Shepherd, and Ann C. Power, *Warrenton, Virginia: A Unique History of 200 Years, 1810 to 2010* (Warrenton: The Partnership for Warrenton Foundation, 2010), 36.

12. James M. McPherson, *Battle Cry of Freedom: The Civil War Era* (New York: Oxford University Press, 1988), 710.

13. Eugene M. Scheel, "The Reconstruction Years: Tales of Leesburg and Warrenton, Virginia," *The History of Loudoun County, Virginia*, https://www.loudounhistory.org/history/loudoun-cw-reconstruction-towns/.

14. *The True Index* (Warrenton), February 27, 1866.

15. *Alexandria Gazette*, October 31, 1865.

16. J. W. Dear to Annie Cross (Dear to Cross); Wrenn/Harrison/Fitzhugh/Cross Family Papers (WHFC); Record Group (RG) 07–05; The Virginia Room, Fairfax County Library (FCL).

17. *Loudoun Mirror*, June 13, 1867.

18. *Alexandria Gazette*, June 14, 1870.

19. WHFC; RG 07–05; Virginia Room, FCL.

20. Dear to Cross, March 9, 1868; WHFC; RG 07–05; The Virginia Room, FCL.

CHAPTER 8

1. Dee Brown, *Bury My Heart at Wounded Knee: An Indian History of the American West* (London: Macmillan, 2001), 86–87.

2. Stan Hoig, *The Sand Creek Massacre* (Norman: University of Oklahoma Press, 2005), 153.

3. Peter Cozzens, *The Earth Is Weeping: The Epic Story of the Indian Wars for the American West* (London: Atlantic Books, 2017), 33.

4. John D. McDermott, *Red Cloud: Oglala Legend* (Pierre: South Dakota Historical Society Press, 2015), 35.

5. Shannon Smith Calitri, "Give Me Eighty Men: Shattering the Myth of the Fetterman Massacre," *Montana: The Magazine of Western History* 54, no. 3 (Autumn 2004), 46.

6. Cozzens, *The Earth Is Weeping*, 40.

7. General Ulysses S. Grant to General William Tecumseh Sherman, March 2, 1868; Letters Sent (LS), Commanding General; RG 108; NAB.

8. Olson, *Red Cloud*, 74–75.

9. Lloyd E. McCann, "The Grattan Massacre," *Nebraska History* 37 (March 1956): 1–25; and Richard A. Serrano, *Summoned at Midnight: A Story of Race and the Last Military Executions at Fort Leavenworth* (Boston: Beacon Press, 2019), 42.

10. Article XI, Fort Laramie Treaty, 1868.

11. Robert M. Utley, *Frontier Regular: The United States Army and the Indian, 1866–1891* (Lincoln: University of Nebraska Press, 1984), 137.

CHAPTER 9

1. James Woodruff Savage and John Thomas Bell, *History of the City of Omaha* (Omaha: Munsell, 1894), 50–60.

2. Ryan Michael Collins, *Irish Gandy Dancer: A Tale of Building the Transcontinental Railroad* (Seattle: Create Space Independent Publishing Platform, 2010), 198.

3. The Right Reverend E. S. Tuttle, *Reminiscences of a Missionary Bishop: Missionary to the Mountain West, 1866–1886* (New York: Thomas Whittaker, 1906), 63.

4. *Collins' Omaha City Directory*, compiler Charles Collins (Omaha: Omaha Daily Herald Book and Job Office, 1868), 7–10.

5. David L. Bristow, *A Dirty, Wicked Town, Tales of 19th Century Omaha* (Caldwell, ID: Caxton Press, 2009), 91.

6. Collins, *Omaha City Directory*, July 1869, 87.

7. Savage and Bell, *History of Omaha*, 122–23.

8. Dee Brown, *Hear That Lonesome Whistle Blow: Railroads of the West* (New York: Holt, Rinehart & Winston, 1977).

9. Margaret I. Carrington, *Absaraka, Home of the Crows* (Chicago: Lakeside Press, 1950), 85–86.

10. DFC.

11. Walter H. Rowley, "Omaha's First Century—Installment IV," http://www.historicomaha.com/ofcchap4.htm.

12. Paul F. Sharp, *Whoop-up Country: The Canadian-American West, 1865–1885* (Minneapolis: University of Minnesota Press, 1955), 33–45.

13. Charles Larpenteur, *Forty Years a Fur Trader on the Upper Missouri: The Personal Narrative of Charles Larpenteur, 1833–1872*, ed. Elliot Coues (Minneapolis: Ross & Haines Inc., 1962), 391–92.

CHAPTER 10

1. Larpenteur, *Forty Years*, 1.

2. Barton H. Barbour, *Fort Union and the Upper Missouri Fur Trade* (Norman: University of Oklahoma Press, 1951), 5–9.

3. "John Jacob Astor," Encyclopædia Britannica, Ninth Edition, 737, https://en.wikisource.org/wiki/Encyclop%C3%A6dia_Britannica,_Ninth_Edition/John_Jacob_Astor.

4. Kathy Weiser-Alexander, "Pierre Chouteau, Jr.—Merchant & Fur Trader," Legends of America, https://www.legendsofamerica.com/pierre-chouteau-jr/.

5. Larpenteur, *Forty Years*, 2, 355.

6. Barbour, *Fort Union*, 16.

7. Larpenteur, *Forty Years*, 2, 360, 366.

8. Sharp, *Whoop-up Country*, 35–45.

9. Larpenteur, *Forty Years*, 2, 91–92.

CHAPTER 11

1. Kathy Weiser-Alexander, "Montana Forts of the Old West," Legends of America, https://www.legendsofamerica.com/mt-forts/.

2. 1870 Federal Census.

3. Joe De Barthe, *The Life and Adventures of Frank Grouard: Chief of Scouts, U.S.A.* (St. Joseph, MO: Combe Printing Company, 1894), 31–177.

4. Steamers *Key West* and *Chippewa* successfully completed the journey and arrived at Fort Benton on July 2, 1860. Clinton Lawson, Research Specialist, State Historical Society, University of Missouri.

5. James Willard Schultz, *My Life as an Indian* (New York: Dover Publications, 1997), 3–5.

6. Sharp, *Whoop-up Country*, 5–6. Permission to use text granted by University of Minnesota Press.

7. Interview with E. H. Durfee of Durfee & Peck. *Leavenworth Daily Conservative*, May 8, 1868.

8. Larpenteur, *Forty Years*, 392.

CHAPTER 12

1. Olson, *Red Cloud*, 86.

2. Auger to Sherman, February 25, 1869, Auger to AG, US Army, March 13, 1860, MARS, RG 98, LS, Department of the Platte (DPR).

3. Jefferson Glass, *Reshaw: The Life and Times of John Baptiste Richard* (Glendo, WY: High Plains Press, 2014), 93.

4. Susan Bordeaux Bettelyoun and Josephine Waggoner, *With My Own Eyes: A Lakota Woman Tells Her People's History*, ed. Emily Levine (Lincoln: University of Nebraska Press, 1999), 41–42.

5. Eli S. Ricker, *Voices of the American West Vol. 2: The Indian Interviews of Eli S. Ricker, 1903–1919* (Lincoln and London: University of Nebraska Press, 2005), 41.

6. Manifest Destiny: A phrase coined in 1845 for the belief that white Americans were superior to other races, that their institutions had special virtues, and that they were destined by God to expand their country's territory for the benefit of all.

7. Kerry R. Oman, "The Beginning of the End: The Indian Peace Commission of 1867–68," *Great Plains Quarterly* 2, no. 1 (Winter 2002), University of Nebraska Press, 38.

8. The Papers of Ulysses S. Grant, ed. John Y. Simon (Carbondale: Southern Illinois University Press, 1994), 18–44.

9. Robert H. Keller Jr., "Episcopal Reformers and Affairs at Red Cloud Agency, 1870–1876," *Nebraska History* 68 (1987): 118.

10. Olson, *Red Cloud*, 92.

11. Chambers to Acting AG, DPR, April 28, 1870.

12. Parker to John A. Burbank, Yankton, South Dakota, May 3, 1870; LS, CoIA; RG75; NAB.

13. Telegram, Chambers to Acting AG, DPR, May 16, 1870; LR, Dept. of the Platte; RG98; NAB.

14. Telegram, Smith to E. S. Parker, May 19, 1870; LR, Upper Platte Agency; RG 75; NAB.

15. *New York Times*, June 1 and 2, 1870.

16. Olson, *Red Cloud*, 101–03.

17. *New York Times*, June 7, 1870.

18. *New York Times*, June 8, 9, 15, 1870.

19. James T. Savage and John T. Bell, *History of City of Omaha, Nebraska* (New York & Chicago: Munsell & Co, 1894), 461.

CHAPTER 13

1. Debbie Robison, "Royal Oaks Chain of Key Events," *Fairfax News*, September 19, 1873, 3; Fairfax Deed Book, 4 (100): 170.

2. Cheryl Repetti, "Celebrating Our Heritage, Royal Oaks: 'The Capitol of All This Country,'" Centreville Community Network, www.centrevilleva.org.

3. *Alexandria Gazette*, June 9, 1870 (Chancery File Folder 1858–007).

4. William Page Johnson II, *Brothers and Cousins: Confederate Soldiers & Sailors in Fairfax County, Virginia* (Athens, GA: Iberian Publishing Company, 1995).

5. Robison, Northern Virginia History Organization, Court Record, July 1, 1870, 487–88.

6. JW to James Cross (Dear to J. Cross), Omaha, November 7, 1870, Lewis Leigh Private Collection (LLPC).

7. DFC.

8. Dear to J. Cross, November 7, 1870, LLPC.

9. *Omaha City Directory*, 1872–1876.

10. *Omaha City Directory*, 1870, 1872–1873.

11. Dear to J. Cross, November 7, 1870, LLPC.

12. Savage and Bell, *History of the City of Omaha*, 461.

13. Dear to J. Cross, February 15, 1872, LLPC.

14. Dear to J. Cross, February 15, 1872, LLPC.

15. David Michael Delo, *Peddlers & Post Traders: The Army Sutler on the Frontier* (Helena, MT: Kingfisher Books, 1998), 174–75.

16. Larpenteur, *Forty Years*, 394.

17. "Sinking of the Ida Rees in the Missouri River," *Sacramento Daily Union*, July 4, 1871, 41, no. 7220, 1.

18. Dear to J. Cross, February 15, 1872, LLPC.

CHAPTER 14

1. Brian Jones, "Those Wild Reshaw Boys," in *Sidelights of the Sioux Wars*, ed. Francis B. Taunton (London: English Westerners' Society, Special Publication no. 2, 1967), 24.

2. Catherine Price, *The Oglala People, 1841–1879: A Political History* (Lincoln and London: University of Nebraska Press, 1996), 92–95; Olson, *Red Cloud*, 118–19; McDermott, *Red Cloud*, 58–59.

3. Olson, *Red Cloud*, 132; Price, *Oglala People*, 98.

4. Dear to J. Cross, February 15, 1872, LLPC.

5. "Fort Fetterman," Wyoming Tales and Trails, http://www.wyomingtalesandtrails .com/fetterman.html.

6. George Rex Buckman, "Ranches and Rancheros of the Far West," *Lippincott's Magazine*, May 1882, from Wyoming Tales and Trails, http://www.wyomingtalesandtrails .com/fetterman.html.

7. Greg Pierce, "Negotiating the West: A History of Wyoming Trading Posts," prepared for the Wyoming State Historic Preservation Office, Planning and Historic Context Development Program, Wyoming State Parks & Cultural Resources, 45–46, https:// wyoarchaeo.wyo.gov/DocsPDFs/Publications/Negotiating%20the%20West_Pierce.pdf.

8. McDermott, *Red Cloud*, 52.

9. Laura Winthrop Johnson, *Eight Hundred Miles in an Ambulance* (Philadelphia: J. B. Lippincott Company, 1889), 74–75.

10. Dear to J. Cross, February 15, 1872, LLPC.

11. Paul L. Hedren, *Fort Laramie in 1876: Chronicle of a Frontier Post at War* (Lincoln: University of Nebraska Press, 1988), 54, 123.

12. Mark E. Miller, *Military Sites in Wyoming, 1700–1920: Historic Context* (Laramie, WY: Wyoming Dept. of State Parks and Cultural Resources, 2012), 52.

13. Merrill J. Mattes, "Guardian of the Oregon Trail," *Annals of Wyoming* 17, no. 1 (January 1945).

14. *The Diaries of John Gregory Bourke*, 2, ed. Charles M. Robinson III (Denton: University of North Texas Press, 2005), 249.

15. Telegram, Joseph W. Wham Indian Agent, Fort Laramie, to Ely S. Parker, CoIA, July 2, 1871; Letters Received (LR), RCA; RG75; NAB.

16. Telegram, Parker, Long Branch, N.J., to Acting Commissioner H. R. Clum, July 7, 1871; LR, RCA; RG 75; NAB.

CHAPTER 15

1. Governor J. A. Campbell to Acting Commissioner H. R. Clum, Washington, DC, Sept. 2, 1871, LR by OIA, 1824–1881; Fort Laramie National Historic Site, WY (FLNH).

2. Trader Licenses 1865–1898, 2; Records of the Miscellaneous Division, Records of the BIA, RG 75; NAB.

3. Dear to J. Cross, February 15, 1872, LLPC.

4. Eric H. Reid, letter to Nebraska Historical Society, pub. Addison E. Sheldon, "The Red Cloud Agency Buildings," *Nebraska History and Record of Pioneer Days* I, no. 8 (December 1918): 4.

5. *The Settler and Soldier Interviews of Eli S. Ricker, 1903–1919: Voices of the American West*, 2, ed. Richard E. Jensen (Lincoln and London: University of Nebraska Press, 2005), 215.

6. "Report of Employees in Red Cloud Agency W. T.," November 10, 1871; LR; RG 75; FLNH.

7. 1870 Federal Census, FLNH.

8. Thomas R. Buecker, "Red Cloud Agency Traders, 1873–1877," *The Museum of the Fur Trade Quarterly* 30, no. 3 (Fall 1994).

9. "Sawyer's and Garnett's of Dixon, California: Information about William 'Billie' Garnett," Genealogy.com, https://www.genealogy.com/ftm/s/a/w/James-N-Sawyer/WEBSITE-0001/UHP-0198.html.

10. *The Saline County Journal* (Salina, Kansas), January 23, 1879, 1, https://www.loc.gov/resource/sn84027670/1879-01-23/ed-1/?sp=1&r=0.239,0.438,0.359,0.3,0.

11. Secretary of Interior Columbus Delano to Acting CoIA H. R. Clum, Washington, DC, October 31, 1871; LR by OIA 1824–81; FLNH.

12. Keller Jr., "Episcopal Reformers," 116–26.

13. Jones, "Those Wild Reshaw Boys," 25.

14. Dear to J. Cross, February 15, 1872, LLPC.

15. Registrar, Virginia Polytechnic Institute, to Dear family, March 27, 1952, confirming Richard Dear's attendance in 1872–1873, DFC.

16. *The Bugle's Echo: A Chronology of Cadet Life at the Military College at Blacksburg, Virginia*, The Virginia Agricultural & Mechanical College & The Virginia Polytechnical Institute, 1 (1872–1900).

17. McDermott, *Red Cloud*, 60.

18. Keller, "Episcopal Reformers."

19. *Cheyenne Daily Leader*, March 19, 1872, 1; Chronicling America: Historic American Newspaper, Library of Congress (CA), https://chroniclingamerica.loc.gov/lccn/sn84022149/1872-03-19/ed-1/seq-1/.

20. McDermott, *Red Cloud*, 63; Robert M. Utley, *The Indian Frontier of the American West, 1846–1890*, rev. ed. (Albuquerque: University of New Mexico Press, 2003), 123.

21. *The Cheyenne Daily Leader*, May 18, 1872 (Cheyenne, WY), CA, https://chroniclingamerica.loc.gov/lccn/sn84022149/1872-05-18/ed-1/seq-1/.

22. *New York Times*, May 20, 1872.

23. Jones, "Those Wild Reshaw Boys," 25.

24. Olson, *Red Cloud*, 152, 154.

25. DFC.

26. DFC.

27. Telegram, Daniels to Commissioner Walker, September 22, 1872; LR, RCA; RG 75; NAB.

28. Olson, *Red Cloud*, 154.

29. DFC.

30. Daniels to Walker, October 25, 1872; LR, RCA; RG 75; NAB; Telegram, Smith to Acting AG, DPR, October 23, 1872; LR, DPR; RG 98; NAB.

31. J. W. Vaughn, "Captain James Egan," *The Westerners Brand Book* 13, no. 1 (New York: Posse, 1966).

32. McDermott, *Red Cloud*, 62.

33. Telegram, Daniels to E. P. Smith, August 2, 1873; Olson, *Red Cloud*, 158.

34. Invitation to James Cross from Richard Dear, July 1873; RG 07–05; FCL.

Chapter 16

1. Kerry R. Oman, "The Beginning of the End," 38; Thomas R. Buecker, *Fort Robinson and the American West, 1874–1899* (Norman: April 28, 2003), 4.

2. Saville's Annual Report (Saville's Report), August 31, 1874, U.S., OIA, *Annual Report of the CoIA to the Secretary of the Interior for the Year 1874* (Washington: GPO, 1874), 251–52.

3. Keller, "Episcopal Reformers," 121.

4. U.S., OIA, *Annual Report of the CoIA to the Secretary of the Interior for the Year 1873* (Washington: GPO, 1874), 243–44.

5. Saville's Report, 1874, 252.

6. Saville to E. P. Smith, August 22, 1873; LR, RCA; RG 75; NAB.

7. Saville's Report, 1874, 252.

8. Olson, *Red Cloud*, 160.

9. Register of Trader Licenses 1847–1873; Records of the BIA; RG 75; NAB.

10. Saville's Report, 1874, 252.

11. Buecker, *Fort Robinson*, 5.

12. "Inventory of Merchandise on Hand by J. W. Dear, RCA, December 20, 1873"; RG 75; Thomas R. Buecker files, accessed June 2010 Fort Robinson Museum (FRM).

13. Oliver Nixon Unthank, telegraph operator at Fort Laramie, to his wife (Unthank to wife), December 5, 1873, Oliver Unthank Correspondence, UON-2, FLNH.

14. Saville to E. P. Smith, December 11 and 29, 1873; LR, RCA; Records of the BIA; RG 75; NAB.

15. Olson, *Red Cloud*, 163.

16. Frank Appleton to his parents, January 7, 1874, Appleton Family, RG 0860.AM-RG 0860, Nebraska State Historical Society (NSHS).

17. Olson, *Red Cloud*, 163–64.

18. Delano to Smith, March 7, 1874, LR, RG 393, DPR.

19. JW to Oliver Unthank, February 2, 1874, (Dear to Unthank), JW Dear Correspondence, FLNH.

20. *Omaha Weekly Bee*, February 25, 1874; *Sioux City Journal*, March 6, 1874.

21. Saville's Report, 1874, 252. The Miniconjou, one of the seven Lakota Sioux tribes, did not sign the Fort Laramie Treaty.

22. Telegram, John E. Smith, February 11, 1874; Buecker, *Fort Robinson*, 8.

23. George E. Hyde, *Red Cloud's Folks: A History of the Oglala Sioux Indians* (Norman: University of Oklahoma Press, 1975), 212–13.

24. Dear to Unthank, February 16, 1874, J.W. Dear Correspondence, FLNH.

25. Unthank to wife, February 13, 1874, Unthank Correspondence, FLNH.

26. Dear to Unthank, February 16, 1874, FLNH.

27. Dear to Colonel J. E. Smith, February 19, 1874, LR by the Office of the AG1871–1880, RG 94, NSHS.

28. Dear to Unthank, February 23, 1874, J.W. Dear Correspondence, FLNH.

29. Buecker, *Fort Robinson*, 14; Vaughn, "Captain James Egan."

30. Roger T. Grange Jr., "Fort Robinson, Outpost on the Plains," *Nebraska History* 39, no. 3, September 1958, 200.

31. U.S., OIA, "Report of the Sioux Commission," *Annual Report of the CoIA, 1874* (Washington: GPO, 1874), 87–97. The Board of Indian Commissioners (BIC) was established as part of Grant's peace policy to supervise agencies.

32. *The Diaries of John Gregory Bourke*, ed. Charles M. Robinson III (Denton, Texas: University of North Texas Press, 2003), 63; Buecker, *Fort Robinson*, 27–42.

33. Ramon Powers and James N. Leiker, "Cholera Amongst the Plains Indians, Causes, Consequences," *Western Historical Quarterly* 29, no. 3 (Autumn 1998): 324–26.

34. Dear to Unthank, November 21, 1874, J. W. Dear Correspondence, FLNH.

35. Ray to Perry, April 27, 1874, LR DPR; Perry to Acting AG, June 16, 1874, LR DP; *Omaha Daily Bee*, June 20, 1874, 4, http://chroniclingamerica.loc.gov/sn99021999/1874-06-20/ed-1/seq-4/.

Chapter 17

1. James B. Cross, Council Bluffs, Iowa, to his sister Lizzie, May 3, 1874; RG 07–05; FCL.

2. *Omaha Daily Bee*, September 13, 1875.

3. Johnson, *Eight Hundred Miles*, 73–76.

4. Claudine Chalmers, "A Year Recording Native American Life in 1874: Jules Tavernier's Artistic Journey," *Incollect, Antiques & Fine Art* (Summer/Autumn 2007).

5. Chalmers, "A Year Recording."

6. Major General William Harding Carter, US Army (Retired), *Sketch of Fort Robinson, Nebraska* (USA: Carter, 1923), 15; Wyoming State Historical Department.

7. Ella Cara Deloria, *Speaking of Indians* (Auckland: Pickle Partners Publishing, 2015), 57–60.

8. Carter, *Sketch of Fort Robinson*, 16.

9. De Barthe, *Grouard*, 77, 172.

10. DFC.

11. Trader Licenses 1865–1898.

Chapter 18

1. Cozzens, *The Earth Is Weeping*, 210–11.

2. Donald Jackson, *Custer's Gold* (Lincoln: University of Nebraska Press, 1966), 28.

3. Jackson, *Custer's Gold*, 26–28; "The Opening of the Black Hills," *Nebraska History* 60 (1979): 524–27.

4. Buecker, *Fort Robinson*, 36–42.

5. Amos Appleton to wife, October 26, 1874; Appleton Family Collection; NSHS.

6. Emmet Crawford's testimony, *Report of the Special Commission Appointed to Investigate the Affairs of the Red Cloud Indian Agency, July 1875* (Washington: GPO, 1875).

7. Major Thaddeus Harlan Stanton, Army Paymaster, to Professor Othniel Charles Marsh, Professor of Paleontology at Yale College, October 1, 1874; Public Domain, Othniel Charles Marsh Papers, Archives of the Peabody Museum, Yale University (YPMNH). O. C. Marsh Correspondence; file 1303; Yale Peabody Museum of Natural History (YPMNH).

8. William Cornelius Wyckoff, "Travels and Adventures in the Indian Country. A Perilous Fossil Hunt," *The Indian Miscellany: Papers on the History, Antiquities, Arts, Languages, Religions, Traditions and Superstitions of the American Aborigines; with Descriptions of their Domestic Life, Manners, Customs, Traits, Amusements and Exploits; Travels and Adventures in the Indian Country; Incidents to Border Warfare; Missionary Relations, etc.*, ed. William Wallace Beach (Albany: Joel Munsell, 1877), 260–66.

9. Olson, *Red Cloud*, 179, footnote 42.

10. Brontotheres collected by JW Dear; catalog no. YPM VP 04271; YPMNH.

11. Minutes of the BIC, April 29, 1875; Records of the BIC, 1869–1933; RG 75.22; NAB.

12. Olson, *Red Cloud*, 179.

13. Marsh to President Grant, July 10, 1875; *Report of the Special Commission*, 1–21.

14. Dear to Unthank, November 21, 1874; FLNH; poem by Henry Wadsworth Longfellow.

15. Harold E. Briggs, "The Black Hills Gold Rush," *North Dakota Historical Quarterly* V (January 1931): 71–99.

CHAPTER 19

1. *Cheyenne Daily Leader*, February 20, 1875, CA.

2. DFC.

3. *Cheyenne Daily News*, January 21, 1875, CA.

4. *Cheyenne Daily News*, March 1, 1875.

5. *Omaha Daily Bee*, March 3, 1875; Watson Parker, *Gold in the Black Hills* (Pierre: South Dakota State Historical Society [SDSH], 1966), 30–36.

6. *Alexandria Gazette*, May 3, 1875, *Virginia Chronicle*, vol. 76, no. 105, Library of Virginia.

7. Trader Licenses, 1865–1898; 2; NAB.

8. *Cheyenne Daily Leader*, April 7, 1875.

9. Olson, *Red Cloud*, 191.

10. George Crook, *General Crook: His Autobiography*, ed. Martin F. Schmitt (Norman: University of Oklahoma Press, 1986), 188–90.

11. *Indian Affairs: Laws and Treaties*, Vol. II (Treaties), comp. ed. Charles Joseph Kapler (Washington: GPO, 1904), 1002.

12. Andrew C. Isenberg, *The Destruction of the Bison: An Environmental History, 1750–1920* (Cambridge: Cambridge University Press, 2020).

13. Congress Bill HR 921 passed in 1874 made the hunting of buffalo by whites illegal.

14. S. C. Gwynne, *Empire of the Summer Moon: Quanah Parker and the Rise and Fall of the Comanches, the Most Powerful Indian Tribe in American History* (New York: Scribner, 2010), 262; Philip H. Sheridan, *Personal Memoirs of P. H. Sheridan*, Vol. II, chapter XII.

15. John Stephens Gray, *Centennial Campaign: The Sioux War of 1876* (Norman: University of Oklahoma Press, 1976), 17.

16. Agnes Wright Spring, *The Cheyenne and Black Hills Stage and Express Routes* (Glendale: Arthur H. Clark Company, 1949), 59.

17. *Cheyenne Daily Leader*, April 3, 1875.

18. Spring, *Stage and Express Routes*, 61.

19. Parker, *Gold in the Black Hills*, 63; Lesta V. Turchen and James D. McLaird, *The Black Hills Expedition* (Mitchell: Dakota Wesleyan University Press, 1975), 9–26.

20. Candy Moulton, *Valentine T. McGillycuddy: Army Surgeon, Agent to the Sioux* (Norman: Arthur H. Clark Company, 2011), 43–45.

21. Olson, *Red Cloud*, 180–89.

22. *Cheyenne Daily Leader*, June 28, 1875.

23. Olson, *Red Cloud*, 185–86; *New York Times*, June 2, 1875.

24. *The Commonwealth*, Washington, May 25, 1875.

25. Spring, *Stage and Express Routes*, 65.

26. *From Our Special Correspondent: Dispatches from the 1875 Black Hills Council at Red Cloud Agency, Nebraska*, ed. James E. Potter (Lincoln: NSHS Books, 2016), 14.

27. *Omaha Daily Bee*, September 13, 1875; Potter, *From Our Special Correspondent*, 120.

28. Homer Stull, Spotted Tail Agency to Editor of *Omaha Daily Herald*, July 6, 1875; Potter, *From Our Special Correspondent*, 36–37.

29. De Barthe, *Grouard*, 173–75.

30. Potter, *From Our Special Correspondent*, 14.

Chapter 20

1. *Report of the Special Commission Appointed to Investigate the Affairs of the Red Cloud Indian Agency, July 1875; Together with the Testimony and Accompanying Documents* (Washington: GPO, 1875).

2. JW Dear's testimony, *Special Commission*, 288.

3. Jules Ecoffey's testimony, *Special Commission*, 213.

4. Dr. J. Saville's testimony, *Special Commission*, 380, 385, 433.

5. Testimonies of Bosler brothers, *Special Commission*, 485.

6. Albert Swalm, RCA, September 14, 1875; *Fort Dodge Messenger*, September 30, 1875; Potter, *From Our Special Correspondent*.

7. Louis Richard's testimony, *Special Commission*, 464.

8. Bishop William Hare's testimony, *Special Commission*, 603.

9. Olson, *Red Cloud*, 204.

10. Little White Clay Creek, Nebraska, was a tributary of the White River, sixty miles upstream from Big White Clay Creek in Dakota Territory.

11. Collins, "Letter from RCA," September 15, 1875, *Omaha Daily Bee*, September 20, 1875; Potter, *From Our Special Correspondent*, 177, 186.

12. Article probably written by JW under the byline "D," September 17, 1875, "Special to the Leader: Red Cloud Agency," *Cheyenne Daily Leader*, September 22, 1875; Potter, *From Our Special Correspondent*, 109.

13. John T. Bell, "Letter from RCA, September 15, 1875," *Omaha Daily Herald*, September 23, 1875, FRM; Potter, *From Our Special Correspondent*, 175.

14. Charles Collins, "Letter from RCA," September 7, 1875, *Omaha Daily Bee*, September 13, 1875, FRM.

15. Charles Collins, "Letter from RCA," *Omaha Daily Bee*, FRM; Potter, *From Our Special Correspondent*, 177.

16. Reuben Davenport, September 15, 1875, *New York Herald*, September 27, 1875; Potter, *From Our Daily Correspondent*, 179–86.

17. *Omaha Daily Herald*, September 28, 1875; Potter, *From Our Special Correspondent*, 226.

18. *Cheyenne Daily Leader*, September 29, 1875, probably written by JW under the byline "D"; Potter, *From Our Special Correspondent*, 246.

19. *Chicago Daily Tribune*, October 1, 1875; Potter, *From Our Special Correspondent*, 243–46.

20. *Omaha Daily Bee*, October 5, 1875; Potter, *From Our Special Correspondent*, 262–63.

21. Olson, *Red Cloud*, 208–12; Hyde, *Red Cloud's Folk*, 244–46; McDermott, *Red Cloud*, 78.

22. *Chicago Daily Tribune*, October 16, 1875; Potter, *From Our Special Correspondent*, 289.

23. Olson, *Red Cloud*, 216, footnote 9; McDermott, *Red Cloud*, 81.

24. De Barthe, *Grouard*, 175–76.

25. Hedren, *Fort Laramie*, 18.

26. Robert W. Larson, *Red Cloud: Warrior-Statesman of the Lakota Sioux* (Norman: University of Oklahoma Press, 1997), 198.

Chapter 21

1. *The Sidney Telegraph*, February 12, 1876.

2. Paul L. Hedren, *Ho! For the Black Hills* (Pierre: SDSH Press, 2012), 60–61; *The Sidney Telegraph*, March 4, 1876.

3. Spring, *Stage and Express Routes*, 81; *The Sidney Telegraph*, February 19, 1876.

4. *The Sidney Telegraph*, January 22, 1876.

5. Norbert R. Mahnken, "The Sidney-Black Hills Trail," *Nebraska History* 30 (1949): 210.

6. *The Sidney Telegraph*, February 26, 1876.

7. Hank Clifford to Professor Marsh, May 2, 1876; OC Marsh Correspondence; Box 7, Folder 262; YPMNH.

8. Snake River Ranch was also known as Snake Creek Ranch.

9. *Cheyenne Daily Leader*, February 15, 1876.

10. *The Sidney Telegraph*, February 19, 1876.

11. *The Sidney Telegraph*, April 22, 1876.

12. *The Sidney Telegraph*, June 4, September 9, 1876.

13. Mahnken, "The Sidney-Black Hills Trail," 215–25.

14. Spring, *Stage and Express Routes*, 80.

15. *Cheyenne Daily Leader*, January 21, 1876, CA.

16. *Wyoming Weekly Leader*, January 22, 1876.

17. Spring, *Stage and Express Routes*, 80.

18. Hedren, *Fort Laramie*, 51.

19. *Cheyenne Daily Leader*, January 21, 1876, CA.

20. Spring, *Stage and Express Routes*, 84–85.

21. *Omaha Daily Bee*, April 1, 1876.

22. Spring, *Stage and Express Routes*, 135–40.

23. De Barthe, *Grouard*, 61.

24. Robert K. DeArment, *Assault on the Deadwood Stage: Road Agents and Shotgun Messengers* (Norman: University of Oklahoma Press, May 2011), 44.

25. William F. Cody and William Lightfoot Visscher, *Life and Adventures of "Buffalo Bill,"* Colonel William F. Cody (Chicago: Stanton and Van Vliet Co, c1917), Chapter XIII.

26. Spring, *Stage and Express Routes*, 134–35.

27. Luke Vorhees, "Personal Recollections of Pioneer Life on the Mountains and Plains of the Great West" (1920); Transcript of Luke Voorhees's talk, undated; Untitled Manuscript file; Wyoming State Archives, Cheyenne, WY.

28. Spring, *Stage and Express Routes*, 135.

29. Paul L. Hedren, "Chamber of Horrors: 'Persimmon Bill' Chambers," *Wild West* (April 2014).

30. *Cheyenne Daily Leader*, May 24, 1876, 4.

31. *Omaha Republican*, May 24, 1876.

32. *Cheyenne Daily Leader*, May 28, 1876.

33. *The Sidney Telegraph*, May 27, 1876, Sidney Public Library.

34. Camp Robinson to Quartermaster, July 1, 1876; DP, RCA; LR by OIA; (roll 720); NAB; *Laramie Daily Sentinel*, June 1, 1876.

35. Buecker, *Fort Robinson*, 80.

36. *Omaha Daily Bee*, February 7, 1909.

37. *Cheyenne Daily Leader*, February 3, 13, and March 9–10, 1876; *The Sidney Telegraph*, February 19, September 9 and 16, 1876; *Cheyenne Daily Leader*, April 10, 1877.

38. *The Sidney Telegraph*, September 2, 1876.

CHAPTER 22

1. Buecker, *Fort Robinson*, 79.

2. Olson, *Red Cloud*, 216–19.

3. De Barthe, *Grouard*, 177–78.

4. Big Horn Expedition, March 1–26, 1876.

5. *Cheyenne Daily Leader*, April 9, 1876.

6. De Barthe, *Grouard*, 205–07.

7. Hedren, *Fort Laramie*, 91–92.

8. Kingsley M. Bray, *Crazy Horse, A Lakota Life* (Norman: University of Oklahoma Press, 2006), 205–14.

9. Hedren, *Fort Laramie*, 123.

10. Thomas Powers, *The Killing of Crazy Horse* (New York: Vintage Books, 2011), 329.

11. *The Cheyenne Daily Leader*, July 6, 1876, CA, https://chroniclingamerica.loc.gov/lccn/sn84022149/1876-07-06/ed-1/seq-1/.

12. Buecker, "Red Cloud Agency Traders," 12.

13. https://articles.historynet.com/buffalo-bills-skirmish-at-warbonnet-creek.htm.

14. *Omaha Daily Bee*, August 7, 1875; "Buffalo Bill Cody," *Wyoming Tales and Trails, Montana, The Magazine of Western History* (Montana Historical Society) 55, no. 1 (Spring, 2005): 16–35.

CHAPTER 23

1. Buecker, *Fort Robinson*, 86.

2. AG's Office to the Secretary of War, November 2, 1876; RG 1517.AM; FRM.

3. Fred Bruning's 1877 correspondence; RG 1517.AM; FRM.

4. *Omaha Daily Herald*, September 1876; reprinted in *Daily Deadwood Pioneer Times*, March 16, 1909.

5. McDermott, *Red Cloud*, 89; Buecker, *Fort Robinson*, 88.

6. *Omaha Daily Herald*, September 1876; *Daily Deadwood Pioneer Times*, March 16, 1909.

7. U.S., OIA, *Eighth Annual Report of the Board of Indian Commissioners for the Year 1876* (Washington: GPO, 1877), 19.

8. Bishop Henry Benjamin Whipple, "The History and Culture of the Standing Rock Oyate," compiler Dr. Wayne G. Sanstead, State Department, *North Dakota Department of Public Instruction, 1995*.

9. "Military Reports on the Red Cloud-Red Leaf Surround," *Nebraska History Magazine* XV, no. 4 (NSHS, October–December 1934), 294.

10. *Omaha Daily Bee*, February 14, 1883, CA.

11. Olson, *Red Cloud*, 233, footnote 69.

12. *Chicago Times*, November 15, 1876; McDermott, *Red Cloud*, 91.

13. Frank H. Goodyear III, *Red Cloud: Photographs of a Lakota Chief* (Lincoln: University of Nebraska Press, 2003), 32.

14. DFC.

15. Cozzens, *The Earth Is Weeping*, 285, 288–91.

CHAPTER 24

1. Richmond L. Clow, "The Sioux Nation and Indian Territory: The Attempted Removal of 1876," *South Dakota History* 6, no. 4 (Fall 1976).

2. *The Sidney Telegraph*, September 16, 1876.

3. *The Sidney Telegraph*, February 1, 1877.

4. "Winter of 1876–1877 at Camp Canby," Fred Bruning Correspondence; FRM: Public Domain, History Nebraska, RG0826.AMA.

5. *Cheyenne Daily Leader*, November 28, 1876, CA.

6. Moulton, *McGillycuddy*, 109, 111.

7. Lieutenant C. A. Johnson, Acting Indian Agent, to CoIA, March 10, 1877; Lieutenant C. A. Johnson's papers and letters; RG 1517.AM, Box 4, FRM.

8. Acting AG to Lieutenant Johnson, June 14, 1877; LS, DP 1877–1879; National Archives, Kansas City, MO (NACPR); FRM.

9. *The Sidney Telegraph*, June 3, 1876.

10. *The Cheyenne Daily Sun*, February 15, 1877.

11. Congressional Act of February 28, 1877, 44th Congress, Session 2, chapter 72, 254.

12. *Dictionary of Canadian Biography* Vol. XI (1881–1890), Library and Archives Canada/MIKAN 3623475.

13. Major Matthew W. Freeburg, "The Northern Cheyenne Exodus: A Reappraisal of the Army's Response" (Master of Military Art and Science, Military History thesis, US Army Command and General Staff College, 2015), 26.

14. *Cheyenne Daily Leader*, no. 180, April 17, 1877.

15. *Cheyenne Daily Leader*, April 29, 1877.

16. Olson, *Red Cloud*, 238–40.

17. Powers, *Crazy Horse*, 262–63.

18. John Gregory Bourke, *On the Border with Crook* 2 (New York: Charles Scribner's Son, 1891) 414–15; Rapherty, *Cheyenne Daily Leader*, May 23, 1877.

19. De Barthe, *Grouard*, 117.

20. *Cheyenne Daily Leader*, May 23, 1877.

21. *Cheyenne Gazette*, May 19, 1877.

22. Buecker, *Fort Robinson*, 126.

CHAPTER 25

1. Buecker, *Fort Robinson*, 97–98.

2. Olson, *Red Cloud*, 240, 247.

3. Interview with James Irwin's great granddaughter, Pat Smith, "Red Cloud Pipe, Livermore, California," *History Detectives*, Episode 1 (Season 2, 2004), pbs.org/historydetectives.

4. Buecker, *Fort Robinson*, 105.

5. *Eyewitnesses to the Indian Wars, 1865–1890: The Long War for the Northern Plains*, 4, ed. Peter Cozzens (Mechanicsburg: Stackpole Books, 2004), 484.

6. Bourke, *On the Border*, 1, 78–83.

7. Olson, *Red Cloud*, 244.

8. Powers, *Crazy Horse*, 416, footnote 3.

9. Stephen E. Ambrose, *Crazy Horse and Custer: The Parallel Lives of Two American Warriors* (New York: Pocket Books, 1975), 477.

10. U.S., OIA, *Annual Report of the CoIA to the Secretary of the Interior for the Year 1877* (Washington: GPO, 1877), 18.

11. Stephen J. Rockwell, *Indian Affairs and the Administrative State in the Nineteenth Century* (New York: Cambridge University Press, 2010), 250.

12. George W. Kingsbury, *The History of Dakota Territory*, 1 (Chicago: The S. J. Clarke Publishing Company, 1915), 802.

13. Olson, *Red Cloud*, 248–52.

14. Luther P. Bradley Diary, October 8, 1877; L. P. Bradley Letters & Diary 1877; RG 1517.AM, Box 4; FRM.

15. Smith, "Red Cloud Pipe."

16. Irwin to CoIA, July 26, 1877; LR, RCA; RG 75; NAB.

17. CoIA to JW Dear, August 22, 1877 (M 21, roll 136, 519); NAB.

18. William E. Lass, *From the Missouri to the Great Salt Lake: An Account of Overland Freighting* (Lincoln: NSHS, 1972), 201–12.

19. JW Dear to Board of Army Appraisers, August 5, 1881; LR, RCA; NAB.

20. Olson, *Red Cloud*, 254.

21. Telegram, Irwin to Hayt, October 24, 1877 (M 21, roll 138); NAB.

22. Commanding General, DP, to Commanding General, Division of the Missouri, December 6, 1877; NAB.

23. *The Sidney Telegraph*, July 20, 1878, SPL.

24. Bettelyoun and Waggoner, *With My Own Eyes*, 112.

25. Irwin to OIA, November 11, 1877; LR; NAB.

26. Telegram, Sheridan to Sherman, December 1, 1877; Doc. File 4163; Sioux War, 1876; RG 94; NAB.

27. *Commissioner's Report to Secretary of the Interior for 1877*, 18.

28. Telegram, Sherman to Sheridan, December 1, 1877; Doc. File 4163; Sioux War, 1876; RG 94, NAB.

29. Olson, *Red Cloud*, 255–56.

30. Bettelyoun and Waggoner, *With My Own Eyes*, 113.

CHAPTER 26

1. Trader Licenses, 1865–1898.

2. Savage and Bell, *History of the City of Omaha*, 80–81.

3. Buecker, "Red Cloud Agency Traders," 12.

4. E. A. Hayt, Commissioner, to James Irwin, U.S. Indian Agent, RCA, November 30, 1874; LR by OIA; RCA 1871–1880 (M234, roll 721); NAB.

5. Hayt to Hammond, May 4, 1877 (M18, 722); NAB.

6. *Daily Press and Dakotaian*, February 7, 1878, CA.

7. Marriage Certificate, March 14, 1878, DFC.

8. Mary Ann's Diary, DFC.

9. E. A. Hayt, Commissioner, to James Irwin, RCA, March 16, 1878; Trader Licenses 1865–1898.

10. JW to Honorable James Keith, Judge of the Circuit Court of Fairfax County, April 11, 1881; Chancery Causes: Tootle, Livingston & Co. vs. J. W. Dear, 1883–013; Fairfax County.

11. *Daily Press & Dakotaian*, April 18, 1878, CA.

12. *Delegation to Select Home in Indian Territory*, Article 4, Chapter 72, August 15, 1876 (19 Stat. 254); Treaty with Sioux Nation, 40th Congress Second Session; Records of the U.S. Senate, NAB, https://www.encyclopedia.com/law/encyclopedias-almanacs-transcripts-and-maps/treaty-sioux-nation.

13. *Helena Weekly Herald*, February 14, 1878, CA.

14. Red Cloud to the President via Major Vroom, Camp Robinson, and General Crook, March 14, 1878; LR by OIA; RCA 1878 (II 976-W2582) (M234, roll 723); NAB.

15. Red Cloud to Major Vroom, Commanding Post near RCA, April 26, 1878; LR by OIA; RCA 1878 (II 976-W2582) (M234, roll 723); NAB.

16. Irwin to OIA, April 27, 1878; RCA 1878 (M18, file 722) (M21, roll 138, 524); NAB.

17. Fanny McGillycuddy's Diary, RG 1517.AM, FRM.

18. Wayne Fanebust, *Outlaw Dakota: The Murderous Times and Criminal Trials of Frontier Judge Peter C. Shannon* (Sioux Falls: The Center for Western Studies, Augustana University, 2016), 207–18, 322.

19. George H. Phillips, *The Indian Ring in Dakota Territory, 1870–1890* 2, no. 4 (SDSH, 1972), 363.

20. Fanebust, *Outlaw Dakota*, 207–18.

21. *Daily Press & Dakotaian*, May 8, 1878, CA.

22. U.S., OIA, "Report of the Sioux Commission," August 28, 1878, *Annual Report of the CoIA, for the Year 1878* (Washington: GPO, 1878), 156.

23. *Daily Press & Dakotaian*, August 7, 1878, newspapers.com.

24. "Sioux Commission Report," August 28, 1878, 156–59.

25. *Daily Press & Dakotian*, August 7, 1878, CA.

26. Governor William A. Howard to the President, August 14, 1878; LR by the OIA, RCA 1878; RCA 1871–1880 (II976-W2582) (M234, roll 723); NAB.

27. Telegram, Hayt to Schurz, August 15, 1878; NAB.

28. Eli S. Ricker, *Voices of the American West*, Volume 1, 76.

29. Ratified by Congress on 28 August (Roll 144, 147); NAB.

30. Dr. James Irwin, United States Indian Agent, "Reports of Agents in Dakota," September 4, 1878, *Commissioner's Report to the Secretary of the Interior: 1878*, 37.

31. Irwin to Carl Schurz, September 5, 1878 (M234, roll 723); RG 75; NAB.

32. *Cheyenne Daily Leader*, September 10, 1878.

33. *The New North-West*, October 11, 1878, CA.

34. *Daily Press and Dakotaian*, October 9, 1878, CA.

CHAPTER 27

1. "General Sheridan's Report: The Causes Which Have Led to the Recent Indian Wars in the West, etc.," *Bozeman Avant Courier*, November 21, 1878, CA.

2. C. Gordon Hewitt, "The Coming Back of the Bison: Under Government and Private Protection Bison Have Increased," *Natural History Magazine*, December 1919, https://www.naturalhistorymag.com/picks-from-the-past/101507/the-coming-back-of-the-bison?page=3.

3. *Cheyenne Daily Sun*, December 7, 1878.

4. U.S., OIA, *Annual Report of the CoIA to the Secretary of the Interior for the Year 1878* (Washington: GPO, 1878), XXXII.

5. Irwin to Schurz, January 4, 1879.

6. U.S., OIA, *Annual Report of the CoIA to the Secretary of the Interior for the Year 1879* (Washington: GPO, 1879), IX–X.

7. U.S., OIA, "Report of Lieutenant-General Sheridan," October 25, 1878, *Annual Report of the Secretary of War for the Year 1878* (Washington: GPO, 1878), 33.

8. *Daily Globe*, December 2, 1878, CA.

9. *The Sidney Telegraph*, February 1, 1879, FRM.

10. *Cheyenne Daily Leader*, December 22, 1878, CA; Patrick D. Simpson, *Whither thou Goest: The true story of two long-lost pioneers whose dream wouldn't die, and how their family found them more than a century later* (Lincoln: Author's Choice Press, 2001), 291; and Isabella L. Bird, *A Lady's Life in the Rocky Mountains* (London: John Murray, 1879), Letter 3, September 8, 1879.

CHAPTER 28

1. *Conners v. United States*, 180 U.S. 271, 21 S. Ct. 362, 45 L. ed. 535 (1901) (Justice Henry Billings Brown for the Court), Wikipedia, https://supreme.justia.com/cases/federal/us/180/271/case.html.

2. Freeburg, *The Northern Cheyenne Exodus*, 26; *Omaha Daily Bee*, April 25, 1877.

3. Stan Hoig, *Perilous Pursuit: The U.S. Cavalry and the Northern Cheyennes* (Boulder: University Press of Colorado, 2002), 8.

4. James N. Leiker and Ramon Powers, *The Northern Cheyenne Exodus in History and Memory* (Norman: University of Oklahoma Press, 2011), 45–48.

5. Cynthia Ann Chamberlain, "Colonel Ranald Slidell Mackenzie's Administration of the Western Section of Indian Territory 1875–1877" (Master's thesis, Texas Tech University, 1971).

6. William Nicholson, Superintendent of Indian Affairs, to CoIA, September 18, 1877; C/A Agency; LR OIA; NAB.

7. "Inquiry into the Cheyenne Outbreak, 1879," Division of the Missouri Special File 905-M-1879 (reel 1 RG 501 1878–79); Records of the War Department United States Army Commands, RG 98, NSHS; and Buecker, *Fort Robinson*, 127–28.

8. Edgar Beecher Bronson, *Reminiscences of a Ranchman* (New York: The McClure Company, 1908), 156.

9. George Bird Grinnell, *The Cheyenne Indians: Their History and Their Ways of Life*, II (Lincoln: University of Nebraska Press, 1972), 5.

10. Buecker, *Fort Robinson*, 134–35.

11. Alan Boye, *Holding Stone Hands: On the Trail of the Cheyenne Exodus* (Lincoln: University of Nebraska Press, 1999), 272.

12. Buecker, *Fort Robinson*, 137.

13. "Inquiry into the Cheyenne Outbreak."

14. Will H. Spindler, "Dull Knife's Cheyennes Fought Finish Fight for Birthright," *Tragedy Strikes at Wounded Knee* (Gordon: Gordon Journal Publishing Company, 1955), 33.

15. Angie Debo, *A History of the Indians of the United States* (Norman: University of Oklahoma Press, 1984), 242.

16. Carter, *Sketch of Fort Robinson*, 25.

17. Spindler, "Dull Knife's Cheyennes," 33.

18. Carter, *Sketch of Fort Robinson*, 26–28.

19. "Inquiry into Cheyenne Outbreak."

20. Lannigan, "Inquiry into Cheyenne Outbreak," 144–45.

21. Hoig, *Perilous Pursuit*, 177.

22. Carter, *Sketch of Fort Robinson*, 26–28.

23. *Cheyenne Daily Sun*, January 23, 1879.

24. Buecker, *Fort Robinson*, 147.

25. *The Cincinnati Daily Star*, January 17, 1879.

26. Thomas R. Buecker and R. Eli Paul, "Cheyenne Outbreak Firearms," *The Museum of the Fur Trade Quarterly* 29, no. 2 (Summer 1993): 8.

27. "Inquiry into Cheyenne Outbreak," 64–66.

28. "Inquiry into Cheyenne Outbreak," 64–66.

Chapter 29

1. James Irwin, U.S. Indian Agent to E. A. Hayt, CoIA, January 1, 1879; LR, RCA; RG 75; FRM.

2. James Irwin, U.S. Indian Agent to Carl Schurz, Secretary of the Interior, January 4, 1879; FRM.

3. E. J. Brooks, Acting Commissioner to the Secretary of the Interior, May 1, 1879; RG 48; FRM; and Olson, *Red Cloud*, 264.

4. On December 31, 1878, the War Department made Camp Robinson a permanent army base and changed its name to Fort Robinson.

5. Moulton, *McGillycuddy*, 153–57.

6. *Press and Daily Dakotaian*, February 1, 1877.

7. *The Saline Journal* (Kansas), January 23, 1879.

8. Mary Ann's Diary, DFC.

9. Fairfax Court records, FXDBX4(102):375; Robison, "Royal Oaks Chain," February 25, 2016; *Cheyenne Daily Leader*, January 29, 1879.

10. Hayt to Irwin, February 3, 1879; LS by OIA 1824–1881 (M 21, Roll 150, 29); NAB.

11. Hayt to McGillycuddy, April 3, 1879; Telegrams Received and Sent, January to December 1879; Pine Ridge Agency (PRA), RG 75; NACPR.

12. Alfred Rasmus Sorenson, *Early History of Omaha: Walks and Talks Among the Old Settlers: A Series of Sketches in the Shape of a Connected Narrative of the Events and Incidents of Early Times in Omaha, Together With a Brief Mention of the Most Important Events of Later Years* (Omaha: Office of The Daily Bee, 1876), 266.

13. Savage and Bell, *History of Omaha*, 81, 111, 577–79.

14. Alvin Saunders to E. A. Hayt, July 23, 1878; RCA, 1878; LR by OIA (M234, roll 723); NAB.

15. Trader Licenses, 1865–1898.

16. Hayt to McGillycuddy, March 4, 1879; LS by OIA, 1824–1881 (M21, roll 150, 93–94); NAB.

17. McGillycuddy to CoIA, December 12, 1879; PRA LR (Roll 2); NAB.

18. Hayt to McGillycuddy, April 3, 1879; Telegrams received and sent, January–December 1879; Records of OIA, PRA; RG 75; NAB.

19. Delo, *Peddlers and Post Traders*, 194.

20. Hayt to Senator Spencer of Alabama, March 4, 1879; LS; NAB.

21. JW's sworn affidavit April 11, 1881, to Fairfax County Court, Fairfax County Records, 1883–013.

22. Mary Ann's Diary, DFC.

CHAPTER 30

1. Hayt to McGillycuddy, March 4, 1879; LS by OIA, 1824–1881 (M 21, Roll 150, 93–94); NAB.

2. Ricker, *Voices of the American West*, Vol. 2, 177–78.

3. Affidavit sworn in Alameda County, California, March 2, 1929; private collection of Daniel Stanton; Moulton, *McGillycuddy*, 160, 162–63.

4. Telegram, Hayt to McGillycuddy, March 24, 1879; Series 11, Box 722; RG 75; NACPR.

5. Affidavit sworn in Alameda County, California, March 2, 1929; private collection of Daniel Stanton.

6. Mary Ann's Diary, 1880: Red Cloud, Stabber, Red Dog, Thunder, Little Wound, Charge in the Shield, Young Man Afraid of His Horses, Hill Bull, Old Day, Crooked Eye, Foam, Grass, Hon Bull [Horn Bull?], Pumpkin Seed, Brave Bear, Trunk, High Wolf, Hat Icon, American Horse, Spider, Little Big Man, Blue Handle, Blue Horse, The Tongue, Feather in the Head, Walking Bear, No Water, Three Star, Eagle, Sword (Police Captain), Two Lance, Afraid of Bear, No Flesh, Three Bears, Black Bear, Swift Bird, Face, Little Bridge, Womans Dress, Three Birds, DFC.

7. McGillycuddy, "Diary."

8. James R. Walker, *Lakota Belief and Ritual* (Lincoln: University of Nebraska Press, 1991), 199, 201.

9. DFC.

10. Red Cloud to Our Great Father, May 1, 1879; PRA Petitions, 1878–1893; Records of OIA; RG 75; NACPR.

11. C. Terry to OIA, 3 June 1879; RCA (roll 724); NAB; McGillycuddy to OIA, September 9, 1879 (roll 724); McGillycuddy to OIA, December 2, 1879; RCA (roll 725); NAB.

12. Brooks to McGillycuddy, June 5, 1879; Series 2, Box 2, RG 75, NACPR.

13. Jeffrey Ostler, *The Plains Sioux and U.S. Colonialism from Lewis and Clark to Wounded Knee* (New York: Cambridge University Press, 2011), 203.

14. *Nebraska Advertiser* (Brownville), November 27, 1879.

15. Bullis to McGillycuddy, May 2, 1879; Series 2, Box 2; RG 75; NACPR.

16. Ostler, *The Plains Sioux*, 204.

17. Schurz to Hayt, September 4, 1879; LS, PRA (MI282, roll 2); NAB; P. E. Northup to McGillycuddy, July 13, 1882; Price to McGillycuddy, July 29, 1882, and James Delano to McGillycuddy, July 13, 1882; Correspondence Received, PRA; NAB.

18. Fanny McGillycuddy, "Diary, 1877–78," FRM.

19. Description of Schurz's visit to Pine Ridge, September 1–4, 1879. McGillycuddy, "Diary."

20. McGillycuddy to Trowbridge, November 15, 1880; LR, RCA; RG 75; NAB.

21. Mary Ann's Diary, DFC.

22. Robert W. Frazer, *Forts of the West: Military Forts and Presidios and Posts Commonly Called Forts West of the Mississippi River to 1898* (Norman: University of Oklahoma Press, 1980), xxii–xxiii.

23. Buecker, *Fort Robinson*, 152.

24. E. D. Townsend, AG to Crook, December 10, 1879; Records of the House of Representatives 49th Congress; Box 13; NAB.

25. Stephens & Wilcox Note to Fairfax County Court, June 15, 1879, "Chancery Causes: Tootle, Livington & Co vs J. W. Dear" (Chancery Causes), CFF94d, part 1 of 2; 1883–013; Fairfax County.

26. Robison, "Royal Oaks Chain," Fairfax Deed Book 4 (102): 375.

27. *National Republican* (Washington, DC), August 1, 1879.

28. T. W. Richards, Attorney to H. W. Thomas, Fairfax Court, September 23, 1879; "Chancery Causes," 79–80.

29. Utley, *Frontier Regulars*, 370.

CHAPTER 31

1. Mary Ann's Diary, DFC.

2. Marble to JW Dear, April 4, 1880; LS OIA (Roll 154, 388); NAB.

3. R. E. Trowbridge to Hollenbeck at Rosebud Landing, April 29, 1880; General Correspondence 1879–1880; Records of BIA; Rosebud Indian Agency 1880, no. 2; Box A-354, RG 75, NAB.

4. Major Upham to OIA, April 19, 1880; LR, RCA; RG 75; NAB; Major J. J. Upham to General John Cook, US Indian Agent, Spotted Tail Agency (STA), May 3, 1880; General Correspondence, Rosebud 1880 no. 3 May-June; Box A-354; RG 75, NAB.

5. Federal Census, 1880, Fort Robinson and Soldier Creek District.

6. P. R. Johnson to Secretary of the Interior, January 20, 1880; RCA Letters (Roll 726), NAB.

7. JW Dear to CoIA, May 6 and 13, 1880; RCA 1880; LR by OIA (M234, roll 726); RG 75; NAB.

8. Mary Ann's Diary, DFC.

9. *The Columbus Journal*, June 23, 1880.

10. McNeil released Clay's goods at Rosebud Landing, August 15, 1879 (Roll 154, 591); NAB.

11. *Press and Daily Dakotaian*, July 30, 1880.

12. McGillycuddy to Trowbridge, July 27, 1880; RCA 1880; LR by OIA (M234, roll 726); RG 75; NAB.

13. *The Black Hills Daily Times*, August 3, 1880.

14. *Black Hills Weekly Pioneer*, August 7, 1880.

15. *The Black Hills Daily Times*, August 6, 1880.

16. Estelline Bennett, *Old Deadwood Days* (New York: J. H. Sears & Company, Inc., 1928), 109.

17. *The Daily Deadwood Pioneer-Times*, August 6, 1880.

18. *Black Hills Weekly Pioneer*, August 14 and 21, 1880.

19. American Horse to Great Father, September 4, 1880; LR, RCA (roll 726); RG 75; NAB.

20. Red Cloud to Great Father, September 4, 1880; LR, RCA (roll 726); RG 75; NAB.

21. Julia B. McGillycuddy, *McGillycuddy Agent* (Stanford: Stanford University Press, 1941), 5.

22. Mary Jacqueline Fear, "American Indian Education: The Reservation Schools, 1870–1900" (PhD Thesis, University College, London, 1978).

23. U.S., OIA, *Annual Report of the CoIA to the Secretary of the Interior for the Year 1880* (Washington: GPO, 1880), 40.

24. Telegram, Marble to McGillycuddy, Pine Ridge via Fort Robinson, September 16, 1880; Series 11, Box 722; RG 75; NACPR.

25. McGillycuddy to CoIA, September 18, 1880; Letter Book Vol. 1, 441; Series 4, Box 35; RG 75; NACPR.

26. McGillycuddy to H. C. Dear, October 2, 1880; PRA Miscellaneous LS, July 22, 1877–1887; Box 53A; RG 75; NAB.

27. Robert S. Gardner, Indian Inspector, to C. Schurz, Secretary of the Interior, October 16, 1880; LR, RCA; RG 75; NAB.

28. McGillycuddy to Clay, Richard, and Luther Dear, November 6, 1880; McGillycuddy to W. H. Bergin, Chief of US Indian Police, PRA, November 12, 1880; PRA Miscellaneous LS, July 22, 1877–1887; Box 53A; RG 75; NAB.

29. McGillycuddy to Trowbridge, November 15, 1880; LR, PRA; RG 75; NAB.

30. Norman Maynard, Postmaster General to The Secretary of the Interior, December 6, 1880; RCA LR; RG 75; NAB.

CHAPTER 32

1. Scheel, "The Reconstruction Years," https://www.loudounhistory.org/history/loudoun-cw-reconstruction-towns/.

2. Mary Ann's Diary, DFC.

3. Mary Ann's Diary, DFC; See also: https://archive.org/stream/NebraskaHistoricBuildingsSurveySiouxCounty/Nebraska%20Historic%20Buildings%20Survey%20Sioux%20County__.djvu.txt.,19, 20.

4. Townsend to Crook, December 10, 1879; Records of the House of Representatives 49th Congress; Box 13; NAB.

5. Mary Ann's Diary, DFC.

6. *Omaha Daily Bee*, July 10, 1880, 4.

7. Mary Ann's Diary, DFC.

8. *Press & Daily Dakotaian*, September 28, 1880, 1.

CHAPTER 33

1. McGillycuddy to R. B. Dear, January 12, 1881; PRA Misc.; LS, July 2, 1877–1887; Box 53A; BIA; RG 75; NACPR.

2. *Alexandria Gazette*, January 24, 1881, 3.

3. JW's sworn statement to Fairfax Court, April 11, 1881, Chancery Causes, Fairfax County; Robison, "Royal Oaks Chain."

4. Horace Maynard, Postmaster General to Secretary of Interior, February 14, 1881; OIA LR 1871–1907; Vol. 2, 1880–1882; RG 75; NAB.

5. Eliza Jane Wilder, "The Long [Dakota] Winter, 1880–1881," *Prologue Magazine* 35, no. 4 (National Archives: 2003).

6. DFC.

7. *Daily Yellowstone Journal* (Miles City, MT), November 30, 1882.

8. McGillycuddy to CoIA, January 14, 1881; LR PRA; case 96; RG 75; NACPR.

9. McGillycuddy to CoIA, March 1 and 8, 1881; LR RCA; RG 75; NAB; and Olson, *Red Cloud*, 272.

10. Red Cloud to President, April 28, 1881, LR RCA; RG 75, NAB; and Olson, *Red Cloud*, 272.

11. Red Cloud to Our Great Father, the President, May 12, 1881; LR RCA; RG 75, NAB.

12. McGillycuddy to OIA, May 1881; LR, RCA; RG 75; NAB.

13. McGillycuddy to Price, May 30, 1881; LR OIA 1871–1909; Vol. 2, 1880–1882; NAB.

14. Transcript of conference held at Sun Dance, June 22, 1881; transmitted by McGillycuddy to Comm of IA, June 23, 1881; LR RCA; RG 75, NAB; and Olson, *Red Cloud*, 274.

15. Olson, *Red Cloud*, 275.

16. U.S., OIA, *Thirteenth Annual Report of the Board of Indian Commissioners, for the year 1881* (Washington: GPO, 1881), 49.

17. John Cook, *Annual Report for the year 1881*, 54–55.

18. Records of the US House of Representatives 49th Congress; Box 13; NAB.

19. JW Dear to Secretary of War, June 8, 1881; Records of the US House of Representatives 49th Congress; Box 13; RG 233; NAB.

20. Major Sumner to General Crook, June 26, 1881; Records of the US House of Representatives 49th Congress; Box 13; RG 233; NAB.

21. Major Sumner to General Sheridan, September 7 and 14, 1881; Board of Officers recommendation to Major Sumner, August 5, 1881; Records of the US House of Representatives 49th Congress; Box 13; RG 233; NAB.

22. *The National Cyclopaedia of American Biography Being the History of the United States*, ed. Distinguished Biographers, Selected from each State, Revised and Approved by the Most Eminent Historians, Scholars and Statesmen of the Day (New York: James T. White & Co., 1920), 99.

23. James M. Love, Co. Commissioner to Fairfax Court, November 17, 1881; Chancery Causes; Fairfax County, 119–22.

24. Chancery Causes, June Term 1883, Fairfax County.

25. Olson, *Red Cloud*, 277.

26. McGillycuddy to Commissioner Price, February 28, 1882; LR OIA; RG 75; NAB.

CHAPTER 34

1. McGillycuddy to Price, March 32 [sic], 1882; Letterbook Vol. 3, 1882, 164; Series 4, Box 35; RG 75; NACPR; and Moulton, *McGillycuddy*, 193, 209.

2. Olson, *Red Cloud*, 276.

3. Moulton, *McGillycuddy*, 160–62.

4. Olson, *Red Cloud*, 282; Cowgill, Edgar, Oldham, Grinnell and others to CoIA, August 21, 1882; Series 2, Box 6; RG 75; NACPR.

5. Moulton, *McGillycuddy*, 211; and Olson, *Red Cloud*, 277.

6. Olson, *Red Cloud*, 278; Red Cloud to Henry M. Teller, Secretary of the Interior, August 13, 1882; LR; RG 75; NAB.

7. Olson, *Red Cloud*, 278; *Press and Daily Dakotaian* (Yankton), August 29, 1882, CA.

8. Olson, *Red Cloud*, 278–81.

9. *New York Times*, August 26, 1882; and Moulton, *McGillycuddy*, 221.

10. McDermott, *Red Cloud*, 105; and Moulton, *McGillycuddy*, 221–24.

11. Pollock to Secretary of Interior, September 15, 1882; LR, Special File 264; RG 75; NAB; and Olson, *Red Cloud*, 283.

12. Telegram, Pollock to H. Teller, October 4, 1882, 8:10 am; Series 4; RG 75; NACPR; and Moulton, *McGillycuddy*, 225.

13. Pollock to Secretary of Interior, October 14, 1882; Special File 264; RG 75; NAB; and Olson, *Red Cloud*, 284.

14. *Omaha Daily Bee*, September 25, 1882; McDermott, *Red Cloud*, 105; and Olson, *Red Cloud*, 283.

15. Townsend to CoIA, October 14, 1882; LR; RG 75; NAB; and Olson, *Red Cloud*, 284.

16. R. V. Belt to Secretary of Interior, November 15, 1882; LR; RG 75; NAB.

17. Hiram Price, CoIA to McGillycuddy, November 25, 1882; *Reports of Committees of House of Representatives for the First Session of the 49th Congress, 1885–86* (Washington: GPO, 1886), 43.

18. Herbert S. Schell, *History of South Dakota* (Lincoln: University of Nebraska Press, 1961), 317; George E. Hyde, *A Sioux Chronicle* (Norman: University of Oklahoma Press, 1956), 115, 187; Olson, *Red Cloud*, 288.

19. Hyde, *A Sioux Chronicle*.

20. Agreement with the Sioux of Various Tribes, 1882–1883, October 17, 1882, to January 3, 1883, Unratified; See H. R. Ex. Doc. 68, 47th Congress, 2d Session, 1065.

21. McDermott, *Red Cloud*, 99–100; Red Cloud, quoted in George Bird Grinnell, "Red Cloud," ca. 1891; George Bird Grinnell Collection MO610; Folder 10, Box 2, Series 3; NSHS.

22. Agreement with the Sioux of Various Tribes, 1882–1883, January 23, 1883.

23. *National Republican* (Washington, DC), December 7, 1882.

24. McDermott, *Red Cloud*, 105–06.

25. *Sunday Globe* (St. Paul, Minnesota), January 21, 1883, CA.

26. *The Evening Star* (Washington, DC), January 31, 1883, CA.

27. *The Evening Critic* (Washington, DC), December 26, 1882, CA.

28. McGillycuddy to CoIA, June 26–27, 1883; LR; RG 75; NAB; and Olson, *Red Cloud*, 291.

29. Olson, *Red Cloud*, 293–94.

CHAPTER 35

1. Fairfax County Records; FXDBX4(102); November Term 1881; Fairfax County.

2. H. Price, Commissioner, to H. C. Dear, April 2, 1883; Misc. LS; RCA; NAB.

3. JW's Letter to Richard, June 29, 1883, DFC.

4. DFC.

5. Fairfax County Records; June Term 1883; Fairfax County.

6. *Loudoun Mirror*, August 16, 1883, Thomas Balch Library, Leesburg, VA.

CHAPTER 36

1. *The Evening Critic*, March 14, 1885; and Olson, *Red Cloud*, 297–98.

2. Bland to Secretary of the Interior, March 16, 1885; LR; RG 75; NAB.

3. *The Council Fire*, VIII (April 1885), 52–53; and Olson, *Red Cloud*, 298.

4. Hyde, *A Sioux Chronicle*, 105–06.

5. U.S., OIA, Report of William H. Waldby to Clinton B. Fisk, Chairman, Board of Indian Commissioners, August 15, 1887, *Nineteenth Annual Report of the Board of Indian Commissioners, 1887* (Washington: GPO, 1888), 24, https://www.nebraskahistory.org/publish/publicat/history/full-text/1998-Young_Man.pdf.

6. Statutes at Large: 49th Congress, Session 1, Chapter 119, Library of Congress; and Olson, *Red Cloud*, 309.

7. Utley, *The Indian Frontier*, 247–49; and Olson, *Red Cloud*, 259.

8. "Lakota Black Hills Treaty Rights," https://www.sbg.ac.at/ges/people/wagnleitner/usa2/lakotas.pdf.

9. *The Saint Paul Daily Globe*, June 19, 1889, CA.

10. Tribal rituals and ceremonies were banned by Commissioner Price in 1883. Department of the Interior, OIA, March 30, 1883, *Rules Governing the Court of Indian Offences*.

11. Robert M. Utley, *The Last Days of the Sioux Nation* (New Haven, CT: Yale University Press, 1963), 61–64, 71–72; and Ostler, *Plains Sioux*, 243–56.

12. McDermott, *Red Cloud*, 115.

13. Olson, *Red Cloud*, 327.

14. Olson, *Red Cloud*, 329–30; and Utley, *Indian Frontier*, 256–57.

15. *The Pittsburgh Dispatch*, January 1, 1891.

16. McDermott, *Red Cloud*, 119.

17. Red Cloud, "I was Born a Lakota," Red Cloud's Abdication Speech, July 4, 1903, *New York Times*, June 17, 1870.

18. Jeffrey Ostler, *The Lakota and the Black Hills: The Struggle for Sacred Ground* (New York: Viking Press, 2010), 129; and Edward Lazarus, *Black Hills White Justice: The Sioux*

Nation Versus the United States, 1775 to the Present (New York: HarperCollins, 1991), 323–24, 375, 401.

19. Olson, *Red Cloud*, 340.

20. "Red Cloud, Sioux Chief Dead," *New York Times*, December 11, 1909.

CHAPTER 37

1. Will Book Vol. 3-F, 1882–1884, 427, Leesburg County Court House.

2. Mary Ann's Diary, DFC.

3. H. Price, Commissioner, to H. C. Dear, April 2, 1883; Misc. LS; RCA; NAB.

4. *Reports of Committees of the Senate of the United States for the First Session of the Forty-Eighth Congress 1883-'84*, February 15 and May 20, 1884 (Washington: GPO, 1884), Vol. 2, 180 and Vol. 5, 563, NAB; Congressional Records, House of Representatives, January 7, 1892, 231; James H. Outhwaite, Chairman of Committee on Military Affairs, House of Representatives U.S., to Secretary of War, February 2, 1892.

5. Federal Censuses, 1900, 1910.

6. Mary Ann's Diary, DFC.

7. Press report, 1894, DFC.

8. "The Milwaukee Road's St. Paul Pass Tunnel," http://www.american-rails.com/st -paul-pass-tunnel.html.

9. *The National Cyclopaedia of American Biography*, 99.

10. *Valentine Reporter*, March 12, 1885; and Olson, *Red Cloud*, 297.

11. *Camp Lee Traveller* (Petersburg, VA) 1, no. 4 (July 23, 1941); and Jane-Raye Smith, *The Review* (Central High School, Washington DC) (Spring 1937).

About the Authors

Marilyn Dear Nelson comes from a military family. Her grandfather was a general and her father a colonel. Both were military doctors, and much of her childhood was spent on military posts and embassies outside the United States. Her career in international marketing allowed her to continue a peripatetic lifestyle, and she has lived and worked on six continents. She met her English husband, **Chris Nelson**, an international businessman, in Hong Kong. They are now retired and live in London, where for much of the last decade, keen to reconnect with Marilyn's American heritage, they have been researching the life of her great-grandfather, JW Dear.